Lecture Notes in Computer S

Edited by G. Goos, J. Hartmanis, and J.

Springer
Berlin
Heidelberg
New York
Hong Kong
London
Milan
Paris
Tokyo

Andreas Butz Antonio Krüger
Patrick Olivier (Eds.)

Smart Graphics

Third International Symposium on Smart Graphics, SG 2003
Heidelberg, Germany, July 2-4, 2003
Proceedings

 Springer

Series Editors

Gerhard Goos, Karlsruhe University, Germany
Juris Hartmanis, Cornell University, NY, USA
Jan van Leeuwen, Utrecht University, The Netherlands

Volume Editors

Andreas Butz
Antonio Krüger
Universität des Saarlandes
FR 6.2 Informatik, Postfach 15 11 50
66041 Saarbrücken, Germany
E-mail: {butz/krueger}@cs.uni-sb.de

Patrick Olivier
Lexicle, Innovation Centre
York Science Park, York, YO10 5DG, UK
E-mail: patrick.olivier@lexicle.com

Cataloging-in-Publication Data applied for

A catalog record for this book is available from the Library of Congress

Bibliographic information published by Die Deutsche Bibliothek
Die Deutsche Bibliothek lists this publication in the Deutsche Nationalbibliografie;
detailed bibliographic data is available in the Internet at <http://dnb.ddb.de>.

CR Subject Classification (1998): I.3, I.2.10, I.2, I.4, I.5, H.5, I.7

ISSN 0302-9743
ISBN 3-540-40557-7 Springer-Verlag Berlin Heidelberg New York

Springer-Verlag Berlin Heidelberg New York
a member of BertelsmannSpringer Science+Business Media GmbH

http://www.springer.de

© Springer-Verlag Berlin Heidelberg 2003
Printed in Germany

Typesetting: Camera-ready by author, data conversion by DA-TeX Gerd Blumenstein
Printed on acid-free paper   SPIN 10929100   06/3142   5 4 3 2 1 0

Preface

The International Symposium on Smart Graphics 2003 was held on July 2–4, 2003 in Heidelberg, Germany. It was the fourth event in a series that started in 1999 as an AAAI Spring Symposium. In response to the overwhelming success of the 1999 symposium, its organizers decided to turn it into a self-contained event in 2000. With the support of IBM, the first two International Symposia on Smart Graphics were held at the T.J. Watson Research Center in Hawthorne, NY. The 2003 symposium was supported by the Klaus Tschira Foundation and moved to the European Media Lab in Heidelberg, thus underlining the international character of the Smart Graphics enterprise and its community.

The core idea behind these symposia is to bring together researchers and practitioners from the field of computer graphics, artificial intelligence, cognitive psychology, and fine art. Each of these disciplines contributes to what we mean by the term "Smart Graphics": the intelligent process of creating expressive and esthetic graphical presentations. While artists and designers have been creating communicative graphics for centuries, artificial intelligence focuses on automating this process by means of the computer. While computer graphics provides the tools for creating graphical presentations in the first place, cognitive sciences contribute the rules and models of perception necessary for the design of effective graphics. The exchange of ideas between these four disciplines has led to many exciting and fruitful discussions, and the Smart Graphics Symposia draw their liveliness from a spirit of open minds and the willingness to learn from and share with other disciplines.

Since the beginning, there have been discussions as to what qualifies as smart graphics and what doesn't. Although the term is intuitively clear to most, there are different interpretations along the outer boundaries of the field. Instead of giving an explicit definition, we decided to have invited papers from researchers to represent certain aspects of the field, and asked these authors to spread word in their respective communities. The result was a large number of submissions with hardly any out of topic, out of which a high quality program with clear focal points could be assembled.

We would like to thank all authors for the effort that went into their submissions, the program committee for their work in selecting and ordering contributions for the final program, the Klaus Tschira Foundation and the European Media Lab for providing space and time for hosting the event, and Springer-Verlag for publishing the proceedings in their Lecture Notes in Computer Science series.

May 2003

Andreas Butz
Antonio Krüger
Patrick Olivier

Organization

Organizing Committee

Conference Chairs: Andreas Butz (Saarland University, Germany)
                      Antonio Krüger (Saarland University, Germany)
                      Patrick Olivier (Lexicle Limited, UK)
                      Michelle Zhou (IBM T.J. Watson Research Center, USA)
Local Organization: Robert Porzel (European Media Lab, Germany)
                      Rainer Malaka (European Media Lab, Germany)

Program Committee

Maneesh Agrawala (Microsoft Research)
Elisabeth Andre (University of Augsburg)
Brian Fisher (University of British Columbia)
Steven Feiner (Columbia University, New York)
Knut Hartmann (University of Magdeburg)
Takeo Igarashi (University of Tokyo)
W. Bradford Paley (Digital Image Design)
Bernhard Preim (University of Magdeburg)
Thomas Rist (DFKI Saarbrücken)
Stefan Schlechtweg (University of Magdeburg)
Massimo Zancanaro (ITC-irst Trento)

Secondary Reviewers

George Popescu, IBM   Holly Rushmeier, IBM
Michelle Kim, IBM   Pengyu Hong, Harvard University

Sponsoring Institutions

The Third International Symposium on Smart Graphics was organized in coope-ration with the European Association for Computer Graphics. It was hosted at the European Media Lab by the Klaus Tschira Foundation. Additional support was provided by Corel Corporation.

Table of Contents

Graphical Interaction

Visualization Techniques

Virtual Characters

Camera Planning

Poster Presentations

Illustrative Interfaces: Building Special-Purpose Interfaces with Art Techniques and Brain Science Findings

W. Bradford Paley

Digital Image Design Incorporated, 170 Claremont Avenue, New York, NY 10027; Columbia University Department of Computer Science, 1214 Amsterdam Avenue, New York, NY 10027
brad@didi.com
http://didi.com/brad

Abstract. Restricting the scope of a user interface allows designers to apply domain-specific and task-specific knowledge, making the interface itself an illustration of the process it is meant to control. Such interfaces may be more easily learned and understood, and perhaps more efficient. This position paper demonstrates how we might apply to interface design findings from the study of human information processing and behavior, from psychophysics to behavioral psychology. It also explores the rationale behind using techniques derived from the fine and graphic arts. It suggests a simplified model of the mind as a "designer's checklist" that might help interface designers take advantage of the power inherent in people's ability to understand illustrations.

1 Introduction

Think of a point in history where technology can provide a single source for almost any kind of information—a channel for culture, education, entertainment, morality, law, and art. One might need to be a trained specialist to use it, but having it in your community (or even better) your home could begin an information explosion that would prove to be a major discontinuity in world culture.

I could be writing about the Internet-connected computer in a modern home, but I'm actually referring to the technology of printing in the years after its widespread deployment, starting with the Gutenberg's famous 42-line Bible, c. 1455. [1] The grand convergence of information in one physical interface wasn't the blessing of the new technology, but the curse of its immaturity.

As printed information technology matured we went from that single volume that needed a trained specialist to interpret—someone who could read—to the incredibly wide variety of form-factors it assumes today. Novels have different sizes and feels, different papers and different fonts than newspapers; labels on spice racks differ greatly from billboards. All for the simple reason that they are used for different purposes and today's well-developed print technology allows us to carefully match the "device" to the need.

A. Butz et al. (Eds.): Smart Graphics 2003, LNCS 2733, pp. 1–11, 2003.

Computers are just beginning to see this sort of physical articulation—calculators and digital watches prefigured personal digital assistants and multi-purpose cell phones by decades. And we are seeing many more unique devices proliferate, if not succeed. The whole field of Ubiquitous Computing addresses the expanding set of physical niches that we can expect to fit hardware information technology.

I suggest a parallel development in the scoping of computer interfaces, whether physical or merely graphical, which identifies specific task or domain niches and allow us to match the interface more closely to the idiosyncratic needs of each niche. As computing technology matures, more and more interfaces will become as specific as calculators and watches. This position paper explores techniques I believe will help make those interfaces more successful, techniques drawn from the arts and supported by an understanding of how the human brain's "protocol" allows artists to direct our attention and give us information.

1.1 Benefits of Restricting the Scope of an Interface

Interfaces that deal with very restricted scopes can be made much more specific than interfaces that must deal with broad ranges of information or many varieties of tasks. They can apply more domain-specific information and take advantage of lexicons and metaphors shared by a small target audience. When an interface looks and feels more like the task that's being accomplished, people can focus more on the task than the tool. The interface can become more "invisible" even if the graphical presentation is more elaborate.

In fact, a more elaborate or less common graphical representation can actually help someone use it more effectively. For example, a spreadsheet program can operate as both a calculator and clock, but seems more awkward to use for either purpose than the "real thing." I suggest that this is true partially because the consistent "numbers in boxes" look of a spreadsheet requires people to do more intellectual work. Realizing that the general purpose keys on a keyboard can serve to enter either passive symbols into a text or active numbers (textual representations of a potentially changing variable) may be an effort hidden from consciousness, but it still requires maintaining and switching to a distinct mental context when those keys used for a spreadsheet instead of a calculator. This mental context, or frame, might be more easily invoked if it can be associated with pre-linguistic, even pre-attentive memories or learning.

The hands on an analog watch have a very specific visual presence. Someone who wants to think about time might be more easily able to mobilize mental forces dealing with time if he's put into that mental frame by visual recognition of the hands on a clock. Physical stimuli can be strongly associated with memories, as Proust's madeline [2] famously demonstrates by sending him into an eight-volume reverie. And they may be just as strongly associated with active mental processes if the physical stimulus brings a whole mental frame including those active processes, to conscious availability (such as figuring out whether you're late or not, or subtracting two times). As interface designers we would like to see concrete evidence from psychological experiments demonstrate that this actually happens, but the lack of such evidence should not curtail design experimentation and innovation. In fact, experimentation in design can help us form new hypotheses for the sciences to test.

1.2 A Simplified Model of the Brain's "Input Protocol"

This position paper will suggest a few plausible connections that have been inspired by writings of people in the brain sciences. But they are presented as a simplification of the real processes, a kind of "designer's checklist" created to explicitly to support the human communication aspects of the process of design. Euclidean Geometry is a model of space proven to be incorrect, but carpenters still get useful work done with it. So our simplified model of the mind might help designers apply and invent new methods because it's easy to apply while we're engaged in the act of architecting information. And it can help individual designers to use some channels into the mind that they may be less familiar with.

A model, even a simplified one, is less useful without some means to apply it to the task at hand. That's where we look to another group of people who have been experimenting with directing attention and representing information for centuries. Artists and graphic artists have been researching human perception in a more ad-hoc way, but fortunately for the designer it's a very applied way. Their techniques can sometimes be disentangling into the myriad individual neurological and psychological processes that combine to, for instance, direct the eye one way or another. This helps us build our model of the mind. But they can sometimes be lifted whole from a painting and applied as an integrated technique. This helps us build interfaces.

The techniques of artists have helped shape our model by providing questions: "why does this mark make me look there?" They also show where simplification is acceptable, letting us group dozens of distinct brain processes into six or nine general categories. Future work includes making a list of artist-derived interface techniques, how they are described by our model, and what sorts of tasks and information they might support. But a listing of those techniques is well beyond the scope of this position paper.

So this paper will outline our still-developing model, a "designer's checklist" that helps describe how people process information, with just enough simplification to make it useful for design. And a technique or two that may have been originally drawn from artists' palettes will be used to demonstrate different parts of the model.

Many of these techniques may have application in building interfaces for general-purpose data exploration or document creation. But the best of them get their strength from tying abstract bits of data to meaning in someone's head by illustrating that meaning—by crafting a user interface widget that has as much of the character of the idea as possible, so it's difficult to mistake for something else. Future work also includes sorting through this growing set of techniques to see which can be applied to all interfaces, and which are best tied to a restricted task domain. But for now the arena of special purpose interfaces seems to be richer in suggesting candidate techniques.

2 A "Knowledge Acquisition Pipeline"

People turn marks on paper and patterns of light on computer screens into living, active ideas in their minds. How does this happen? Contemporary brain sciences have identified dozens or hundreds of distinct neurological processes that participate in this remarkable transition. As interface designers, we can group and simplify them into a few categories that help us do design. In creating this simplified model we should keep the purpose of the model in mind. We're trying to support the design process—to help us figure out how ideas come from information displays and how those displays can suggest actions that will help people modify the information.

The following breakdown has proven useful for me to organize my own exploration of what kinds of displays might evoke what ideas. It will undoubtedly improve with time, and I welcome thoughts from those reading this initial attempt. Let's use the visual modality for our examples, though this model might as easily be applied to others (e.g. auditory or tactile).

- The first step in the process of reading, for example, is a sensory input: the eye sees areas of light and dark; color variations of hue and saturation. Call this a *sensory* process.
- That raw sensory data feeds into processes that integrate or differentiate the sensory input—some starting immediately in the retina itself, such as the lateral inhibition of the retinal ganglion cells which helps us identify boundaries and see lines. Other processes identify things like line orientation and surface texture, the building blocks needed to segment a scene into pieces. Call these *perceptual* processes.
- Some of these lines and textures help us recognize objects, a *cognitive* process.
- Some objects, like the letters on this page, are associated with ideas beyond the object itself; a *symbolic* process.
- Symbols can be assembled into larger structures; like words, sentences, or topics; a *linguistic* process.
- And finally we can understand and commit to memory the propositions carried in language; a *semantic* process—the ideas we as information designers are trying to evoke.

This relatively cold way to think of a person ignores issues critical to careful interface design, such as behavioral, emotional, and social processes. Though they don't fit nicely into the simplified linear pipeline, they're valuable in our checklist, so at this point we just add them as free-floating reminders, to make our final interface designer's checklist:

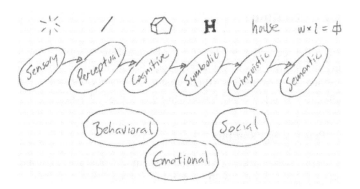

Fig. 1. A "Knowledge Acquisition Pipeline" and other reminders (Intentionally rendered as a sketch, to visually indicate work in progress)

Each set of processes can be thought of as a channel by which we can get information into someone's mind. [3] The most remarkable thing to be exposed by this breakdown is a serious asymmetry in how these channels are used. The vast majority of information in most current interfaces—especially those built with standardized tables, input fields, lists, and scrollbars—are decoded by people's symbolic and linguistic processes, very late in the process. It has to be decoded by the forebrain often with specific, concentrated attention. Even icons are symbols, and the colors used in many visualization displays must be processed as symbols, too—if you need a key, it's a symbolic mapping. Some specific applications; like computer games, computer-based art, and scientific visualization tools; have made better use of the earlier channels but they remain isolated oases of visual sophistication in a desert of text and rectangles.

The ironic thing about that is the forebrain is only three to five million years old, compared with some 125 million years of evolution behind the human visual system; and it's "single-threaded" since we can only attend to one thing at a time, compared to the hundreds or millions of things going on simultaneously in the earlier processes. [4] Worse, we may not even be using it for what it was evolved for: the convoluted logical manipulations needed in a lot of modern tasks developed well after many scholars think evolution stopped for humans. At this point in the maturity of computer interfaces we are squeezing huge amounts of data into a narrow channel: a johnny-come-lately, single-threaded, possibly misused fraction of our brain.

This asymmetry is exciting because it points to a gross inefficiency in how we currently work with computers, and suggests how to fix it. If we find ways to feed some of the data into earlier channels we can greatly improve the man/computer synergy. An intuitive recognition of this asymmetry may be what fueled the mass media's great hopes for virtual reality, and to a lesser extent for scientific visualization. I believe that we have barely delivered on the promise of these fields partially because it's difficult to thread meaning all the way through the pipeline, from sensory input to semantic value. The techniques of "Illustrative Interface Design" provide a first gesture towards exploring and codifying techniques that have been explicitly developed to make that end-to-end connection.

3 Example Techniques

In this section I'll describe applications of visual techniques that fall into the categories in our simplified Knowledge Acquisition Pipeline above. In this short paper I will concentrate on the first three channels: sensory, perceptual, and cognitive processes, since the final two channels are in more common use.

3.1 Sensory Processing Examples

Sensory processing is the earliest of the channels in our pipeline, and one of the oldest in evolutionary terms. Along with perceptual processesing, it may be the most effective in triggering what biologists call "orienting behavior," associated with the release of adrenaline, faster heart rate, and alertness. This state is well suited to directing attention toward important events, where "important" must be determined by the business rules or prioritized task list of the person using the system.

Fig. 2. Detail from a design for an Equities Sales Trading system. A similar system has been working for three years on the New York Stock Exchange trading floor. [5]

In Figure 2, a detail from a design for an equities sales trader's workstation, let's look for the most striking visual features: features that will still be visible even if the image is blurred, shrunken, or displayed for a small fraction of a second. The default colors for the interface were picked to have a relatively bland and flat look so that we could make new information stand out. Here, newly arriving information is one of the most important things a sales trader needs to manage, so new things are distinguished from the rest of the interface by several visual sensory attributes: they are darker, higher in contrast, letters in them are reversed to light on a dark background, and colors are more saturated.

A quick scan of this interface will cause someone's attention to be drawn immediately to the fifth and eighth objects in the list, large areas accentuated by all of the above attributes. A finer-grained scan may draw attention to the first, ninth, and tenth objects, each of which has a smaller rectangle painted with these attributes.

The rest of the interface is intentionally less visually demanding to provide a quiet background for the important information. But information is still immediately available for the trader as soon as they look in the right place. For instance all of the other objects are closer to the background color, drawn with a medium level of contrast. The window borders, including the scrollbar, are drawn with the lowest contrast; appropriate for something that should draw the least visual attention.

In this interface the scrollbar is always there, so it should be available but barely visible—the trader always knows it's there to use so there's no need to call attention to it. It's ironic that in most contemporary windowing interfaces some of the strongest visual cues we can provide on a computer screen—contrast, color, and a 3D appearance—are being squandered; directing the user's attention *away* from the real information in the documents they're creating.

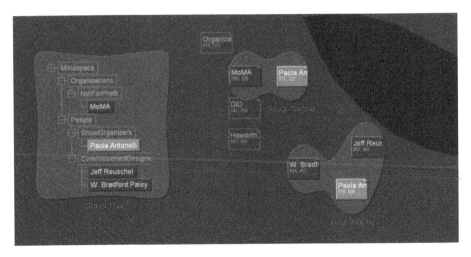

Fig. 3. Detail from a knowledge management concept design, commissioned for the 2001 WorkSpheres exhibition, by the Museum of Modern Art, New York [6] [7]

Figure 3 shows the same sort of attention-directing visual attributes—differences in lightness, saturation, and 3D appearance—at work in another design. This design supports two different views on the same database, or "Model" as described in the Model View Controller paradigm. [8] One view, a hierarchically structured view, is on the left, labeled "Ellipsis Tree." The other view covers the rest of the image and lets people make less structured, ad-hoc arrangements of the information objects.

The highlighting not only draws attention to the selected object (labeled "Paola Antonelli"), but it makes is clear that the object is represented in three places: one in each of two ad-hoc "blobs" and once in the hierarchy. When any object is selected, it and all of the other objects representing the same entity in the Model database acquire the most visually demanding attention-directing visual attributes: bright orange with 3D edges.

This method of highlighting can be distinguished from standard highlighting by its conscious use of low level sensory input. Typical highlighting schemes do not necessarily take into account the colors or attributes on the rest of the screen. A selection color is chosen and represents the locus of attention by a more symbolic mapping: selection color means user focus. Since the colors used in the rest of the screen are not rigorously controlled to provide a low-level sensory contrast with the highlight color, it may take an active change in the user focus to distinguish exactly what is highlighted and what is in the background. It may not be obvious from a still image, as it is here. A case sometimes seen in a standard text list illustrates the point: if half of the items are selected it's often not clear which half is selected unless you know the selection color, or watched (or did) the selection yourself. Your eye is not immediately told what's on and what's off.

It can also be distinguished from an unfortunate technique of using one visual attribute per information channel. Especially in early scientific visualization systems, designers became enamored of how much information could be written on the screen, with the goal of the highest data-density possible. This approach ignored the point of many data representations: that the goal was *reading* the display, not writing it. Reading a display can be made much more difficult by treating visual channels that have deep links in our minds as separate ways in. For instance, having three different ways to highlight things represented as red, green, and blue channels in an RGB display does allow one to have orthogonal selection sets. But people don't experience yellow as R+G, so the complex overlapping of three selection sets becomes an even more complex task of decoding a symbolic proposition that allows eight variations of highlight and keeping it in mind over potentially disjoint spatial areas and thousands of objects. Visual attributes evolved in richly-connected webs of dependence and mutual support, and there is evidence that they are best used in concert [9], as the redundant-encoding of highlight state is accomplished with several visual attributes in Figure 2 and especially Figure 3.

In the MoMA system, a less-demanding color is also used as a clue to show what objects might be important to look at for the next step in the task: dark green, with lightness almost matching the lightness of the background, medium saturation, and medium-lightness labels. This two-level "Selected/Related" highlighting scheme is useful when the system has rules that can help people with the next step in their thought processes. Here, it is assumed that ad-hoc "blob" relationships are telling the system "whenever I select one of these objects, remind me that I have associated the other ones with it."

3.2 Perceptual Processing Examples

There are three kinds of lines in Figure 2: (a) an implied line between two areas painted different colors, (b) a simple line drawn on a background of a different value or color, and (c) the highlight and shadow lines used to create the 3D appearance of the "information objects." They are used to indicate and distinguish three different kinds of entities in the interface

The implied line (a) may be the least visually demanding (at least when drawn in the very close colors we use here). It is used for the interface elements with the least freedom—the background behind the objects and the edge between the background and the window borders. These edges serve to distinguish different areas, but can not be clicked or dragged; they are not affordances.

The simple line (b) is used to outline more active interface elements: the scrollbar, and the thumb and arrow areas that are parts of it. These are clickable or draggable affordances of the scrollbar, but can only be moved (if at all) within tight constraints. This is also true of the small vertical rectangle inside the objects: it acts as a clickable affordance that will bring up a "details window" for that object, so it is generally drawn with the same sort of line. (The exception is when the details window is dark to indicate new information, but in that case there's a more important message being given to the trader. It's okay to override our convention for distinguishing affordances to allow the more important cue to dominate visually.)

In Figure 3, perceptual cues are at work in one additional way: information objects are drawn with straight lines, and relationships are drawn with curved lines. Even before there's a distinction in the viewer's brain between objects and background, there's a distinction between the ways we encode data and relationships. I suggest that this may make it easier to understand the differences later on in the Knowledge Acquisition Pipeline: when earlier processes are supporting later processes, and the signals all encode the same information, we have a very strong redundant encoding of that information.

The highlight, "low-light", and shadow lines (c) in both figures 2 and 3 create the illusion of 3D objects, leading us to the next step in our pipeline, the cognitive processes.

3.3 Cognitive Processing

The human visual system devotes a great deal of effort to finding the borders of things, splitting the world into objects and background. This may be because finding food, threats, and possible mates has a high survival value, and these goals are generally embodied in objects. It also helps us to identify things that we can grasp and manipulate. The cognitive process of distinguishing objects may be even more developed because we're constantly using our hands with nearby objects and the plasticity in the human brain allows it to devote more neurons to processes that are used more or require finer distinctions, even after nature applies the genetic blueprint.

To take advantage of this, we design information objects out of entities that are important to the trader rather than leaving them listed as abstract labels in a standard table format. Our rule of thumb: if something is an object in the trader's head it should look and act like one on the screen.

"Orders" are requests from a customer to buy or sell a financial instrument, the central thing in a sales trader's job, things that have powerful character and cohesion as entities. An order can be urgent, dangerous, unexpected, far out of the market, completely new, or partially updated with new information. Putting it into a standard table requires taking a living, articulated idea and disaggregate it into abstract attributes written as words or numbers in columns. This data normalization completely ignores the emotional and physical capabilities of the mind which help to distinguish, enhance, and identify objects and give them meaning to the trader. Each order must be mentally reassembled by scanning across the table, logically realizing that each row is an entity—despite the fact that a typical table makes no distinction between rows and columns, and despite the fact that columns may have a stronger visual cohesion than rows do since they're adjacent along the longer side of each rectangular cell. By drawing something as an object on the screen we may be making it easier to associate the information on the screen with the entity in the trader's mind.

There are two visual pathways in the human brain, called by some the "what" and "where" (or "how") pathways. [10] The *how* pathway is the earlier one in terms of evolution, and connects with the motor system to control our hands and motions when we manipulate objects. The *what* pathway connects to our conscious processing, letting us the understand things about an object. I suggest that when an object is rendered in 3D it might engage both pathways more firmly, making the 3D object easier to focus on and manipulate mentally as well as physically. In Figure 2 the scrollbar, title bar and resizing edges remain flat, while the order objects are 3D, since they are the usual target of manipulation.

In other systems, such as in Figure 3, I have left many information objects flat, as context for the few 3D objects that are needed for the current manipulation or thought process. Objects become 3D when they need to be manipulated, and the previously 3D objects flatten out to become the new context. The dramatic visual difference makes it feel easier to focus on and manipulate the 3D objects, but actual efficiency increases have to be tested and proven.

In the sales trader's system the more an object "looks like" an order the easier it is for him to associate it with his mental order. In this design the order object's triangular end makes it read as an arrow, implying the "flow" of shares from one party to another. This clearly distinguishes sell (right-pointing) from buy (left-pointing) orders—a very important distinction to traders—while keeping them all looking like they're members of the same family. The visual "objectness" helps the trader's mind to be ready to manipulate this order as a whole and distinct entity, and the shape itself implies some of the actions that might be taken.

Likewise in Figure 3, ad-hoc relationships are fluid blobs that change when their member objects are moved, while the structured tree is more rectilinear. I suggest that this shape difference is a useful mnemonic that suggests the permanence and structure of the hierarchy and the transitory, less explicit associations in the blobs.

3.4 Symbolic and Linguistic Processing

Even the symbolic and linguistic information can be visually articulated in ways that make it more understandable and readable to the trader. In figure 2, for example, we draw the most important information in the largest fonts, and strike through numbers that are not operational but historical. At a lower level this font variation provides visual landmarks to help people locate specific pieces of data.

4 Illustrating Information

There are many ways to make an information object look like an entity in someone's mind, and the exploration of how to do this most effectively is one of the central issues in developing Illustrative Interfaces. Here, we've touched on a basic first principle—associate a visual object with a mental entity. More refined principles all developed along similar lines: the visual object should depict as much of the character of the mental entity as possible. This is where we start seeing the luxuries a designer has in a restricted application scope: more restricted scopes often have more of the idiosyncrasies and details that can be represented in a more evocative way.

To accomplish this while designing an interface for an individual or group, we can first make a list of their language, structures, notational conventions, and shared metaphors. Then we can try to illustrate them: make some kind of drawing (or sound, or tactile event) that captures some of the character of the mental entity by using their own language or notation.

Specific techniques we use to capture character vary widely.

- We can simply copy previously used artifacts to the screen. This is very useful because people recognize them. It may be one of the reasons the Quicken personal finance system became so popular: there are concrete recognizable checks on the screen, not just numbers in columns.
- We can simplify existing objects and redraw them.
- We can draw completely new objects based on the entity distinctions in the minds of the group. And we can shape and decorate them to display

information in a way that resonates with how people think of them—a kind of applied "visual data poetics."

This last technique is the one demonstrated in the sales trader's system example in Figure 2. I believe it holds great promise for showing the widest range of information, since drawn information objects can be shaped to take advantage of the fluid representational abilities of the computer. Once people have a concrete representation of their current thoughts in front of them their minds are freer to build new levels of ideas on that foundation. These new ideas may suggest another round of information objects, acting as bricks in an iterative climb towards more complex yet more understandable structures of ideas.

5 Conclusion

I suggest that the use of an interface designed to reflect people's thoughts about their work, leveraging the illustration-interpreting capabilities of the mind might have several very positive effects: It might speed learning of the system by people in the group. It might help a group teach and integrate new colleagues. It might help a group share a stronger, more concrete mental model of the activity they're all engaged in. And perhaps the most profound effect is that if that group's shared mental model is flawed, its new concreteness might make it easy to identify the flaws and focus on how to repair them or create a wholly new mental model.

This new mental model might be useful in itself, as a new scientific understanding. Or it could be the basis of the creation of a new work process, with fewer errors or costs, or greater efficiencies. Of course then we have to design a new interface, but iteration is the heart of any good design process—this approach to interface design just might make it easier to include the user's own work or though process in the iterations.

References

1. Blumenthal, Joseph: Art of the Printed Book 1455-1955, Godine, Boston, MA (1973) 2
2. Proust, Marcel: Remembrance of Things Past, Volume I, Vintage Books (1982)
3. Kosslyn, Stephen M., Elements of Graph Design, W. H. Freemen & Co. (1994)
4. Minsky, Marvin, The Society of Mind, Simon and Schuster (1986)
5. Abrams, Jan, Stock Options, ID Magazine, June 2000, F&W Publications, New York, volume 47, number 4, (2000) 48–51
6. Paola Antonelli, Ed., Workspheres, Design and Contemporary Work Styles, The Museum of Modern Art, New York (2001) 215
7. Paley, W. Bradford, Web site with MindSpace production notes and working Java applet, http://didi.com/brad/mindspaceAtMoMA (2001)
8. Glenn E. Krasner and Stephen T. Pope. A Cookbook for Using the Model-View-Controller User Interface Paradigm in Smalltalk-80. Journal of Object-Oriented Programming, 1(3):26–49, August/September 1988.
9. Zakia, Richard D., Perception & Imaging, Focal Press, Woburn, MA, (2002) 61
10. Ramachandran, V.S., Phantoms in the Brain: Probing the Mysteries of the Human Mind, Quill, New York (1998) 77–82

The Effect of Motion in Graphical User Interfaces

Paul U. Lee[1], Alexander Klippel[2], and Heike Tappe[3]

[1]San Jose State University
NASA Ames Research Center, Mail Stop 262-4
Moffett Field, CA 94035-1000 USA
plee@mail.arc.nasa.gov
[2]Universität Bremen - Cognitive Systems Group
Department for Informatics and Mathematics, PO box 330
440 Bremen GERMANY
klippel@informatik.uni-bremen.de
[3]Humboldt University at Berlin
Department of English and American Studies
10099 Berlin GERMANY
heike.tappe@rz.hu-berlin.de

Abstract. Motion can be an effective tool to focus user's attention and to support the parsing of complex information in graphical user interfaces. Despite the ubiquitous use of motion in animated displays, its effectiveness has been marginal at best. The ineffectiveness of many animated displays may be due to a mismatch between the attributes of motion and the nature of the task at hand. To test this hypothesis, we examined different modes of route presentation that are commonly used today (e.g. internet maps, GPS maps, etc.) and their effects on the subsequent route memory. Participants learned a route from a map of a fictitious town. The route was presented to them either as a solid line (static) or as a moving dot (dynamic). In a subsequent memory task, participants recalled fewer pertinent landmarks (i.e. landmarks at the turns) in the dynamic condition, likely due to the moving dot that focused equally on critical and less important parts of the route. A second study included a combined (i.e. both static and dynamic) presentation mode, which potentially had a better recall than either presentation mode alone. Additionally, verbalization data confirmed that the static presentation mode allocated the attention to the task relevant information better than the dynamic mode. These findings support the hypothesis that animated tasks are conceived of as sequences of discrete steps, and that the motion in animated displays inhibits the discretization process. The results also suggest that a combined presentation mode can unite the benefits of both static and dynamic modes.

1 Introduction

Animations have become an important design tool in recent graphical user interfaces, as they motivate interactions and draw attention to specific contents. However, the efficacy of animated displays has been questioned by many researchers (e.g. Hegarty, 1992; Palmiter & Elkerton, 1993; Tversky, Morrison, & Betrancourt, 2002). This seems surprising since many graphic representations of physical spaces (e.g. weather

A. Butz et al. (Eds.): Smart Graphics 2003, LNCS 2733, pp. 12–21, 2003.

maps) or devices (e.g. pulley systems) have an intrinsic dynamic component. Hence, the representation of the dynamic aspects through animation should have facilitated information processing.

Tversky and her colleagues (2002) have reviewed animation research and concluded that animated graphics failed to show an advantage over static graphics in facilitating learning and comprehension when the information content and the level of interactivity were equated. They hypothesized that the drawback of animation was due to perceptual and cognitive limitations in the processing of a changing visual situation. They proposed a potential cognitive constraint that people conceive continuous events as composed of discrete steps (Zacks et al., 2001). The discretizations of events occur systematically and the break points of the events (i.e. points where events are segmented) are better remembered than other points within an event. If this is true, then a sequence of static graphics that focuses on the correct set of discrete steps may be more effective than an animated graphics.

Although animation research has failed to show increased learning and comprehension, the property of motion in animated graphics has shown some promise as an effective mechanism for visually organizing complex information by grabbing user's attention and perceptually grouping otherwise dissimilar objects (Bartram & Ware, 2002). The motion can also embed certain temporal components of actions, such as speed, which may be more difficult to infer from a sequence of static graphics. Based on these benefits and costs associated with motion, we hypothesize that the efficacy of static vs. animated graphics depends on the match between the attributes of the presentation mode and the nature of the task. If the motion in an animated display can effectively draw user's attention to the task relevant information, then it may facilitate learning. Otherwise, it can distract the user from attending to the task-relevant information and thereby inhibit the learning process.

2   Dynamic vs. Static Presentation of Route Information

To test this hypothesis, we compared the efficacy of motion in conveying route information by maps. Recently, route maps have become widely available through the Web and through handheld and on-board navigation systems (e.g. Agrawala & Stolte, 2001; Baus et al., 2001). Despite the ubiquitous status of route maps, optimal visual presentation methods are still a matter of research. For example, route maps integrated in on-board navigation systems present routes dynamically with a moving arrow that traverses the map to simulate an imagined navigator. In contrast, internet maps present information statically with lines or arrows representing a route (Fig. 1). Differences in the presentation modes are induced by technical constraints of each medium, rather than by considering cognitive processes.

When people recall route information, they decompose the route into a set of discrete route parts, consisting of only minimal information such as turns and landmarks at the turns, in congruence with effective wayfinding aids (Jackson, 1998). The turns in route directions are key decision points in which the user has to remember to re-orient himself in order to remain on the route. Analogous to event break points, the turning points (decision points with a direction change or DP+) are better remembered than the non-turning points (decision points with no direction change or DP-). Most of the landmarks and intersections along the route are omitted

(Ward et al., 1986; Denis, 1997; Lee & Tversky, in preparation), or parts of the route are chunked to higher order route (direction) elements (Klippel et al., in press).

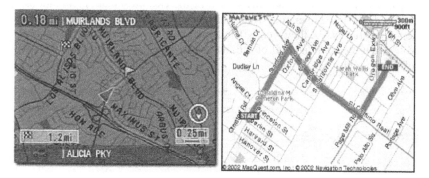

Fig. 1. Examples of dynamic (left) and static (right) route maps

Based on these findings, we predict that dynamically presented route information would hinder subsequent route memory. Given that the key components of route directions are turns and landmarks at the turns, we predict that a static route would allow users to allocate their attention according to the task goals, resulting in a better memory for the landmarks at the turns. In contrast, dynamically presented route information directs users to pay attention to the motion itself, resulting in more equal allocation of attention and subsequent memory to the landmarks at turning (DP+) and non-turning (DP-) points on the route.

By studying how various presentation modes affect the acquisition of route information, especially landmarks, this study aims to shed light on appropriately designing user interfaces to best support cognitive processes. Since landmarks at decision points (i.e. DP+ and DP-) are critical components of route information, we will focus on participants' recall of these landmarks.

2.1 Method

Participants. Forty-three undergraduates, 21 male and 22 female, from Stanford University participated individually in partial fulfillment of a course requirement. The minimum criterion of 30% recall rate eliminated the data of three men and one woman. The data of the remaining thirty-nine participants were analyzed.

Materials and Procedure. We employed a map of a fictitious town consisting of a street network and various landmarks, such as McDonald's and gas stations. We restricted the design to the following functions and appearances of landmarks:

- We chose only instantly recognizable landmarks, such as McDonalds and Seven Eleven, thereby eliminating the need for a legend.
- The landmarks were placed only at decision points – (DP+) and (DP-).
- There were an equal number of landmarks at the turns (DP+) and at the crossing paths along the route (DP-).
- We restricted ourselves to point-like landmarks and avoided street names.

The route in the map was presented statically or dynamically. The static condition presented the complete route between a start and a destination point as a solid line (Fig. 2). In contrast, the dynamic condition conveyed the route by a moving dot. The participants were assigned randomly to one of the two presentation conditions. They were asked to remember the route as they viewed the map for 3 minutes. Immediately afterwards, they were given a map with only the street network and were asked to draw the route and all of the landmarks that they could remember, both on and off of the route.

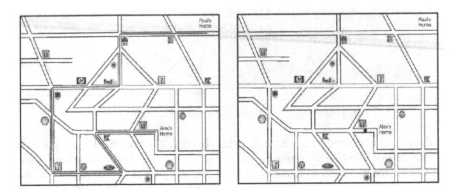

Fig. 2. Route map with a static (left) or a dynamic (right) presentation of the route

2.2 Results

The recalled landmarks were analyzed for static and dynamic route presentation according to the following three categories: landmarks at the turns (DP+), landmarks at the crossing paths (DP-), and landmarks not on the route. The accuracy of the recalled landmarks and the route were coded for each participant. Partial credits were given for partially correct recalls. Whenever a landmark was recalled but placed on a wrong intersection along the route, 0.25 credits were assigned. A quarter credits were also assigned when a wrong landmark was placed on a correct location. When a correct landmark was placed on a correct intersection but was placed on a wrong corner (e.g. on the left side instead of on the right), 0.75 credits were assigned.

The participants remembered very few landmarks that were not on the route (4% for the static route; 2% for the dynamic route); these were excluded from subsequent analyses. Using repeated measures design, the results showed that the DP+ landmarks were recalled better (72.4%) than the DP- landmarks (27.0%). $F(1,37) = 87.9$, $p < 0.001$. This finding confirmed that the participants overwhelmingly remembered the landmarks at the turns than other landmarks since they were most pertinent to route directions.

More relevant results were whether the presentation mode (i.e. static vs. dynamic) affected the recall memory. If the motion in the dynamic route guided participants' attention equally to the DP+ and DP- landmarks, it would increase the recall of landmarks along the route (DP-) and decrease the recall of landmarks at the turns

(DP+) relative to the static route. Additionally, the dynamic condition revealed the route piecemeal, taking away the "big picture" of the overall route and forcing the participants to attend to the moving dot to gather the route information. Despite the lack of "big picture" in the dynamic condition, the overall recall rate did not vary significantly across conditions (52.3% for static and 47.3% for dynamic). $F(1,37) = 1.53$, $p > 0.2$. The accuracy of the generated route seemed slightly better for the dynamic (85%) than for the static condition (74%) but the results were not significant. $\chi_1 = 0.77$, $p > 0.38$.

The results (Fig. 3) confirmed our hypothesis that the presentation mode would affect the type of landmarks recalled. $F(1,37) = 4.1$, $p < 0.05$. The difference in the recall rate between DP+ (turns) and DP- (non-turns) landmarks were greater for the static condition (80.0% for DP+; 24.6% for DP-) than for the dynamic condition (65.2% for DP+; 29.4% for DP-). As predicted, the dynamic route presentation reduced the recall rate of landmarks at the turns and increased the recall of landmarks along the route, suggesting that it guided the participants to attend less to the route relevant landmarks. However, the dynamic presentation did not completely override the task goals since they recalled the DP+ landmarks more often than the DP- landmarks.

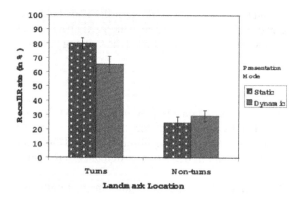

Fig. 3. Effects of presentation modes on the landmark recalls

In summary, the participants had a significantly greater recall of landmarks at the turns in the static condition, which suggests that they could freely allocate their attention to pertinent route information, which happened to be landmarks at turns (DP+). In the dynamic condition, however, the motion of the "imagined navigator" dot and the lack of the complete route information constrained the participants to allocate their attention more evenly along the route, resulting in a relatively even distribution of the recall rate for DP+ and DP- landmarks. As predicted, the mismatch between the attributes of motion in the dynamic route map and the route direction task, which requires selective attention to the turns, resulted in an inferior memory of the relevant route information in the dynamic presentation mode.

3   Combined Presentation Mode with Verbalization

The previous experiment demonstrated that animated objects in a dynamic display can reduce the task efficacy when the motion distracts the user from attending to the task relevant information. However, the experimental design raises further questions. The conclusion that the motion itself was the source of the memory difference between the static and dynamic condition was confounded by the fact that without the knowledge of the complete route in the dynamic condition, the participants did not have a choice of attending to the upcoming turn instead of the current location of the moving dot.

Hence, in this follow up study, we tried to overcome this shortcoming in two ways. First, we added a condition that combined the static and dynamic components of the route presentation by superimposing a moving dot on a solid line. In this presentation mode, the participants could take a divergent strategy to attend to either the static route or the moving dot. This combined mode is also closer to the actual presentation mode used in the current on-board navigations systems which have a "you are here" arrow that moves along a static route (see Fig. 1).

Second, we increased the speed of the presentation and let the participants view it multiple times. The increased speed seemed more "natural" to the users and the multiple presentations meant that the users could minimize the inherent disadvantage of the dynamic presentation since they could gain the knowledge of the overall route after the first presentation. To make sure that the participants attended to the route, we required them to give route directions during the viewing sessions.

3.1 Method

Participants. Sixty-one undergraduates, 26 male and 35 female, from Stanford University participated individually in partial fulfillment of a course requirement. The minimum criterion of 30% recall rate eliminated the data of three men and four women. The data of the remaining fifty-four participants were analyzed.

Materials and Procedure. We used the same map stimuli as in the previous experiment. The route in the map was presented statically, dynamically, or both. The combined condition presented static and dynamic route information by superimposing a moving dot on a solid line. The participants were assigned randomly to one of the three presentation conditions. They were asked to remember the route as they viewed the map. They were also asked to give route directions during the viewing sessions. They viewed it three times, for 1.5 minutes each. After they finished the verbalizations, they were given a map with only the street network and were asked to draw the route and all of the landmarks they could remember.

3.2 Results

The participants recalled landmarks at the turns (DP+) (57.7%) better than the landmarks at the non-turns (DP-) (48.2%). $F(1,51) = 5.33$, $p < 0.025$. However, the recall ratio between the DP+ and DP- landmarks was greatly reduced compared to the previous experiment. As in the first experiment, we had concerns that the dynamic condition was significantly harder than the static condition because participants had to reconstruct the route from a moving dot in dynamic condition. However, the total number of recalled landmarks did not differ significantly between conditions (51.6%, 51.4%, 56.1% for dynamic, static, and combined conditions, respectively; $F(2,51) = 0.56$, $p > 0.5$), suggesting that multiple presentations further minimized the recall difference between conditions. The accuracy of the generated route also did not vary significantly across conditions (78%, 68%, 71% for static, dynamic, and combined conditions, respectively). $\chi_2 = 0.44$, $p > 0.8$.

Fig. 4 illustrates the percentages of recalled landmarks when the route was shown statically, dynamically, or both. Analogous to the previous experiment, the DP+ and DP- landmarks were recalled more equally for the dynamic condition (52.0% for the turns; 50.9% for the non-turns) than the static condition (57.2% for the turns; 46.1% for the non-turns). Interestingly, when a moving dot was superimposed on top of a static route, participants recalled even more landmarks at turns (64.7%) than non-turns (47.5%). However, the interaction between landmark types (i.e. turns vs. non-turns) and presentation mode (i.e. static, dynamic, and combined) was not significant. $F(1,51) = 1.23$, $p > 0.3$. It seemed that the multiple presentations of the route and/or the verbalization of the route shifted the task focus to attend more to landmarks at non-turns across all conditions. Further investigation is needed to determine which factor(s) contributed to this shift.

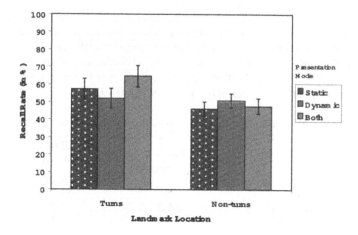

Fig. 4. Recall of landmarks for different presentation modes

Although the presentation mode did not significantly affect the recall memory, verbalization data supported the hypothesis that the static condition would allow more efficient allocation of attention to the pertinent landmarks than the dynamic condition. As expected, most of the landmarks at the turns (DP+) were verbalized in all conditions (80.6%, 90.7%, 91.2% for static, dynamic, and combined condition, respectively), confirming that the important landmarks in route directions were the ones at the turns. Interestingly, the static condition had fewer verbalizations of DP+ landmarks than the other two conditions. $\chi_2 = 7.01$, $p < 0.03$. A closer look at the data revealed that the reduction occurred because participants did not pace themselves properly during the session such that the time ran out before they could complete the verbalization of the route. The preset pace of the dynamic and combined presentations seemed to be an advantage over the static presentation mode.

Similarly, the landmarks at the non-turns (DP-) were verbalized at a lower rate in the static condition (30.6%) than in the dynamic (56.5%) or the combined condition (69.6%). $\chi_2 = 33.4$, $p < 0.001$. Low verbalization rate of DP- landmarks in the static condition was expected since route directions in general omitted these landmarks. Higher verbalization rate of DP- landmarks in the dynamic condition suggested that the verbalization of the route traced by the moving dot prompted the participants to mention more of the DP- landmarks. Interestingly, the combined condition resulted in the most verbalizations of DP- landmarks. The verbalization data suggest that the combination of static route and motion may have drawn more attention to all aspects of the route, including both DP+ and DP- landmarks, although this finding was not reflected in the recall data.

Although the verbalization rate for the DP- landmarks was the lowest for the static condition, the verbalized DP- landmarks were recalled better in the static condition (84.8%) than the dynamic (63.9%) or the combined condition (54.2) (see Table 1). $\chi_2 = 9.22$, $p < 0.01$. The participants in the static condition seemed to verbalize fewer DP- landmarks because these landmarks were less pertinent to route memory. The DP- landmarks that were verbalized may have been deemed important by the participants since they were recalled at a fairly high rate. In contrast, the dynamic and the combined conditions had higher verbalization rate of DP- landmarks, likely due to the motion. However, since the DP- landmarks were less important for the route, they were recalled less despite the higher rate of verbalizations. We failed to see a similar pattern for the DP+ landmarks, as the verbalized landmarks at the turns were not recalled differently across conditions (54.0%, 53.1%, and 62.4% for static, dynamic, and combined condition, respectively. $\chi_2 = 1.99$, $p > 0.39$.

Table 1. Verbalization and recall of verbalized DP- landmarks (non-turns)

	Verbalized DP- Landmarks	Recall of Verbalized DP- Landmarks
Static	**30.6**	**84.8**
Dynamic	**56.5**	**63.9**
Combined	**69.6**	**54.2**

The verbalization data suggest that the static condition was most efficient for the route memory task since participants verbalized (and presumably attended to) mostly the landmarks that they recalled later. Given this finding, we would have expected that the static condition would have the best recall of landmarks at turns, but the data suggest that the combined presentation mode showed potentially the highest recall of the landmarks at the turns, perhaps due to greater attention to all aspects of the route in this mode. We originally predicted that the combined condition would yield results that were somewhere between those of dynamic and static condition, since the availability of both the complete route and the moving dot would give participants a choice to segment either by following the moving dot or by using the static route. This potential benefit of combined presentation mode is noteworthy because the combined condition did not provide any additional information over the static or dynamic condition. Instead, the benefit resulted from directing attention to the route and providing a preset pace of learning as in the dynamic mode but also providing overall route structure like the static route.

4   Conclusions

We varied the presentation mode of routes in maps (i.e. dynamic vs. static) to examine how it affected the memory for landmarks at intersections. We predicted and found that landmarks at the key decision points (DP+) were remembered better after the static presentation of routes than the dynamic presentation, which constrained users to remember all landmarks more equally. Therefore, we concluded that static display of route information was preferable over dynamic display.

In the second study, the route was presented multiple times so that an inherent disadvantage of the dynamic route presentation was minimized. A combined static and dynamic presentation mode was also added to test if the users could take advantage of each mode. Verbalization data supported the claims in the first experiment. In the static presentation mode, the user attended mostly to the pertinent landmarks and the landmarks at the non-turning points were attended selectively for subsequent recall. In contrast, participants in the dynamic and combined presentation modes verbalized more often and indiscriminately, suggesting that the verbalization were driven partly by the motion in the display rather than the underlying task. The recall data failed to show significant interaction between presentation modes and landmark types, likely due to multiple presentations of the stimuli, but the data were consistent with the first experiment. The recall of DP+ landmarks also suggested that the combined presentation mode was more effective in directing users' attention to important cues.

The combined presentation mode can unite benefits of both types of displays. The static display allows users to organize the spatial information at hand more freely, applying principles acquired by everyday interaction with the environment, and it encourages a planning component. On the other hand, dynamically displayed information guides users along their way, reducing the stress to self–organize the amount of time available. The combination of different presentation modes and the resulting memory improvement for vital information add to findings regarding the benefits of redundant information display (Hirtle, 1999). In summary, the findings in this paper demonstrate the need for selectively choosing the appropriate presentation mode for the task at hand and encourage further research on the interaction of various information sources, especially their display by different modalities.

Acknowledgements. This research was supported by DAAD PKZ A-01-49336 to the first author and by the Deutsche Forschungsgemeinschaft (DFG) HA 1237-10, (Conceptualization processes in language production), and FR, 806-8 (Aspect maps) to the second and the third author.

References

Agrawala, M. & Stolte, C. (2001). Rending effective route maps: improving usability through generalization. *Proceedings of SIGGRAPH 2001*.

Baus, J., Ding, Y, Kray, C., & Walther, U. (2001). Towards adaptive location-aware mobile assistants. Workshop notes on the IJCAI 2001 workshop on Artificial Intelligence in Mobile Systems.

Bartram, L. & Ware, C. (2002). Filtering and brushing with motion. *Information Visualization*.1(1), 66–79.

Denis, M. (1997). The description of routes: A cognitive approach to the production of spatial discourse. *Cahiers de Psychologie Cognitive, 16,* 409–458.

Hegarty, M., Quilici, J., Narayanan, N. H., Holmquist, S., & Moreno, R. (1999). Multimedia instruction: Lesson from evaluation of a theory-based design. *Journal of Educational Multimedia and Hypermedia, 8,* 119–150.

Hirtle, S. C. (1999). The use of maps, images, and "gestures" for navigation (pp. 31–40). In C. Freksa, W. Brauer, C. Habel, K.F. Wender (eds.). *Spatial cognition II, integrating abstract theories, empirical studies, formal methods, and practical applications.* Springer: Berlin.

Jackson, P. G. (1998). In search for better route guidance instructions. *Ergonomics, 41*(7), 1000–1013.

Klippel, A., Tappe, H., & Habel, C. (in press). Pictorial representations of routes: Chunking route segments during comprehension. In C. Freksa, W. Brauer, C. Habel & K. Wender (eds.), *Spatial Cognition III.* Berlin: Springer.

Palmiter, S., & Elkerton, J. (1993). Animated demonstrations for learning procedural computer-based tasks. *Human-Computer Interaction, 8*(3), 193–216.

Tappe, H., & Habel, C. (1998). Verbalization of dynamic sketch maps: Layers of representation in the conceptualization of Drawing Events. *Poster at Cognitive Science Conference.* Madison WI.

Lee, P. U. & Tversky, B. (in preparation). Keeping the "goodness" in good directions and maps.

Tversky, B., Morrison, J. B., & Betrancourt, M. (2002). Animation: can it facilitate? *International Journal of Human-Computer Studies, 57,* 247–262.

Ward, S.L., Newcombe, N., & Overton, W.F. (1986). Turn left at the church or three miles north: A study of direction giving and sex differences. *Environment and Behavior, 18,* 192–213.

Zacks, J., Tversky, B., & Iyer, G. (2001). Perceiving, remembering, and communicating structure in events. *Journal of Experimental Psychology: General, 130,* 29–58.

Pointing and Visual Feedback for Spatial Interaction in Large-Screen Display Environments

Barry A. Po, Brian D. Fisher, and Kellogg S. Booth

Department of Computer Science, University of British Columbia
201-2366 Main Mall
Vancouver, British Columbia, Canada
{po, fisher, ksbooth}@cs.ubc.ca

Abstract. The two visual systems hypothesis in neuroscience suggests that pointing without visual feedback may be less affected by spatial visual illusions than cognitive interactions such as judged target location. Our study examined predictions of this theory for target localization on a large-screen display. We contrasted pointing interactions under varying levels of visual feedback with location judgments of targets that were surrounded by an offset frame. As predicted by the theory, the frame led to systematic errors in verbal report of target location but not in pointing without visual feedback for some participants. We also found that pointing with visual feedback produced a similar level of error as location judgments, while temporally lagged visual feedback appeared to reduce these errors somewhat. This suggests that pointing without visual feedback may be a useful interaction technique in situations described by the two visual systems literature, especially with large-screen displays and immersive environments.

1   Introduction and Background

Two-dimensional pointing plays a central role in our day-to-day interaction with desktop user interfaces. Three-dimensional pointing enables spatial interaction with objects in non-desktop interfaces such as large-scale collaborative workspaces. Designers rely on pointing as an interaction technique because it is commonly believed that the usability of complex applications is enhanced by employing interactions that mirror familiar gestures.

Common intuition tells us that visual feedback helps make pointing an effective method of interaction. Current design practices reflect a belief that pointing becomes unreliable when it is uncoupled from visual feedback in display environments, especially when there are multiple potential targets. However, studies from psychology tell us that our intuition is not always correct, and in particular that visual feedback can degrade pointing performance if certain circumstances exist.

Our research has examined the influence of varying levels of visual feedback on target selection in a large-screen graphical display environment. The first

A. Butz et al. (Eds.): Smart Graphics 2003, LNCS 2733, pp. 22–38, 2003.

step in our research was a pilot study that successfully reproduced the previous laboratory findings of Bridgeman et al. [2], but in a setting more representative of collaborative and immersive display environments. This demonstrated that a displaced frame surrounding a target will cause some participants to make systematic errors in verbally reported location judgments but not in pointing without visual feedback (also known as "open-loop" pointing in experimental psychology). The classic work on this is known as the Induced Roelofs Effect [2, 18], part of the theoretical framework for our research.

After our pilot study, we designed a larger study with four conditions, the first two the same as in Bridgeman's work, in order to examine the impact of multiple visual representations on two additional interaction conditions: pointing with a fast-response visible cursor and pointing with a slow-response (temporally lagged) visible cursor. These conditions were identified as pointing with visual feedback and pointing with lagged visual feedback respectively.

We tested for the presence of the Induced Roelofs Effect and found differences across the four conditions consistent with the theoretical predictions. In the remainder of this section, we provide background material on the problems that we are addressing, related work, and the theoretical framework for our research. We then describe our study and results, followed by a closing discussion and future work, with implications for the design and implementation of spatial interaction techniques in large-screen display environments.

1.1   Feedback in Spatial Interaction

Contrary to our intuition, there is considerable evidence to suggest that visual feedback may not positively affect user performance in all display environments and interactive situations. A study of object selection and positioning by Poupyrev et al. [17] indicates that visual feedback does not always improve user performance, particularly in situations where users are in close proximity to the display. Hayne et al. [6] report that the use of visual feedback has potential drawbacks in shared display systems, where visual feedback may take the form of multiple cursors that compete for valuable display space and obscure informative parts of the display. Wolf and Rhyne [22] further observe that maintaining real-time visual feedback significantly increases the workload of network and processor resources.

Even if we believe that these particular disadvantages are insignificant compared to the apparent advantage of visual feedback, there are other potential concerns that should give us pause when we consider the use of visual feedback in large-screen display environments. In instances where a large group of users are concurrently interacting with a large-scale display, it is possible that the presence of a multiplicity of cursors may make it difficult for users to keep track of a particular user's cursor. Additionally, the presence of one or more visible cursors may draw attention away from other, more important display items, especially when the cursors move or change state.

Thus, it seems that the presence of visual feedback of pointer position has potential drawbacks, and that removing that feedback might alleviate those concerns. Unfortunately, it is not known how the removal of visual feedback would affect overall user performance in large-screen display environments. While most users achieve similar and adequate levels of performance when pointing with visual feedback, it is reasonable to expect higher error and greater individual differences in the accuracy and precision of pointing without visual feedback. Thus, the current practice of providing visual feedback at least appears to help equalize performance across a larger user population with a wide range of pointing abilities.

1.2   Voice as a Substitute for Pointing

Given the difficulties that surround pointing and other gestural interactions, we might attempt to sidestep these kinds of issues altogether by using alternative methods of interaction. One alternative that has been proposed for advanced applications is voice command, using voice recognition technology to support system interaction. For many years, researchers have worked toward introducing reliable voice input technology into user interfaces [9]. There is a substantial body of literature that documents advancements in speech and voice recognition technology, and a variety of user studies that report enhanced performance of voice-activated interfaces relative to, and in conjunction with, conventional input devices such as keyboards and mice [3,16].

Assuming that the speed and accuracy of voice recognition technology continues to advance, Oviatt and Cohen [15] suggest that vocal interaction may someday be more efficient and accessible. They advocate a mixed approach to interaction, where users can choose between vocal localization and spatial interaction in complex multimodal interfaces. However, aside from the many existing technical concerns, there are also open questions about the inherent effectiveness and reliability of voice-based interfaces. As we will see, verbally reported location judgments can be subject to visual illusions, more than some motor responses, so pointing still seems to be our best choice for interaction in large-screen display environments.

1.3   Pointing for Large-Screen Displays

The use of laser pointers as tools for interaction in large-scale collaborative environments has established pointing as an important research topic, particularly for shared displays and large-scale systems. Kirstein and Muller [10] demonstrate how a camera-based approach can be used to acquire laser projections for display interaction. Oh and Stuerzlinger [13] expand upon this work, describing a system that permits multiple laser pointers to be used in a Single Display Groupware (SDG) environment. In a comparison with other devices for spatial interaction, including touch-screen styli and conventional mice, Myers et al. [12] note that laser pointers present serious technical and user performance challenges.

Limitations with laser pointers, and presumably other similar pointing devices, are most apparent in the difficulties that surround object selection through button press and the reduction of individual hand jitter [14,21]. Fortunately, continual advances in our understanding of gesture interaction and improvements in physical device design (grip style, form factor, etc.) should eventually make it possible for laser pointers and other pointing devices to overcome many of these physical limitations.

1.4   Cognitive Factors in Spatial Interaction

Formal predictive models of user interaction such as Fitts Law [5] have provided us with an understanding of the spatial and motor factors that limit users' abilities to perform spatial interactions in a variety of situations. We have a comparatively poorer understanding of the cognitive perceptual factors that affect our capacity to execute motor movements in complex display environments. It is clear that the impact of visual feedback on spatial interaction is complex. Previous studies have provided evidence of a strong connection between the perceptual structure of visual information in an interactive display environment and the control structures of the input devices that facilitate interaction [8,20]. Other perceptual phenomena associated with control actions, such as kinesthetic and proprioceptive feedback, also affect spatial interactions in large-screen display environments [1,7].

Research in experimental psychology and functional neuroanatomy provides substantial evidence for cognitive relationships between visual perception and motor action that could affect performance in interactive systems. Central to this is a model of human cognition and motor processes that is known as the two visual systems hypothesis [2,11,19]. The hypothesis claims that visually-guided action can be mediated by either or both of two separate mental representations of space: a cognitive representation, which generates a world-relative view of visually-perceived objects in surrounding space, and a sensorimotor representation, which generates an egocentric view of these same objects. These representations have been isolated in different areas of the brain, primarily through work with brain-damaged patients who lack one of the two systems [11].

The two visual systems hypothesis states that the process of spatial motor interaction draws from two independent mental representations of the visual world, with different performance characteristics. The cognitive representation of space is susceptible to a large set of visual illusions and perceptual phenomena (i.e. the Induced Roelofs Effect, described below) that may bias performance based upon visual representation. In contrast, the sensorimotor representation of space is believed to be less susceptible to these illusory artifacts, but is also thought to have less information overall. The hypothesis further postulates that the two representations of space are informationally encapsulated, and that only one of the representations of space is typically active in configuring the execution of a particular spatial interaction.

Past studies in experimental psychology show that the choice of mental representation that is used in a particular spatial motor interaction, such as pointing, is strongly influenced by the level of visual feedback that is provided to participants [2,11]. These studies also suggest that spatial references to objects through a non-motor interaction will consistently draw from the cognitive representation of space, with the result that non-motor interactions are highly subject to perceptual biases by a broad range of visual illusions.

Perhaps one of the best examples of how the two visual systems influence task performance is the classic experiment by Milner and Goodale [11] with "blindsight" patients who could do reaching and grasping tasks accurately even in the presence of cues that would ordinarily override the sensorimotor system with the inaccurate cognitive system. Without access to the normally dominant cognitive representation of space, "blindsight" patients rely solely on the sensorimotor representation of space and thus are not affected by these cues.

1.5   The Induced Roelofs Effect

The Induced Roelofs Effect [18] is one example of a much larger class of visual display illusions that have been found to selectively bias cognitive representations of visual space. Other illusions such as apparent motion and the motion aftereffect often produce similar effects. Because of the simplicity and effectiveness of the Induced Roelofs Effect we chose to use it as the basis for our current study. This illusion affects the ability of individuals to correctly perceive the spatial positions of presented targets in relatively sparse environments.

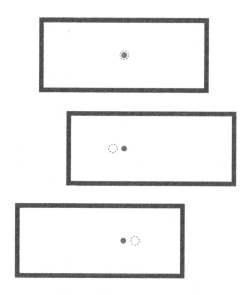

Fig. 1. The Induced Roelofs Effect. When a frame is offset, it appears that a target within the frame is more to the left or right than it really is. Solid circles are actual target positions, while dashed circles are observed reports of target position.

The illusion can be described as a systematic bias in the perceived location of targets that are presented within a rectangular frame that is offset to the left or to the right of a target. When a target and rectangular frame are presented simultaneously, and the frame is offset to the left, there is a tendency to perceive the presented target to be further to the right than it actually is. Likewise, when the frame is offset to the right, there is a tendency to perceive the presented target as being further to the left than it actually is. When the frame is centered, there is no effect. Figure 1 illustrates this by showing the relationship between targets (solid circles) and their perceived locations (dashed circles) in the presence of offset frames.

Because the basic characteristics of the Induced Roelofs Effect are present in many graphical applications (either explicit frames, or display objects that may be perceived as implicit frames), it is possible that this visual illusion may exert some influence in large-screen display environments where the position of the frame varies over time. Related illusions such as apparent motion and the motion after-effect can also be created when virtual camera motion creates large visual flow fields (e.g. in a flythrough with an off-axis point of interest or a long pan).

From the two visual systems hypothesis, we can predict that a cognitive visual system response measure such as verbal report of target location will be more sensitive to the Induced Roelofs Effect than will a sensorimotor visual system response measure such as pointing with no cursor and an unseen hand. The first two conditions in our study test this prediction and essentially replicate Bridgeman et al. [2], but in a setting more typical of large-screen collaborative environments.

1.6   Predictions for HCI

The classic empirical studies of the two visual systems hypothesis in psychology laboratories were conducted in environments devoid of visual feedback to more clearly differentiate between the two systems and demonstrate their autonomy. In applying this theory to HCI we focus instead on the impact of multiple visual representations on the performance of tasks that are characteristic of large display systems, such as pointing with a cursor that may or may not lag the pointer position in time.

Thus, in our extension of earlier psychology studies we predict that pointing will draw from the cognitive representation (and hence exhibit the illusion) only if sufficient visual feedback is provided, in our case by a visible cursor. This prediction is counterintuitive, as it postulates poorer performance with visual feedback present than with it absent. A lagged cursor can be considered an intermediate condition, since the correspondence between pointer motion and cursor motion is less convincing. This leads to our second counterintuitive prediction, that a cursor with a large temporal lag may in fact improve user performance relative to more responsive feedback. We note that these predictions are true only under a specific set of display conditions that are described by the two visual systems hypothesis.

If our mapping of the two visual systems hypothesis onto HCI is correct, then the choice of interaction method and the perceptual feedback that is provided to users are influential components in determining which of the two visual representations is used. If this is borne out by experimental evidence, we may wish to choose interaction techniques that selectively utilize the sensorimotor representation in conditions where visual illusions are likely. This should lead to more precise performance in some cases, despite the lower overall accuracy of the sensorimotor system. We might then investigate ways to improve the accuracy of that system. These will be discussed later in this paper. First, we present our experimental study.

2   Method

Our study tested our predictions with a within-subjects methodology by using a large-scale display environment that is typical of collaborative situations and interactive large-screen display environments. We used a simple target acquisition task to provide a situation where vocal localization and spatial motor interaction might be equally feasible methods of interaction.

Participants completed four blocks of trials that required them to acquire targets through either voice selection or motor pointing in the presence of a centered or an offset frame. The voice selection versus pointing without visual feedback conditions replicate Bridgeman et al. [2] in our experimental setup, while the pointing with visual feedback and lagged visual feedback conditions extend the methodology to more familiar interactive systems. We are currently unaware of any studies, from experimental psychology or elsewhere, that have looked at pointing with rendered visual feedback in the context of this cognitive-motor model.

2.1   Design

Each participant attended a single, individual session between one and a half hours to two hours in duration. There were four blocks of 54 trials each, with each block characterized by a different method of interaction that changed how a participant indicated the perceived position of a displayed target. The first block (i.e. condition) did not involve pointing.

– A simple voice protocol for selecting specific targets was used. Since this technique was considered inherently cognitive, interaction of this kind was called cognitive report. All of the participants started their sessions with this method of interaction.

The other three conditions used continuous spatial pointing with varying degrees of visual feedback.

– A spatial pointing measure without visual feedback of any kind was called pointing without visual feedback. The lack of visual feedback eliminated any possibility of making cognitive corrections to the pointing gestures that were being made, effectively breaking the relationship between action and visual perception of that action.

- A spatial pointing measure with visual feedback in the form of a small cursor was called pointing with visual feedback. This is similar to what is normally provided in typical interactive environments.
- As a final exploratory measure, we tested the effects of spatial pointing in the context of unreliable visual feedback. This was done by inducing a one-half second lag to the same rendered cursor that was used in the previous pointing with visual feedback condition, effectively creating a pointing with lagged visual feedback condition. The reason for using such a large amount of lag was not to simulate the interactive lag seen in typical interactive systems, but rather to identify any potential influence of lag on cognitive performance.

To ensure that there would be no unwanted order effects between the pointing without visual feedback and pointing with visual feedback conditions, the order of these two methods of interaction were counterbalanced across participants. All participants ended their sessions with the pointing with lagged visual feedback condition.

2.2   Participants

We recruited fourteen participants between the ages of 17 and 31 to participate. Seven of the participants were male, and seven of the participants were female. All of the participants had normal or corrected-to-normal vision. Twelve of the participants were right-handed, while the remaining two participants were left-handed.

2.3   Apparatus

For each session, participants were seated and centered in front of a three-screen projection display arranged in an angled configuration at a distance of two and a half meters. During this study, only the center screen of the three screens was used. Figure 2 is a photograph of the experimental environment. The active display screen was forward-projected, with a width of 2.75 meters and a height of 2.15 meters. With the exception of illumination from the active screen, all other light sources were extinguished during the sessions. An experimenter was present at all times during all of the sessions.

A PC workstation and a custom software application were used to render trials, to control the flow of each session, and to record quantitative data from participating participants. A six degree-of-freedom Polhemus Fastrak with an attached stylus and a second passive receiver was used to provide spatial interaction for the study. The stylus was used as a pointing implement that was similar in size and shape to a pen or laser pointer. The passive receiver was attached to a plastic helmet as a head-tracking device. To ensure that the performance of the Fastrak would not be impeded by environmental interference, most of the equipment used in the experiment was non-metallic in nature, and all possible sources of metallic interference were kept away from the display environment.

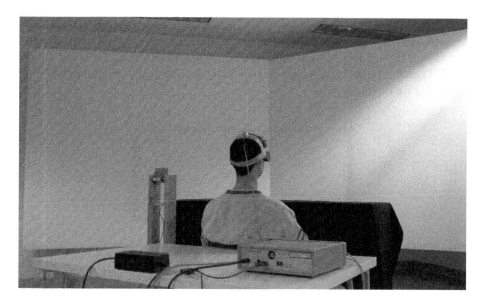

Fig. 2. The room set up that was used during the user study. Participants kept their hands and arms underneath a table set directly in front of them. They also wore a pair of stereo glasses and a head tracker. Spatial interaction was provided by a Polhemus Fastrak and an attached stylus. During the actual sessions, all ambient lighting was extinguished and an experimenter was always present.

In order to limit visual feedback to only the feedback provided on the display, participants were asked to keep their arms and hands out of their own sight at all times by placing them underneath a large, wooden table with a width of 1.2 meters, a length of 0.80 meters, and a height of 0.95 meters. Although no stereoscopic imagery or head-coupled perspectives were used in the present study, participants were required to wear a pair of active stereo glasses and the head-tracked plastic helmet at all times. This particular requirement is intended to support comparison between this study and future planned investigations using stereo and head coupling; similarly, the presence of three screens is for consistency with future studies of wide-angle displays.

2.4   Procedure

Trials began with the presentation of a small circular target, 0.5 degrees of visual angle in diameter, in one of three positions on the display. Targets were either directly ahead of participants or displaced 1.5 degrees to their left or right. The circular targets were surrounded by a rectangular frame, 21.0 degrees in width, 9.0 degrees in height, and 1.0 degree in line thickness. The frame also appeared in one of three offsets: aligned symmetrically to participants' midline, or offset asymmetrically by 4.0 degrees to the left or to the right. Both target and frame were rendered on a black background. This simultaneous presentation of frame and target lasted for a period of exactly one second, after which all stimuli were extinguished and the task was performed. Participants were asked to specify the location of the previously presented target either immediately, or after a four second delay. Figure 3 illustrates the five targets used in practice trials (color is not accurate in the figure).

Fig. 3. The five target positions used in our study. Targets were 0.5 degrees in visual angle and were spaced apart by 1.5 degrees from one another. These targets were surrounded by a rectangular frame, 21.0 degrees in width, 9.0 degrees in height, and 1.0 degree in line width. Only one of the five targets was displayed for any given trial.

These conditions resulted in eighteen trial types: three target positions by three frame offsets at two response delays. All trial types were repeated three times in random order for a total of 54 trials per block.

Each block of 54 experimental trials was preceded by a set of practice trials that gave participants an opportunity to familiarize themselves with the possible responses for each condition. Practice trials had five possible targets, the three used in the experimental trials and two additional locations 1.5 degrees to the left of the left target (Far Left), and 1.5 degrees to the right of the right target (Far Right). The far left and far right responses were provided to give participants practice responding to experimental targets that might appear to be at a greater eccentricity than their actual positions as a result of the Induced Roelofs Effect (see below). Practice trials began with a set of randomized target-only presentations, followed by successive sets of randomized target presentations with a frame fixed in the non-offset position. Participants were provided with a minimum of fifteen practice trials for each interaction technique.

Cognitive Report Condition. Cognitive report interaction was simulated in a Wizard of Oz fashion by the experimenter. After presentation of a particular target and frame offset, participants would respond with one of five verbal responses: "Far Left," "Left," "Center," "Right," and "Far Right." Upon hearing a participant's response, the experimenter recorded the response using the experiment software.

The Far Left and Far Right responses were provided to allow participants to respond naturally in conditions where the Induced Roelofs Effect might make it appear as if the targets were at a greater eccentricity than their actual positions (i.e. when target and frame offsets were in opposing directions).

Pointing Conditions. Pointing was performed with the Fastrak stylus. When asked to respond after the presentation of particular target and frame offsets, participants would respond by making an aiming response. When participants were satisfied with their final aiming position, they were asked to hold the stylus position until an audible indication was provided after a period of approximately two seconds. Such a "point-and-dwell" mechanism has been previously suggested to reduce artifacts that result from button presses related to object selection with laser pointers and other pointing implements (the "pen-drop" phenomenon [14]).

3   Results

Participant data that were collected during the study were analyzed in two ways. We explain each analysis before presenting the data. We initially performed a 4 (report) x 3 (target) x 3 (offset) x 2 (response delay) analysis of variance on the data for each subject. No effects were found for response delay, which was a condition included for compatibility with Bridgeman's earlier study [2]. We therefore collapsed the response delay conditions, resulting in six trials for every cell instead of just three.

3.1   Primary Analysis

Two-way ANOVAs tested participant response against independent factors of target position and frame offset and a single dependent factor of participant response. These analyses were run for each participant for the collapsed response delay and each interaction technique to enable inter-subject comparison of the presence or absence of an effect.

For cognitive report, participant responses were one of the five previously described verbal choices. For the pointing measure, participant responses were recorded as the position on the screen where a line projected along the axis of the pointing device would intersect the screen. We note that this measure was some transformation of the intended position, as participants typically point in a body-centric frame (e.g. shoulder or head-centered) rather than an artifact-centric one. In an interactive system it is possible to rescale these measures to translate between user and system coordinates. Only the horizontal (x) coordinate was used in the analysis.

The two-way ANOVAs enabled us to statistically test for the presence or absence of the Induced Roelofs Effect in each participant and condition. In this analysis, presence of the visual illusion would be reflected in a main effect for frame offset that was not complicated by a significant interaction with target position. Presence of a main effect for frame offset in most subjects would support our hypothesis.

3.2   Secondary Analysis

We performed an alternate analysis that set an absolute threshold criterion for the number of trials in which participants were deemed to exhibit the Induced Roelofs Effect. This was done as follows.

For the cognitive report condition, the categorical data was used directly. For each of the three pointing conditions, a separate analysis was made for each participant of the errors in target location for trials that involved offset frames. This was performed in two stages. The first stage, repeated for each of the three pointing conditions, considered only the trials for which the frame was not offset. The mean and standard deviation of a participant's response (the x-coordinate of where the participant pointed on the screen) were computed for each of the three presented target positions (recall that "Far Left" and "Far Right" were never presented in experimental trials).

The second stage used these values to categorize the remaining trails (those with offset frames) as being either a Roelofs trial or a non-Roelofs trial. An offset trial was considered to be Roelofs if the participant's response (x-coordinate) was more than one standard deviation to the left (when the frame is offset right - but to the right when the frame is offset left) of the mean non-offset response for that participant for that target position in that condition. A similar categorization was used for trials without offset frames, which were considered to be non-Roelofs if the response was not within one standard deviation of the mean.

A participant was considered to have exhibited Roelofs behavior if more than 50% of the offset trials were Roelofs and less than 50% of the non-offset trials were non-Roelofs. This criterion can be paraphrased by saying that the participant had to make an error at least half of the time in the predicted direction when the frame was offset and had to be close to the correct position at least half of the time when no error was anticipated. The choice of a 50% threshold and the choice of one standard deviation for categorization is arbitrary, but its application is automatic, involving no subjective judgments by the experimenter.

By setting an arbitrary cutoff for the presence or absence of the Induced Roelofs Effect for particular participants, we have a rough indication of which of the two mental representations of space was probably used for the task. We predicted that cognitive report and pointing with visual feedback would demonstrate an Induced Roelofs Effect due to their common use of the cognitive representation of space. We also predicted that pointing without visual feedback would not demonstrate an effect of the illusion, since lack of visual feedback should motivate use of the sensorimotor representation of space.

3.3   Summary of the Data

All of the participants under all of the different interaction techniques were observed to have highly significant main effects of target position, as would be expected if they were performing the task as instructed. Figure 4 presents a summary of the results of the ANOVAs (the primary analysis) and the proportion of trials where responses were consistent with an Induced Roelofs Effect (the

secondary analysis). The figure gives individual p-values from the ANOVAs and
the percentage of trials that were judged to show the effect.

Participant Number	Cognitive Report (Vocal Interaction)		Pointing Without Visual Feedback		Pointing With Visual Feedback		Pointing w/ Lagged Visual Feedback	
1	0.454	5.6%	0.577	30.6%	0.834	27.8%	0.291	27.8%
2	0.465	8.3%	0.821	25.0%	0.838	13.9%	0.359	22.2%
3	0.387	5.6%	0.789	33.3%	0.838	27.8%	0.898	38.9%
4	0.178	16.7%	0.936	33.3%	0.834	30.6%	0.084	36.1%
5	0.001 *	100.0%	0.923	33.3%	0.037 *	41.7%	0.961	25.0%
6	0.001 *	75.0%	0.011 *	33.3%	0.488	19.4%	0.021*	33.3%
7	0.001 *	100.0%	0.841	27.8%	0.002 *	55.6%	0.074	27.8%
8	0.001 *	100.0%	0.084	38.9%	0.001 *	63.9%	0.008*	86.1%
9	0.001 *	94.4%	0.001 *	44.4%	0.037 *	77.8%	0.094	41.7%
10	0.001 *	88.9%	0.126	47.2%	0.001 *	83.3%	0.005*	94.4%
11	0.001 *	100.0%	0.001 *	38.9%	0.001 *	75.0%	0.030*	38.9%
12	0.001 *	83.3%	0.177	47.2%	0.001 *	61.1%	0.021*	77.8%
13	0.001 *	88.9%	0.281	30.6%	0.028 *	52.8%	0.147	36.1%
14	0.001 *	88.9%	0.013 *	38.9%	0.294	44.4%	0.002*	44.4%
Means		67.9%		35.9%		48.2%		45.0%

Fig. 4. A summary of individual participant performance in the study. The p-values
with asterisks (*) indicate that a particular participant had an observed main effect of
frame position for a particular interaction technique. Corresponding numerical values
indicate the percentage of frame-displaced trials that were judged to exhibit the Induced Roelofs Effect for a particular participant with a particular interaction technique.
Statistically significant values are highlighted in bold.

In the discussion that follows, we follow a standard practice in experimental psychophysics and report the smallest F-values for significant results, and
the largest F-values for non-significant results. For main effects of target position, we have $[F(2, 18) > 4.214, p < 0.032]$, indicating that each participant's
trial responses were consistent and reliable across all conditions. The interesting
analyses were for frame offset.

Cognitive report was found to be most sensitive to the Induced Roelofs Effect,
with ten of the fourteen participants exhibiting significant main effects of frame
offset $[F(2, 18) > 4.460, p < 0.027]$. For these participants, the mean magnitude
of the effect was measured to be roughly one discrete target position from the
actual presented target positions. These results were echoed in the percentages
of trials that were judged to exhibit the visual illusion, where these participants
were observed to easily surpass the defined criteria.

Those four participants who did not exhibit an Induced Roelofs Effect in
cognitive report also consistently exhibited no significant illusory effects in any

of the other remaining conditions. There is a particularly interesting division between those participants who either did or did not exhibit the effect. Participants who exhibited a significant effect quite consistently did so, while those who did not quite consistently did not. These observations suggest that despite expected differences in individual participants susceptibility to the illusion, the observed effects are consistent for each participant, and are not due to noise in participant responses.

Of the ten participants who exhibited an Induced Roelofs Effect for cognitive report, six were found to have no effect when asked to respond by pointing without visual feedback $[F(2,18) < 2.845, p > 0.084]$. This is consistent with our hypothesis that some participants utilize different representations of space for different interaction techniques. The remaining four participants who did show significant effects may have continued to draw from their cognitive representation of space to accomplish the target acquisition task (earlier research also observed some subjects who failed to exhibit any effect [2]). Nevertheless, the percentage of trials that were judged to exhibit the Induced Roelofs Effect demonstrates that there is a marked drop in the number of participant responses that were affected by the visual illusion. In particular, a chi-square test against the trials from cognitive report across all of the participants confirms that there is a highly significant difference $[(1, N = 14) = 12.6, p < 0.001]$ in illusory influence between cognitive report and pointing without visual feedback.

Interestingly, of the six participants who exhibited an Induced Roelofs Effect for cognitive report but not for pointing without visual feedback, all six exhibited a significant effect when asked to respond by pointing with visual feedback $[F(2,18) > 3.850, p < 0.05]$. This appears to suggest that pointing with visual feedback is more susceptible to illusory effects than pointing without visual feedback, which is entirely consistent with our hypothesis that visual feedback motivates the use of the cognitive representation of space. Once again, these effects are reflected by the percentage of trials that were judged to exhibit the Induced Roelofs Effect, which is noticeably higher than the count observed in pointing without visual feedback. A chi-square test against the trials from vocal interaction across all of the participants found no significant difference between vocal interaction and pointing with visual feedback $[(1, N = 14) = 1.4, p = 0.237]$, suggesting that these two interaction techniques share similar susceptibility to the illusion.

If we distinguish between accuracy and precision of different interaction techniques, another interesting result strongly indicates that pointing without visual feedback is consistent and reliable - it is reasonably precise, although its overall accuracy is generally much poorer than pointing with some level of visual feedback. In an analysis of individual pointing data without visual feedback, it was apparent that most of the errors could be attributed to a consistent bias along the horizontal axis, and that these errors of variance can be characterized as rescaled versions of the variance seen in the corresponding pointing trials with visual feedback. This may reflect participants' choice of a particular body-centered frame for the pointing task.

Our final analysis looked at pointing with lagged visual feedback. We found that only three participants out of the six who showed effects in pointing with and without visual feedback also showed an Induced Roelofs Effect with this interaction technique. A chi-square test against the trials from vocal interaction also demonstrates a significant difference $[(1, N = 14) = 5.6, p = 0.018]$. This suggests that the susceptibility of lagged visual feedback to the Induced Roelofs Effect is intermediate between pointing with purely reliable visual feedback and no visual feedback at all, and it is less susceptible than vocal interaction. However, there are several other factors, especially the lack of counterbalancing between this interaction technique and the other studied techniques, which could have contributed to this finding, and so we cannot reach firm conclusions about interactive lag based on these data.

3.4   Sex Differences

One unexpected finding was a sex difference between participants who exhibited an Induced Roelofs Effect for cognitive report. Only three of the seven male participants demonstrated a significant Induced Roelofs Effect in this condition, while all seven female participants demonstrated the effect. Subsequent t-tests testing gender against the different interaction conditions confirmed this effect for vocal interaction (t=2.828, p=0.030), but were not significant for other interaction techniques. We might interpret such a difference as the result of different levels of contextual influence in the environment. It seems possible that males may be less sensitive than females to context in location judgments under some conditions.

4   Discussion and Future Work

Our results suggest that the selection and implementation of spatial interaction techniques should take into account cognitive factors that may introduce performance errors. Such errors may be unacceptable for safety-critical applications, or where errors of interaction are not easily correctable, or where such errors may go unnoticed.

Visual illusions are an increasing concern when we move away from desktop environments to other, less-constrained environments, such as large-screen displays. The Induced Roelofs Effect is one example of an influential visual illusion, and other illusions that affect motion or size-contrast perception may have stronger effects. Being aware of these cognitive factors may help us design future environments and applications that are robust against such effects.

Our study manipulated frame offset to obtain an Induced Roelofs Effect. We believe that perceptual effects similar to this particular visual illusion are possible in a variety of display situations. For example, an Induced Roelofs Effect might occur when large background objects, perceived as framing a scene, move as a result of changes in rendered data or changes in viewpoint. In collaborative display applications, where interaction is shared by multiple users, instances may arise where one individual user moves an object that serves as a perceived frame for another user.

In exocentric target acquisition environments, such as advanced air traffic control displays, multiple targets may be grouped within a very small display area, surrounded by contextual cues that might bias perceived spatial position. For these displays, updates may not occur at fully interactive rates, nor necessarily synchronously, and users may attempt to acquire targets by using past spatial perceptions as predictors to improve target tracking, thereby creating an environment that is similar in many key respects to the experimental one we have used. Situations such as these effectively create stimuli whose underlying perceptual effects are similar to those used in this study. Thus, at least where voice command or pointing with visual feedback are concerned, we can expect to see the kinds of errors that occurred in the present study.

Our findings suggest that pointing without visual feedback is a potentially viable technique for spatial interaction with large-screen display environments that should be seriously considered. Pointing without visual feedback solves the problems with multiple cursors that can arise from collaborative interaction with large-scale shared displays. Pointing without visual feedback also appears to minimize the impact of perceptual artifacts and visual illusions on user performance. Compensating for the relatively poor accuracy of pointing without visual feedback is the most significant obstacle to using it as a spatial interaction technique. Our finding that much of the error in pointing without visual feedback has a consistent bias suggests that future work might examine how we can correct for individual differences in order to make pointing without visual feedback a more useful spatial interaction technique.

5   Conclusion

Our comparison of different techniques for spatial interaction with a large-scale interactive display suggests that pointing without visual feedback may be a viable technique that should be considered when developing applications for large-screen display environments. Using the Induced Roelofs Effect as an example of a class of illusions described by the two visual systems hypothesis, we established a differential impact of the illusion on different interaction conditions and for different individuals. Inherently non-motor interactions, such as cognitive report (voice response), were most susceptible to this illusion, while pointing without visual feedback was least susceptible. Several issues remain to be explored, motivating future investigations into interaction techniques that minimize the use of visual feedback in large-screen environments where these kinds of perceptual illusions are likely to occur.

References

1. Balakrishnan, R., Hinckley K.: The Role of Kinesthetic Reference Frames in Two-Handed Input Performance. UIST 1999, ACM Symposium on User Interface Software and Technology (1999) 171–178

2. Bridgeman, B., Peery, S., Anand, S.: Interaction of Cognitive and Sensorimotor Maps of Visual Space. Perception and Psychophysics, Vol.59, No. 3 (1997) 456–469
3. Christian, K., Kules, B., Shneiderman, B., Youssef, A.: A Comparison of Voice Controlled and Mouse Controlled Web Browsing. ASSETS 2000, 72–79
4. Cooper, C.: Visual Dominance and the Control of Action. Proceedings of the 20th Annual Conference of the Cognitive Science Society (1998), 250–255
5. Fitts, P. M.: The Information Capacity of the Human Motor System in Controlling Amplitude of Movement. Journal of Experimental Psychology, Vol. 47 (1956) 381–391
6. Hayne, S., Pendergast, M., Greenberg, S.: Gesturing Through Cursors: Implementing Multiple Pointers in Group Support Systems. Proceedings of the Hawaii International Conference on System Sciences (1993)
7. Hinckley, K., Pausch, R., Proffitt, D.: Attention and Visual Feedback: The Bimanual Frame of Reference. 1997 ACM Symposium on Interactive 3D Graphics (1997) 121–126
8. Jacob, R. J. K., Sibert, L. E., McFarlane, D. C., Mullen, M. P.: Integrality and Separability of Input Devices. ACM Transactions on Computer-Human Interaction, Vol. 1, No. 1 (1994) 3–26
9. Karl, L., Pettey, M., Shneiderman, B.: Speech Activated Versus Mouse-Activated Commands for Word Processing Applications: An Empirical Evaluation. International Journal of Man-Machine Studies, Vol. 39, No. 4, October (1993) 667–687
10. Kirstein, C., Muller, H.: Interaction with a Projection Screen Using a Camera-Tracked Laser Pointer. Proceedings of Multimedia Modeling (1998) 191–192
11. Milner, A. D., Goodale, M. A.: The Visual Brain in Action. Oxford Psychology Series, Vol. 2, (1995) New York: Oxford University Press.
12. Myers, B. A., Bhatnagar, R., Nichols, J., Peck, C. H., Kong, D., Miller, R., Long, A. C.: Interacting at a Distance: Measuring the Performance of Laser Pointers and Other Devices. Proceedings of CHI 2002, 33–40
13. Oh, J., Stuerzlinger, W.: Laser Pointers as Collaborative Pointing Devices. Proceedings of Graphics Interface 2002, 141–149
14. Olsen, D. R., Neilsen, T.: Laser Pointer Interaction. Proceedings of CHI 2002, 17–22
15. Oviatt, S., Cohen, P.: Multimodal Interfaces that Process What Comes Naturally. Communications of the ACM, March, Vol. 43, No. 3 (2001) 45–53
16. Poock, G. K.: Voice Recognition Boosts Command Terminal Throughput. Speech Technology, Vol. 1, No. 2 (1981) 36–39
17. Poupyrev, I., Weghorst, S., Billinghurst, M., Ichikawa, T.: A Framework and Testbed for Studying Manipulation Techniques in Immersive VR. VRST 1997, ACM Symposium on Virtual Reality Software and Technology (1997) 21–28
18. Roelofs, C.: Optische localisation [Optical localization]. Archiv für Augenheilkunde, 109 (1935) 395–415
19. Trevarthen, C. B.: Two Mechanisms of Vision in Primates. Psychologische Forschung, Vol. 31 (1968) 299–337
20. Wang, Y., MacKenzie, C. L., Summers, V. A., Booth, K. S.: The Structure of Object Transportation and Orientation in Human-Computer Interaction. Proceedings of CHI 1998, 312–319
21. Winograd, T., Guimbretiere, F.: Visual Instruments for an Interactive Mural. Abstracts, Proceedings of CHI 1999, 234–235
22. Wolf, C. G., Rhyne, J. R.: Gesturing with Shared Drawing Tools. ACM Conference on Human Factors and Computing Systems (1993)

Freeform User Interfaces for Graphical Computing

Takeo Igarashi

Department of Computer Science, The University of Tokyo / PRESTO, JST
7-3-1 Hongo, Bunkyo-ku, Tokyo 113-0033, Tokyo, JAPAN
takeo@acm.org
http://www-ui.is.s.u-tokyo.ac.jp/~takeo

Abstract. It is difficult to communicate graphical ideas or images to computers using current WIMP-style GUI. Freeform User Interfaces is an interface design framework that leverages the power of freeform strokes to achieve fluent interaction between users and computers in performing graphical tasks. Users express their graphical ideas as freeform strokes using pen-based systems, and the computer takes appropriate actions based on the perceptual features of the strokes. The results are displayed in an informal manner to facilitate exploratory thinking. This paper explores the concept of Freeform UI and shows its possibilities with four example systems: beautification and prediction for 2D geometric drawing, a stroke-based 3D navigation, an electronic office whiteboard, and a sketch-based 3D freeform modeling. While Freeform UI is not suitable for precise, production-oriented applications because of its ambiguity and imprecision, it does provide a natural, highly interactive computing environment for pre-productive, exploratory activities in various graphical applications.

1 Introduction

Graphical User Interface (GUI) has been the predominant user interface paradigm for almost 30 years. But because the purpose of computing is changing, we clearly need next-generation user interface framework. In the near future, computers' main application will no longer be as a tool for supporting knowledge workers in office environments. As they become smaller and still less expensive, they will become ubiquitous and their goal will be to support every aspect of human life. At that stage, a new form of user interfaces, post-WIMP [16] or non-command [13] user interfaces, will be needed. In [13], Nielsen argued that current GUI is essentially the same as command-line user interface in that users have to translate their tasks into machine-understandable sequences of commands. Pressing buttons or selecting items in menus in GUI is essentially identical to typing commands in command-line user interface. In non-command user interfaces, computers take appropriate action based on the users activity, allowing the user to concentrate on the task itself without worrying about commands.

Candidates for post-WIMP, non-command user interface include virtual realities and augmented realities, multi-modal and multi-media interfaces, natural language

A. Butz et al. (Eds.): Smart Graphics 2003, LNCS 2733, pp. 39–48, 2003.

interfaces, sound and speech recognition, portable and ubiquitous computers. Each new interface is designed to support specific new uses of computers. The increasing number of applications dealing with three-dimensional information require virtual reality techniques and various three-dimensional input devices. The need to support people in situations where one cannot use hands or keyboards has spurred the growth of voice input technologies. Highly complicated, spatial applications gave birth to the idea of physical (graspable or tangible) interfaces that can provide more affordable, space-multiplexed input channels. The essence of the next-generation user interface is its diversity. While current user interfaces are characterized simply as "WIMP-style GUI," post-WIMP or non-command user interfaces will be characterized as collections of task-oriented, tailored interfaces. An important task for user interface research is to identify an emerging application domain and find the ideal user interface for that domain beyond WIMP-style GUI.

This paper explores a user interface framework, Freeform User Interfaces, as a post-WIMP, non-command user interface in the domain of graphical interaction. Current point-click-drag style interaction is suitable for specific kinds of graphical interaction, namely object-oriented graphics such as block diagrams or flow charts. However, the point-click-drag interface does not work well for expressing arbitrary graphical ideas or geometric shapes in computers. The user has to do this manually by placing many control points one by one or combining editing commands in a nested menu. On the other hand, people have been using pen and paper to express graphical ideas for centuries. Drawing freeform strokes is a convenient, efficient, and familiar way to express graphical ideas. Freeform UI is an attempt to bring the power of freeform strokes to computing.

Section 2 introduces the concept of Freeform UI, a pen-based non-command user interface for graphical applications. We define the concept with three properties: stroke-based input, perceptual processing, and informal presentation. Section 3 briefly introduces four independent example systems embodying the idea of Freeform UI. They as a whole form a concrete basis for discussing the nature of Freeform UI. Section 4 discusses the limitation of Freeform UI and several design principles to mitigate the problems.

2   Freeform User Interfaces

Freeform UI is an interface design framework using pen-based input for computer-supported activities in graphical domains. In Freeform UI, the user expresses visual ideas or messages as freeform strokes on pen-based systems, and the computer takes appropriate action by analyzing the perceptual features of the strokes. This is based on the observation that freeform sketching is the most intuitive, easiest way to express visual ideas. The fluent, lightweight nature of freeform sketching makes Freeform UI suitable for exploratory, creative design activities. Freeform UI embodies a non-command user interface for two- and three-dimensional graphical applications in that the user can transfer visual ideas into target computers without converting the ideas into a sequence of tedious command operations.

Specifically, Freeform UI is characterized by the following three basic properties: the use of pen-based stroking as input, perceptual processing of strokes, and informal presentation of the result. We describe each property in detail in the following subsections.

2.1   Stroke-Based Input

Freeform UI is characterized by its use of strokes as user input. A stroke is a single path specified by the movement of a pen and is represented as a sequence of points internally. Stroking is usually recognized as a dragging operation in a standard programming environment: it is initiated by "button press" event, followed by a sequence of "mouse move" event, and terminated by "button release" event. However, stroking is actually a significantly different interface model than dragging. In short, stroking corresponds to physical drawing activity using real pen and paper, while dragging corresponds to a physical grab-and-move operation of objects. During a stroking operation, the trajectory of the pen's movement is shown on the screen, and the system responds to the event when the user stops stroking by lifting the pen. The system's reaction is based on the entire trajectory of the pen's movement during the stroking, not just the pen's position at the end (Fig. 1). In contrast, in a typical dragging operation, the current cursor position is shown on the screen. Possibly, the object shape specified by the current cursor position is shown as a feedback object, but the trajectory of the cursor movement is not shown. The system's action is based on the final cursor position and possibly the starting position of dragging. In stroking, the user first imagines the desired stroke shape and then draws the shape on the screen at once, while the user constantly adjusts the cursor position observing the feedback objects during dragging.

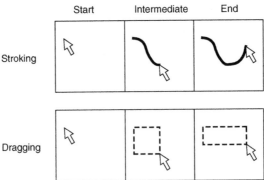

Fig. 1. Stroking vs. dragging.

Pen-based stroking is an intuitive, fast, and efficient way to express arbitrary graphical ideas in computing environments. This is because a pen-based stroking operation, or sketching, has been for centuries the primary interaction technique for expressing graphical ideas, and is therefore familiar to us. Specifically, stroking is suitable for quickly entering rough images that internally consist of many parameters from the computer's point of view. On the other hand, mouse-based dragging is suitable for more-delicate control of simple parameters. Dragging has been the dominant interaction technique because traditional computer-based drawing applications are designed for the careful construction of precise diagrams. The argument of this paper is that graphical computing in the future should support informal drawing activities and thus require a pen-based stroking interface.

2.2   Perceptual Processing

The next important property that characterizes Freeform UI as a non-command user interface, and that makes Freeform UI different from plain pen-based scribbling systems, is its advanced processing of freeform strokes inspired by human perception. Scribbling programs such as those used in commercial electronic whiteboards simply convert the user's pen movement into a painted stroke on the screen without any further processing. Character-recognition and gesture-recognition systems convert a stroke into a predefined character or command, using pattern-matching algorithms. In these recognition systems, the output of the recognition is represented as a single symbol. The stroking operation in these systems is essentially equivalent to key-typing and button-pressing. "Perceptual processing" refers to mechanisms that infer information from simple strokes that is richer than mere symbols. The idea behind perceptual processing is inspired by the observation that human beings perceive rich information in simple drawings, such as possible geometric relations among line primitives, three-dimensional shapes from two-dimensional silhouettes (Fig. 2). Perceptual processing is an attempt to simulate human perception at least in limited domains.

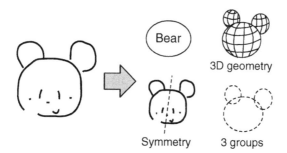

Fig. 2. Human beings perceive rich information in a simple drawing.

The goal of perceptual processing is to allow the user to perform complicated tasks with a minimum amount of explicit control. In traditional command-based interfaces, the user must decompose a task into a sequence of machine-understandable, fine-grained command operations, then input the commands one by one. As we discussed in Section 1, non-command user interfaces try to avoid this process and allow the user to directly interact with tasks without worrying about low-level commands. Freeform UI frees users from detailed command operations by this perceptual processing of freeform strokes. For example, Pegasus (Section 3.1) frees the user from tedious geometric operations such as rotation and duplication by automatically inferring desired geometric constraints, and Teddy (Section 3.4) eliminates the manual positioning of many vertices in 3D space by automatically constructing 3D geometry from the input stroke. This simplicity also significantly reduces the effort spent on learning commands. In traditional command-based systems, the user has to learn many fine-grained editing commands to do something simple. In Freeform UI, on the other hand, the user can do a variety of things simply after learning a single operation.

2.3   Informal Presentation

The last property of Freeform UI is informal presentation of contents. The system displays the materials to manipulate or the result of computation in an informal manner, using sketchy representation without standard, cleaned-up graphics. This informal presentation is important not only for an aesthetically pleasing appearance, but also to arouse appropriate expectations in the user's mind about the system's functionality. If the system gives feedback in precise, detailed graphics, the user naturally expects that the result of computation will be precise and detailed. In contrast, if the system's feedback is in informal presentation, the user can concentrate on the general structure of the information without worrying about the details too much. The importance of informal presentation in exploratory design activities has been discussed in many papers [1,2,13,17].

Several experimental systems implemented sketchy presentation techniques. Strothotte et al. introduced a non-photorealistic renderer for an architectural CAD system [15]. The system used irregular curves for representing straight line segments to make them appear hand-drawn. The SKETCH system [18] also used non-photorealistic rendering to give a sketchy appearance to a 3D scene being constructed. The system intentionally displaced the vertex position when rendering projected 2D line segments. Teddy uses a real-time pen-and-ink rendering technique developed by Markosian et al. [10]. It efficiently detects the silhouette lines of a 3D model, and renders the silhouettes in various styles.

While these systems are designed for 3D graphics, some systems introduced sketchy rendering for 2D applications. The EtchaPad system [11] used synthesized wiggly lines for displaying GUI widgets in order to give them an informal look. Other systems employ the user's freeform strokes as-is to represent recognized primitives without cleaning up the drawings. SILK [9] allows the user to interact with the GUI widgets sketched on the screen. The Electronic Cocktail Napkin system [3] also retains and displays the as-inked representation of hand-drawn graphical primitives. Pegasus used intentionally thick line segments to show beautified drawings to give them an informal look.

3   Example Systems

This section presents four independent example systems embodying the idea of Freeform UI. While each of these systems contributes independently to the improvement of existing applications, taken as a whole they form a concrete basis for discussing the nature of Freeform UI, including its strengths and limitations.

3.1 Pegasus: Beautification and Prediction for 2D Geometric Drawing [5,6]

Pegasus is a system that allows the user to construct precise illustrations such as shown in Fig. 3 without using complicated editing commands such as copy, flip, and move. The idea is to automate complicated drawing operations by having the computer infer possible geometric constraints and the user's next steps from the user's freeform strokes. Interactive beautification receives the user's free stroke input and beautifies it by considering possible geometric constraints among line segments such as connection, parallelism, and congruence. The system generates multiple alternatives to prevent recognition errors. Predictive drawing predicts the user's next drawing operation based on the spatial relationships among existing segments on the screen.

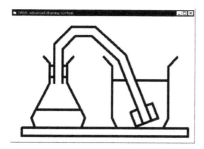

Fig. 3. A diagram drawn using interactive beautification and predictive drawing.

3.2 Path-Drawing Technique for Virtual Space Navigation [7]

This technique allows the user to navigate through a virtual 3D space by drawing the intended path directly on the screen. After drawing the path, the avatar and camera automatically move along the path (Fig. 4). The system calculates the path by projecting the stroke drawn on the screen onto the walking surface in the 3D world. Using this technique, with a single stroke the user can specify not only the goal position, but also the route to take and the camera orientation at the goal. This is faster and more intuitive than to turn and advance using arrow buttons or a joystick.

3.3 Flatland: An Electronic Office Whiteboard for Informal Activities [4, 12]

Flatland is an augmented whiteboard interface designed for informal office work. Our research has investigated approaches to building an augmented whiteboard in the context of continuous, long-term office use. In particular, the system is characterized by the following three features: techniques for the efficient management of space on the board, the ability to flexibly apply behaviors to support varied domain specific

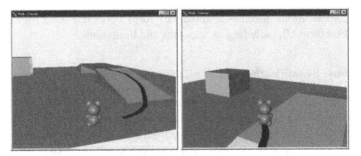

Fig. 4. An example of a path-drawing walkthrough.

activities, and mechanisms for managing history on the board. We implemented a calculator that takes hand-written numbers as input, map drawing program that takes freeform strokes and turns them into streets and intersections, to-do list manager that organizes handwritten to-do items. These facilities provide support for pre-productive activities, rather than final production work, in an office setting.

Fig. 5. Flatland example.

3.4 Teddy: A Sketch-Based 3D Freeform Modeling System [8]

This technique allows the user to quickly and easily design freeform models, such as stuffed animals and other rotund objects, using freeform strokes. The user draws several 2D freeform strokes interactively on the screen and the system automatically constructs plausible 3D polygonal surfaces. Our system supports several modeling operations, including the operation to construct a 3D polygonal surface from a 2D silhouette drawn by the user: the system inflates the region surrounded by the silhouette, making wide areas fat and narrow areas thin. Teddy, our prototype system, is implemented as a Java program, and the mesh construction is done in real-time on a standard PC. Our informal user study showed that a first-time user typically masters the operations within 10 minutes, and can construct interesting 3D models within minutes.

Fig. 6. Teddy in use on a video tablet (left). Example 3D models designed using Teddy (right).

4 Discussions

4.1 Fundamental Limitations of Freeform UI

Freeform UI achieves fluent interaction that is not possible with traditional GUI, but several difficulties are inherent in it. This section discusses three major difficulties (ambiguity, imprecision and learning), and the next section proposes possible solutions to mitigate the problems.

Freeform UI is characterized by its indirect interaction style. Traditional command-based interfaces accept explicit command input and perform the command directly without any hidden processing. In contrast, Freeform UI accepts highly ambiguous freeform strokes as input, and performs complicated processing internally to infer the user's intention from the strokes. The indirect operation is inherently associated with the problem of *ambiguity*. It is difficult to infer appropriate interpretation from the user's ambiguous freeform strokes, and the behavior of perceptual processing can be seen as ambiguous from the user's perspective.

Imprecision is another problem inherent in Freeform UI. While mouse-based careful manipulation of each control point in traditional GUI is suitable for editing precise diagrams, handwritten freeform strokes are not good at precise control. Perceptual processing and informal presentation are also incompatible with precise manipulation.

The indirect nature of Freeform UI also requires a *learning* process by the novice user. Because a simple stroke can transform to a variety of results, the user has to try many strokes and accumulate experience to master the operation. In other words, Freeform UI imposes certain implicit rules to infer complicated information from simple strokes, and the user has to learn the implicit rules through experience.

4.2 Guidelines to Mitigate the Limitations

Based on our implementation and user study experience, we found several techniques and design guidelines to mitigate these problems. Although it is impossible to remove these difficulties entirely because they are strongly associated with the essential nature of Freeform UI, the following tips work as basic guidelines to design a good Freeform UI system.

First, it is important to give users an appropriate impression that the system is not designed for precise, detailed editing; this will help prevent frustration over ambiguous, imprecise operation. In addition to informal presentation describe in Section 2, a designer can install similar tricks in many places, such as in the introduction to the system, in the system's feedback messages and in the user manuals.

From a technical point of view, construction of multiple alternatives is an effective way to mitigate ambiguity. This strategy is commonly used in Japanese text input systems to type thousands of Chinese characters using a limited alphabet. Pegasus constructs multiple alternatives as a result of beautification and prediction; this feature turned out to be essential to making beautification and prediction perform practically.

As for the problems of learning and ambiguity, it is important to make the interface quick-responding and to ensure that changes can be easily undone so as to encourage trial-and-error experience. For example, Teddy deliberately uses simple algorithms to calculate geometry quickly sacrificing surface quality, instead of using more advanced, time-consuming algorithms. Construction of multiple alternatives is definitely an important feature one should consider when developing a system based on Freeform UI.

Finally, it is necessary to give explanatory feedback for each operation so that the user can easily understand why the system returned the unexpected result. This kind of informative feedback is not very important in traditional command-based interfaces because the system response is always predictable. However, well-designed informative feedback is a crucial feature to prevent frustration and to facilitate the learning process in Freeform UI. For example, Pegasus displays small marks indicating what kinds of geometric constraints are satisfied by the beautified segment. We believe that informative feedback can allow the user to learn how to use the system without having to read manuals or tutorials beforehand.

4.3 User Experience

Although we have a limited amount of user experiences with the prototype systems, it is our future work to obtain further insight by accumulating more experience with real users. Initial user feedback has been quite positive. Users are excited by the demonstrations given by the authors and they successfully start playing around after a minutes of practice. However, the prototype systems are not designed to handle large problems and it is not clear to what extend the Freeform UI approach scales. The scalability problem is actually serious in the Pegasus system; the system generates too many candidates as the diagram becomes complicated. We are currently exploring various ways to solve the problem.

Fortunately, the Teddy system is now widely used as a commercial modeling software and a video game. The users (mostly children) have created various interesting 3D models with them. We believe that the reason for this success is the choice of right application domain: video games do not require precise or large, complicated models which is a perfect match for Freeform UI.

5 Summary

We proposed an interface design framework for graphical computing based on pen-based input, and named it Freeform UI. It uses freeform handwriting strokes as input, recognizes the configuration of the strokes and performs appropriate actions automatically, and presents the result of computation using informal rendering. We introduced four example user interface systems embodying the concept of Freeform UI and discussed its strengths and limitations.

References

1. Black, A.: Visible Planning on Paper and on Screen: The Impact of Working Medium on Decision-making by Novice Graphic Designers. *Behavior & Information Technology.* Vol.9 No.4 (1990) 283–296
2. Goel, V.: Sketches of Thought. The MIT Press (1995)
3. Gross, M.D., Do, E.Y.L.: Ambiguous intentions: A Paper-like Interface for Creative Design. *Proceedings of UIST'96* (1996) 183–192
4. Igarashi, T., Edwards, W.K., LaMarca, A., Mynatt, E.D.: An Architecture for Pen-based Interaction on Electronic Whiteboards. *Proceedings of AVI 2000* (2000) 68–75
5. Igarashi, T., Matsuoka, S., Kawachiya, S., Tanaka, H.: Interactive Beautification: A Technique for Rapid Geometric Design. *Proceedings of UIST'97* (1997) 105–114
6. Igarashi, T., Matsuoka, S., Kawachiya, S., Tanaka, H.: Pegasus: A Drawing System for Rapid Geometric Design. *CHI'98 summary* (1998) 24–25
7. Igarashi, T., Kadobayashi, R., Mase, K., Tanaka, H.: Path Drawing for 3D Walkthrough. *Proceedings of UIST'98* (1998) 173–174
8. Igarashi, T., Matsuoka, S., Tanaka, H.: Teddy: A Sketching Interface for 3D Freeform Design. *SIGGRAPH 99 Conference Proceedings* (1999) 409–416
9. Landay, J.A., Myers, B.A.: Interactive Sketching for the Early Stages of User Interface Design. *Proceedings of CHI'95* (1995) 43–50
10. Markosian, L., Kowalski, M.A., Trychin, S.J., Bourdev, L.D., Goldstein, D., Hughes, J.F.: Real-time Nonphotorealistic Rendering. *SIGGRAPH 97 Conference Proceedings* (1997) 415–420
11. Meyer, J.: EtchaPad - Disposable Sketch Based Interfaces. *CHI'96 Conference Companion* (1996) 195–198
12. Mynatt, E.D., Igarashi, T., Edwards, W.K., LaMarca, A.: Flatland: New Dimensions in Office Whiteboards. *Proceedings of CHI'99* (1999) 346–353
13. Nielsen, J.: Noncommand User Interfaces. *Communications of the ACM* Vol.36 No.4 (1993) 83–99
14. Schumann, J., Strothotte, T., Raddb, A., Laser, S.: Assessing the Effect of Non-photorealistic Rendered Images in CAD. *Proceedings of CHI'96* (1996) 35–41
15. Strothotte, T., Preim, B., Raab, A., Schumann, J., Forsey, D.R.: How to Render Frames and Influence People. *Proceedings of Eurographics'94* (1994) 455–466
16. van Dam, A.: Post-WIMP User Interfaces. *Communications of the ACM* Vol.40 No.2 (1997) 63–67
17. Wong, Y.Y.: Rough and Ready Prototypes: Lessons From Graphic Design. *Proceeding of CHI'92* (1992) 83–84
18. Zeleznik, R.C., Herndon, K.P., Hughes, J.F.: SKETCH: An Interface for Sketching 3D Scenes. *SIGGRAPH 96 Conference Proceedings* (1996) 163–170

A Sketching Interface for Modeling the Internal Structures of 3D Shapes

Shigeru Owada[1], Frank Nielsen[2], Kazuo Nakazawa[3], and Takeo Igarashi[1]

[1] Department of Computer Science, The University of Tokyo,
7-3-1 Hongo, Bunkyo-ku, Tokyo 113-8654, JAPAN,
{ohwada|takeo}@is.s.u-tokyo.ac.jp
[2] Sony Computer Science Laboratories,Inc.,
Takanawa Muse Bldg., 3-14-13, Higashigotanda,
Shinagawa-ku, Tokyo 141-0022, JAPAN,
nielsen@csl.sony.co.jp
[3] National Cardiovascular Center,
5-7-1 Fujishiro-dai, Suita, Osaka 565-8565, JAPAN,
nakazawa@ri.ncvc.go.jp

Abstract. This paper presents a sketch-based modeling system for creating objects that have internal structures. The user input consists of hand-drawn sketches and the system automatically generates a volumetric model. The volumetric representation solves any self-intersection problems and enables the creation of models with a variety of topological structures, such as a torus or a hollow sphere. To specify internal structures, our system allows the user to cut the model temporarily and apply modeling operations to the exposed face. In addition, the user can draw multiple contours in the Create or Sweep stages. Our system also allows automatic rotation of the model so that the user does not need to perform frequent manual rotations. Our system is much simpler to implement than a surface-oriented system because no complicated mesh editing code is required. We observed that novice users could quickly create a variety of objects using our system.

1 Introduction

Geometric modeling has been a major research area in computer graphics. While there has been much progress in rendering 3D models, creating 3D objects is still a challenging task. Recently, attention has focused on sketch-based modeling systems with which the user can quickly create 3D models using simple freehand strokes rather than by specifying precise parameters for geometric objects, such as spline curves, NURBS patches, and so forth [15,6]. However, these systems are primarily designed for specifying the external appearance of 3D shapes, and it is still difficult to design freeform models with internal structures, such as internal organs. Specifically, the existing sketch-based freeform modeling system [6] can handle 3D models only with spherical topology. This paper introduces a modeling system that can design 3D models with complex internal structures,

A. Butz et al. (Eds.): Smart Graphics 2003, LNCS 2733, pp. 49–57, 2003.

while maintaining the ease of use of existing sketch-based freeform modelers. We used a volumetric data structure to handle the dynamically changing topology efficiently. The volumetric model is converted to a polygonal surface and is displayed using a non-photorealistic rendering technique to facilitate creative exploration. Unlike previous systems, our system allows the user to draw nested contours to design models with internal structures. In addition, the user can cut the model temporarily and apply modeling operations to the exposed face to design internal structures. The underlying volumetric representation simplifies the implementation of such functions. Moreover, our system actively assists the user by automatically rotating the model when necessary.

The heart of our technique is automatic "guessing" of 3D geometry from 2D gestural input, and it is done by making certain assumptions about the target geometry. To be specific, the system assumes that the target geometry has a rotund, smooth (low curvature) surface [6] other than the places where the user explicitly defined the geometry by the input strokes. In other words, the user specifies the information about important features (silhouette, intersection, and sweep path) and the system supplies missing information based on the above assumption.

Our system is designed to facilitate the communication of complicated geometric information, such as surgical plans. Like other sketch-based modeling systems, however, our system is not suitable for creating the final output of any serious production, because of its lack of accuracy.

2   Previous Work

Three-dimensional shape modeling systems that use a volumetric data structure directly are relatively new [14,4] as compared with other popular modeling primitives, such as polygons, NURBS, and subdivision surfaces. Recently, a scripting language [2], octree [11], subdivision volume [10], and level set [1] have been used as volumetric modeling methodologies. Some systems use 3D haptic input devices [4,3,5,10].

Sketch-based modeling using standard mouse operations became popular in the past decade. Instead of creating precise, large-scale objects, a sketching interface provides an easy way to create a rough model to convey the user's idea quickly. One of the earliest sketching systems was Viking [12], which was designed in the context of prototypic CAD models. Later works include SKETCH [15] and Teddy [6]. The SKETCH system is intended to sketch a scene consisting of simple primitives, such as boxes and cones, while the Teddy system is designed to create rotund objects with spherical topology. Although improvements to the original Teddy system have recently been proposed [7], extending the topological variety of creatable models is still an unsolved problem.

Although the user interface of our system is based on the Teddy system, our system is free from topological limitations, provides multiple interfaces for specifying internal structures, and actively assists the user by automatically rotating a model when necessary.

3   User Interface

The entire editing operation is performed in a single window. Modeling operations are specified by freeform strokes drawn on the screen and by pressing buttons on a menu bar. The freeform strokes provide necessary geometric information and the buttons apply specific modeling operations using the strokes as input. The drawing of strokes is assigned to the left mouse button and rotating the model is assigned to the right mouse button. The current implementation uses four buttons, as shown in Fig. 1. The leftmost button is used to initialize the current scene; the second one is to create items; the third is for the extrusion/sweep function; and the last is for undo.

Fig. 1. Buttons in our system

3.1   Create

Objects are created by drawing one or more contours on the canvas and pressing the "Create" button. This operation inflates the intermediate region between the strokes leaving holes (Fig. 2).

Fig. 2. Nested contours are allowed in the Create operation.

3.2   Extrusion

Extrusion is an operation that generates a protuberance or a dent on a model. The user draws a single closed stroke on the object's surface specifying the contour (Fig. 3 (b)) and presses the "Extrusion/sweep" button. After rotating the model (Fig. 3 (c)), the user draws a second stroke specifying the silhouette of the extruded area (Fig. 3 (d, f)). The user should place each end of the silhouette stroke close to each end of the projected surface contour (otherwise the second stroke is interpreted as a sweep path; see Section 3.4.) A protuberance is created if the second stroke is drawn on the outside of the object (Fig. 3 (d,e)). The user can also create a hole by drawing a stroke into the object (Fig. 3 (f,g)). Volumetric representation automatically prevents self-intersection problems, where specialized care must be taken when using a polygonal representation. A hidden silhouette is rendered as broken lines.

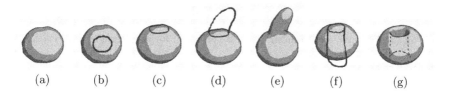

(a)   (b)   (c)   (d)   (e)   (f)   (g)

Fig. 3. Examples of Extrusion

3.3   Loop Extrusion

In addition, it is also possible to create a hollow object using extrusion. To do this, the user first cuts the model to expose the internal region (Fig. 4 (a-c)), then draws a contour on the exposed plane (Fig. 4 (d)), and finally draws a circular stroke that entirely surrounds the contour (Fig. 4 (e)). We call this operation "Loop Extrusion". The cutting operation that we use differs from the standard Cut operation in the Teddy system [6] in that the removed region is just deactivated temporarily. The system distinguishes these two operations by checking whether there is a corner at the end of a stroke. The system performs a standard cutting operation when there is no corner, while the system deactivates a region when there is a corner. The direction of the stroke end is used to determine which area to deactivate. The silhouette of the deactivated parts is rendered as broken lines.

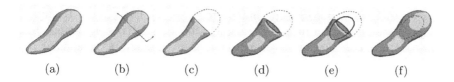

(a)   (b)   (c)   (d)   (e)   (f)

Fig. 4. An example of creating a hollow object: first, the user defines the desired cross-sectional plane by deactivating part of the object (a-c). Then, the user draws a contour on the cut plane (d). Finally, the user draws a extruding shape surrounding the contour, which we call "Loop Extrusion" (e). This creates a hollow object (f).

Deactivation is provided in order to make the inside of an object accessible. The user can draw a contour and have it extrude on an internal surface in exactly the same way as done on an external surface (Fig. 5). The following sweep operation can also be used in conjunction with deactivation.

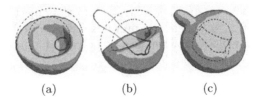

(a)   (b)   (c)

Fig. 5. An extrusion from an internal surface of an object using deactivation

3.4 Sweep

After pressing the "Extrusion/Sweep" button, the user can also draw an open stroke specifying the sweep path. If a single contour is drawn in the first step, both ends are checked to determine whether they are close to the projected contour. Unlike extrusion, the user can draw multiple contours to design tube-like shapes (Fig. 6).

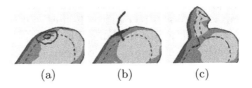

(a)   (b)   (c)

Fig. 6. Sweeping double contours: drawing contours on the surface of an object (a) and sweeping them (b) produces a tube (c).

3.5 Animation Assistance

In extrusion or sweep, the model must be rotated approximately 90 degrees after pressing the "Extrusion/Sweep" button to draw the last stroke. To automate this process, our system rotates the model after the "Extrusion/Sweep" button is pressed; the contours are then moved so that they are perpendicular to the screen (Fig. 7 (a-c)). This animation assistance is also performed after a Cut operation, because it is likely that a contour will be drawn on the cut plane in the next step. When a model is cut, it is automatically rotated so that the cut plane is parallel to the screen (Fig. 7 (d-f)).

4 Implementation

We use a standard binary volumetric representation. The examples shown in this paper require approximately 400^3 voxels. The volumetric data are polygonized using the Marching Cubes algorithm [9]. The polygonized surface is then smoothed [13] and displayed using a non-photorealistic rendering technique [8]. The silhouette lines of invisible or deactivated parts are rendered as broken lines.

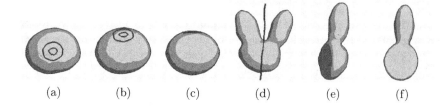

Fig. 7. Examples of animation assistance: as soon as the user presses the "Extrusion/Sweep" button, the model is rotated so that the contours are perpendicular to the screen (a-c). When the user cuts a model, the /model is automatically rotated so that the cut plane is parallel to the screen (d-f).

The Create and Extrusion operations can be implemented using the algorithms described in the original Teddy system, converting the resulting polygonal model into a volumetric model and performing a CSG operation. In Extrusion, our system adds the additional geometry to the original model when an outward stroke is drawn and subtracts it when an inward stroke is drawn. Note that complex "sewing" of polygons is not necessary and no self-intersection will occur because of the volumetric data structure. Loop Extrusion applies the standard inward (subtract) extrusion in both directions. The Sweep operation in our system requires two-path CSG operations to add a new geometry to the original model. First, the sweep volume of the outermost contour is subtracted from the original model (Fig. 8 (a-c)). Then, the regions between the contours are swept and the sweep volume is added to the model (Fig. 8 (d)). This avoids the inner space being filled with the original geometry.

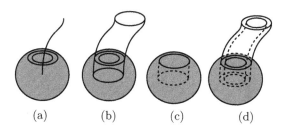

Fig. 8. Handling the sweep operation. The outmost contour is swept along the specified path (a,b) and extracted from the original model (c). Then, every contour is swept and added to the model.

The volumetric representation significantly simplifies the implementation of the Cut operation and enables the change in topology. A binary 2D image is computed from the cutting stroke in the screen space to specify a "delete" region and a "remain" region. Both ends of the cutting stroke are extended until they intersect or reach the edges of the screen. Then, one of the separated regions is set as the "delete" region (usually the region to the left of the stroke, following the original Teddy convention). Each voxel is then projected to the screen space to check whether it is in the deleted region; if so, the voxel is deleted. This process is significantly simpler than traversing the polygonized surface and remeshing it.

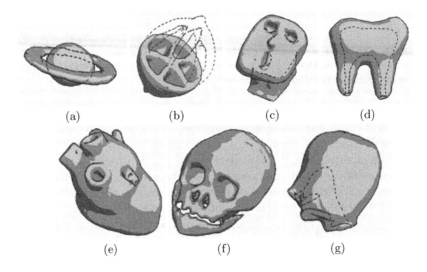

(a)   (b)   (c)   (d)

(e)   (f)   (g)

Fig. 9. Examples created using our system. (a-c) were created by novices, while (d-g) were created by an expert.

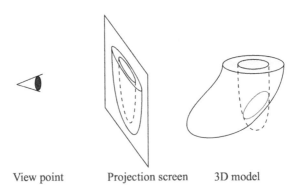

View point   Projection screen   3D model

Fig. 10. An undesired effect caused by the lack of depth control. Since there is no depth information in the original model, the newly created cavity can pierce the wall.

5   Results

We used a Dell Dimension 8200 computer that contained a Pentium 4 2-GHz processor and 512 MB of RAM. The graphics card was an NVIDIA GeForce3 Ti500 with 64 MB of memory. Users can create models interactively on this machine. We also used a display-integrated tablet as an input device, with which the user can edit an object more intuitively. However, some users found it difficult to rotate an object because they needed to press a button attached to the side of the pen and move the pen without touching the display.

Figure 9 shows some models created using our system. Fig. 9 (a-c) were created by novices within fifteen minutes of an introductory fifteen-minute tutorial; the others were created by an expert. Our observations confirmed that users could create models with internal structures quickly and easily. Nevertheless, one limitation also became clear. The users occasionally found the behavior of Extrusion unpredictable because there was no depth control. Specifically, when a user tried to create a cavity in an object, the hole sometimes penetrated the wall of the original model (Fig.10).

6   Conclusions and Future Work

We presented a sketch-based modeling system for creating objects with internal structures. The underlying volumetric data structure simplifies the handling of a dynamically changing topology. The user can modify the topology easily in various ways, such as by cutting an object, forming a extrusion, specifying multiple contours with create or sweep operations, or specifying internal structures in conjunction with temporal deactivation. In addition, automatic rotation of the object frees the user from tedious manual labor.

Our system is designed for the rapid construction of coarse models and is not appropriate for precise modeling. Currently, it is difficult to modify shapes locally and we are exploring ways to add small details. As mentioned above, the absence of depth control causes difficulty. Finally, our current implementation can produce only binary volumetric data and we plan to explore a new interface in which the user can define the internal volumetric textures of a model.

References

1. Bærentzen, J.A. and Christensen, N.J.: Volume Sculpting Using the Level-set Method. Proc. 2002 International Conference on Shape Modeling and Applications (2002) 175–182
2. Cutler, B., Dorsey, J., McMillian, L., Müller, M. and Jagnow, R.: A Procedural Approach to Authoring Solid Models. ACM Transactions on Graphics **21** 3 (2002) 302–311
3. Ferley, E., Cani, M.P. and Gascuel, J.D.: Practical Volumetric Sculpting. The Visual Computer **16** 8 (2000) 469–480
4. Galyean, T.A. and Hughes, J.F.: Sculpting: An Interactive Volumetric Modeling Technique. In Computer Graphics (Proc. SIGGRAPH 91) **25** 4 (1991) 267–274

5. Hua, J. and Qin, H.: Haptics-based Volumetric Modeling Using Dynamic Spline-based Implicit Functions. In Proc. 2002 IEEE Symposium on Volume Visualization and Graphics (2002) 55–64
6. Igarashi, T., Matsuoka, S. and Tanaka, H.: Teddy: A Sketching Interface for 3D Freeform Design. In Computer Graphics (Proc. SIGGRAPH 99) (1999) 409–416
7. Karpenko, O., Hughes, J.F. and Raskar, R.: Free-form Sketching with Variational Implicit Surfaces. Computer Graphics Forum **21** 3 (2002) 585–594
8. Lake, A., Marshall, C., Harris, M. and Blackstein, M.: Stylized Rendering Techniques for Scalable Real-Time 3D Animation. In Proc. Symposium on Non-Photorealistic Animation and Rendering (NPAR 2000) (2000) 13–20
9. Lorensen, W.E. and Cline, H.E.: Marching Cubes: A High Resolution 3D Surface Construction Algorithm. In Computer Graphics (Proc. SIGGRAPH 87) **21** 4 (1987) 163–169
10. McDonnell, K.T. and Qin, H.: Dynamic Sculpting and Animation of Free-Form Subdivision Solids. The Visual Computer **18** 2 (2002) 81–96
11. Perry, R.N. and Frisken, S.F.: Kizamu: A System for Sculpting Digital Characters. In Computer Graphics (Proc. SIGGRAPH 2001) (2001) 47–56
12. Pugh, D.: Designing Solid Objects Using Interactive Sketch Interpretation. Computer Graphics (1992 Symposium on Interactive 3D Graphics) **25** 2 (1992) 117–126
13. Taubin, G.: A Signal Processing Approach to Fair Surface Design. In Computer Graphics (Proc. SIGGRAPH 95) (1995) 351–358
14. Wang, S.W. and Kaufman, A.E.: Volume Sculpting. Computer Graphics (1995 Symposium on Interactive 3D Graphics) (1995) 151–156
15. Zeleznik, R.C., Herndon, K.P. and Hughes, J.F.: SKETCH: An Interface for Sketching 3D Scenes. In Computer Graphics (Proc. SIGGRAPH 96) (1996) 163–170

Smart Sketch System for 3D Reconstruction Based Modeling

Ferran Naya[1], Julián Conesa[2], Manuel Contero[1], Pedro Company[3], and
Joaquim Jorge[4]

[1] DEGI – ETSII, Universidad Politécnica de Valencia, Camino de Vera s/n,
46022 Valencia, Spain
{fernasan, mcontero}@degi.upv.es
[2] DEG, Universidad Politécnica de Cartagena, C/ Dr. Fleming
30202 Cartagena, Spain
julian.conesa@uptc.es
[3] Departamento de Tecnología, Universitat Jaume I de Castellón, Campus Riu Sec
12071 Castellón, Spain
pcompany@tec.uji.es
[4] Engª. Informática, IST, Av.Rovisco Pais
1049-001 Lisboa, Portugal
jorgej@acm.org

Abstract. Current user interfaces of CAD systems are still not suited to the initial stages of product development, where freehand drawings are used by engineers and designers to express their visual thinking. In order to exploit these sketching skills, we present a sketch based modeling system, which provides a reduced instruction set calligraphic interface to create orthogonal polyhedra, and an extension of them we named quasi-normalons. Our system allows users to draw lines on free-hand axonometric-like drawings, which are automatically tidied and beautified. These line drawings are then converted into a three-dimensional model in real time because we implemented a fast reconstruction process, suited for quasi-normalon objects and so-called axonometric inflation method, providing in this way an innovative integrated 2D sketching and 3D view visualization work environment.

1 Introduction

User interfaces of most CAD applications are based on the WIMP (Windows, Icons, Menus and Pointing) paradigm, that is not enough flexible to support sketching activities in the conceptual design phase. Recently, work on sketch-based modeling has looked at a paradigm shift to change the way geometric modeling applications are built, in order to focus on user-centric systems rather than systems that are organized around the details of geometry representation. To this end, the aim of our research is to develop expeditious ways to construct geometric models. We want to generate solid

A. Butz et al. (Eds.): Smart Graphics 2003, LNCS 2733, pp. 58–68, 2003.

and surface models from two-dimensional freehand drawings, using a digitizing tablet and a pen, an approach we have termed *calligraphic interfaces*. These rely on interactive input of drawings as vector information (pen-strokes) and gestures.

The present text describes work at the user interface, where the main objective is keeping the number of low level interactions to a minimum, as well as the command set, in order to provide support for the preliminary phases of design, where it is not necessary to build complex CAD models but to express the visual thinking in a fast way. This implies to choose a compromise between geometric complexity and fast interaction. This is accomplished by working in a particular geometric domain (quasi-normalon objects) that opens the possibility to implement three-dimensional reconstruction algorithms that operates in real-time. This environment differs from previous sketch systems in that the speed of execution and timely feedback are more important than the ability to produce models from vectorized bitmaps in one step, as has been typical of previous efforts in computer vision.

2   Related Work

There are two main approaches to sketch-based modeling. The first one is based in the calligraphic interface concept that uses gestures and pen-input as commands [1, 2, 3]. These systems rely on gestures as commands for generating solids from 2D sections. Some *gestural modeling* systems are:
- Sketch [4]: the geometric model is entered by a sequence of gestures according to a set of conventions regarding the order in which points and lines are entered as well as their spatial relations.
- Quick-Sketch [5]: system oriented to mechanical design that consists of a 2D drawing environment based on constraints. From these it is possible to generate 3D models through modeling gestures.
- Teddy [6]: oriented to free-form surface modeling using a very simple interface of sketched curves, pockets and extrusions. Users draw silhouettes through a series of pen strokes and the system automatically proposes a surface using a polygonal mesh whose projection matches the object contour.
- GIDeS [7]: allows data input from a single-view projection. In addition the dynamic recognition of modeling gestures provides users with contextual menus and icons to allow modeling using a reduced command set.

The second approach, which we call *geometric reconstruction*, derives from computer vision, uses algorithms to reconstruct geometric objects from sketches that depict their two dimensional projection. The systems we surveyed use two main techniques. The first is based on Huffman-Clowes labeling scheme [8], [9]. The second approach deals with reconstruction as an optimization problem [10]. This enables us to obtain what, from the point of view of geometry, is unrealizable: a three-dimensional model from a single projection. However, for the psychologists it is well known that humans can identify 3D models from 2D images by using a simple set of perceptual heuristics [11]. Authors such as Marill [12], Leclerc and Fischler [13], and Lipson and

Shpitalni [14] provide interesting references in the development of this field. Some recent examples are:

- Digital Clay [15], which supports basic polyhedral objects, and, in combination with a calligraphic interface for data input, uses Huffman-Clowes algorithms to derive three-dimensional geometry.
- Stilton [16], where a calligraphic interface is directly implemented in a VRML environment and the reconstruction process uses the optimization approach based on genetic algorithms.

3   Overview of Operations

In contrast to surveyed work, our application, we have called CIGRO (Calligraphic Interface for Geometric Reconstruction), provides an integrated 2D-3D environment, where users sketch and can immediately switch the point of view and see the corresponding 3D model. Real-time sketching is supported by implementing a minimal gesture alphabet, automatic line-drawing beautification, and a fast and robust axonometric-inflation engine. Previous reconstruction-based applications include a preliminary offline 2D reconstruction stage, where the input sketch is adjusted before proceeding with the 3D reconstruction. To implement a true interactive sketching system we have developed an automatic online 2D reconstructor that operates in real time. Thus, whenever the input sketch is changed, because edges are added or deleted, the sketch is adjusted and a 3D model is automatically built and offered to the user for review. The only constraint on drawing is that the reconstruction algorithm requires a single orthogonal axonometric projection of the model as input. The user interface is designed to minimize the interaction with menus or icons in an attempt to emulate the traditional use of pen and paper.

3.1   Gesture Alphabet

CIGRO processes strokes generated by the user directly onto the screen of a Tablet-PC or LCD tablet, supported by the Wintab API (http://www.pointing.com), an open industry interface that directly collects pointing input from a digitizing tablet and passes it to applications in a standardized fashion. This API allows retrieving additional information as the pressure the user applies at each point of the stroke over the tablet. Raw strokes are then processed by the CALI library [3], which provides some components to develop calligraphic interfaces. It is based on a recognizer of elemental geometric forms and gestural commands that operates in real time using fuzzy logic. The recognized gestures are inserted in a list, where they are ordered according to the degree of certainty, and returned to the application. CALI recognizes the elemental two-dimensional geometric shapes (like triangles, rectangles, circles, ellipses, lines, arrows, etc.), and some gestural commands, such as delete, move, copy, etc. At the current development level, the CIGRO application only supports sketched segments, which can be recognized as entities of the *line* type or as a gestural command of the *delete* class. Using a pressure threshold defined by the user, line strokes are classified as real or auxiliary line. The gesture alphabet is reduced to the following commands: new edge, new auxiliary edge and remove edge (auxiliary or not).

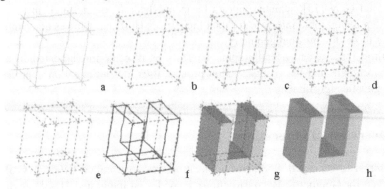

Fig. 1. Modeling sequence in CIGRO. Orange color represents raw strokes corresponding to auxiliary lines. Cyan dashed lines represent adjusted auxiliary lines. Blue raw strokes in f correspond to real geometry that is snapped to auxiliary-lines skeleton in e.

3.2 Sketching Procedure

Many engineers draw a set of auxiliary lines (see Figure 1.a to 1.e) to define main geometric features of objects and then, using this framework as a drawing template, the sketch is refined by applying pressure with the pencil and drawing over the previous template (see Figure 1.f). CIGRO supports this sketching paradigm allowing over-sketching of real geometry lines over auxiliary lines, which are intented to provide a set of references for snapping purposes.

Users generate faces, drawing a sequence of straight edges. It is not relevant in which order edges are drawn, since the three-dimensional reconstruction method only looks at connectivity and perceptual constraints. As soon as the system detect a complete face it is shaded and presented to the user (working in shaded mode).

Edges and segments can be removed using a scratching gesture. This not only allows errors to be corrected but also enables more complicated shapes to be drawn by refining "simpler" forms as illustrated in Figure 2. When drawing a scratch gesture, the application detects the edge(s) that the user wants to delete as being those intersecting the smallest quadrilateral enclosing the scratching gesture.

3.3 Line Drawing Beautification and 3D Sketchy Wireframe

Previous reconstruction-based applications usually include an offline 2D reconstruction stage, where the input sketch is adjusted. In our system we propose an online 2D reconstruction [17]. Online reconstruction provides an immediate feedback to the user, because it operates as the user draws the sketch, and it offers better integration in the calligraphic interface. This concept of 2D reconstruction is similar to drawing beautification proposed by Igarashi [6], [18] and it is aimed to adjust drawing entities provided by the CALI recognizer to be used at the 3D reconstruction stage.

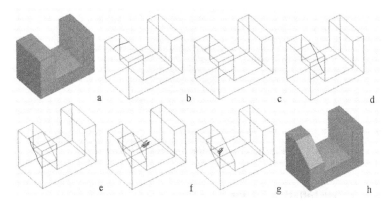

Fig. 2. Refining geometry from simple shapes

Correct work of the 3D reconstruction algorithm needs to clean up input data and adjust edges to make sure they meet precisely at common endpoints in order to get geometrically consistent figures. The "beautification" process has to filter all defects and errors of the initial sketches that are inherent to their inaccurate and incomplete nature. At present, the stage of 2D reconstruction receives geometric shapes of the *line* or *auxiliary line* type as input data. In order to provide an adequate database for the 3D geometric reconstructor, the application supports the following drawing aids:

- Automatic line slope adjustment: consists of checking whether the new line is parallel to any of the principal axes of the sketch by considering a slope tolerance. In case where the straight line is nearly parallel to one axis, then we adjust one or both endpoints so that the resulting line is now parallel to one of the main axes.
- Vertex point snap: it looks for vertices close to the line endpoints, again taking into account a vertex proximity tolerance. Should there be several such vertices, we select the one closest to that line endpoint.
- Vertex on line snap and automatic line breaking: for endpoints of the new line which do not lie close to a model vertex, the system analyzes whether the points are close to an existing edge, taking into account a given edge proximity tolerance. If several edges match this criterion, we select the edge that lies closest to the given endpoint. Then, the selected edge is broken at the contact point; in order to easy later delete operations, like in figure 2.e.

Snapping and adjustments are performed in real time. Other previous systems perform these analyses offline, when the user has finished sketching and before launching 3D reconstruction. A general tolerance parameter controls the beautification action, because some users prefer a less automatic drawing control. After this stage, all the 2D data are stored in a database consisting of a list of vertices and a list of edges.

The user can change the point of view and shading mode at all moment. There are three visualization modes: wireframe (fig. 3.b), shaded (fig. 3.c) and sketchy wireframe (fig 3.a and 3.d). This last mode is used to provide a hand-made look to the reconstructed model, and it is generated simply adding the z coordinate obtained from the reconstruction process in the raw 2D original sketch.

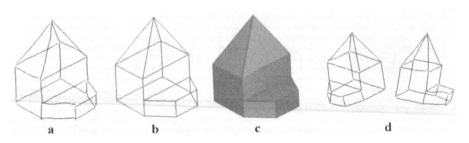

a   b   c   d

Fig. 3. Visualization modes in CIGRO

3.4 Axonometric Inflation Engine

To provide a real-time experience, we have implemented a fast reconstruction algorithm whose clearest antecedents are presented by Sugihara [19], Kanatani [20], and Lamb and Bandopadhay [21]. The shape domain supported by Axonometric Inflation is restricted to normalon objects. Where a *normalon* is rectangular trihedral polyhedron, whose corners consist of three mutually perpendicular edges (this name is an extension to 3D of Dori's definition of a normalon [22]). Other reconstruction strategies, with a wider universe of objects, have been discarded because they are not fast enough, since they rely on optimization or labeling algorithms.

Our implementation is similar to Kanatani's, and details on the approach can be found in [20]. In brief, the spatial orientation of an arbitrary corner (with one central a three lateral vertices) is analytically determined (see Figure 4.a, where D is the central vertex and A B C are the lateral ones). From this analytical relation, coordinates of all lateral vertices are obtained. Next, the process is repeated through a propagation tree that converts already determined lateral vertices into new central vertices of neighbor corners, ensuring in this way that a topologically consistent 3D model is constructed. We use a particular version of Kruskal algorithm to obtain a spanning tree formed by all edges connecting the successive central vertices.

The algorithm requires the concurrence of three orthogonal edges in each central vertex. Nevertheless, information about faces is not required and the restriction applies to central vertices only. The valence (the number of edges concurring in a vertex) of lateral vertices is irrelevant. Consequently, the approach will work if a spanning tree can be obtained where all central vertices have a valence of three, and all vertices of other valences can be determined as laterals. Moreover, only edges contained in the spanning tree must be parallel to main directions. Hence, the shape domain supported by CIGRO extends to *quasi-normalon* objects, which are objects that can be reduced to normalons by deleting all edges running non-parallel to the three main directions, without losing any vertices in the model. For practical purposes, we do distinguish two classes of quasi-normalon objects:

- Class 1: when a connected graph is obtained after simplification.
- Class 2: when a not connected graph is obtained after simplification.

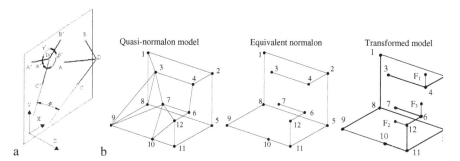

Fig. 4. a) Inflation method b) Transformation of a quasi-normalon model

3.4.1 Managing Class 1 Quasi-normalon Objects

Axonometric inflation can be applied to the class 1 quasi-normalon models as described above, provided than the spanning tree is determined in the equivalent normalon, obtained after the temporary elimination of all line-segments that are non-parallel to any of the three main directions. The equivalent normalon is valid if no vertex is deleted and the graph remains connected.

Sometimes, in spite of getting an equivalent normalon, axonometric inflation cannot be applied if certain vertices are not accessible through some valid spanning tree. This is the case when some junctions are only connected to other junctions with a valence below three. For instance, in Figure 4.b, vertex 3 is only connected to vertex 4, which cannot be central because its valence is two. Nevertheless, the assumption of the model to be a normalon has already been made. Hence, adding fictitious line-segments is coherent with the assumption and solves the problem. These fictitious line-segments are defined by unit length and oriented in accordance with those main directions still not present in the vertex. In Figure 4.b, fictitious edges 4-F1, 12-F2 and 6-F3 allow vertices 3, 6 and 7 to be determined. When vertices with a valence above three appear, the approach will still work if a valid spanning tree can be obtained; i.e. a tree where those vertices are not central. When this is not possible, we have limited ourselves to obtaining one of the potential models by randomly choosing three of the edges that converge in the vertex. But, moreover, for the method to be able to spread throughout the whole graph that defines the projection of the model, this graph must be connected. However, what sometimes occurs is that when the equivalent normalon of a quasi-normalon-type of model is obtained, the resulting graph is not connected resulting a class 2 object.

3.4.2 Managing Class 2 Quasi-normalon Objects

In these cases, and if the user has not drawn them, our system generates enough automatic auxiliary lines (fig. 6.a) to allow the reconstruction of the model. This algorithm essentially consists of joining the graphs that have been isolated as a consequence of

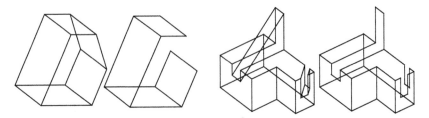

Fig. 5. Examples of Class 1 quasi-normalon-type 1 objetcs and their equivalent models

Quasi-normalon model   Equivalent normalon

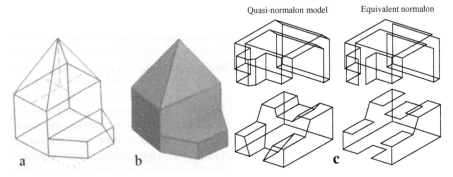

a   b   c

Fig. 6. Automatic auxiliary lines (dashed cyan lines in a) and class 2 quasi-normalon models

their conversion into equivalent normalons. Nevertheless, the graphs cannot be joined in a random fashion and the operation must comply with the following points:
1. The connecting edges must be parallel to the directions that define the xyz-axis (in order to ensure that the axonometric inflation method can spread).
2. The connecting edges and the vertices that are used to connect the graphs must be coplanar. This coplanarity condition obviously requires faces to be detected in the input 2D drawing, which is itself an encouraging task. Currently, to detect faces automatically, we make use of an adapted version of Courter and Brewer's [23] algorithm.

To determine the automatic auxiliary lines it is first selected a connecting edge that links the independent graphs resulting from the transformation into equivalent normalon (we call it hypotenuse). The selection is made at random from the set of candidate edges, although this does not mean losing the generality of the method. The second step is to replace the connecting edge with two edges that are parallel to one of the xyz-axis (we call them the cathetus), thus giving rise to a new vertex on the initial graph. The choice of two directions from the three offered by the xyz-axis is conditioned by the coplanarity criterion: i.e. the process begins by detecting a face that contains the connecting edge and at least two edges that run parallel to two of the directions belonging to the main trihedron. This is a necessary and adequate condition for the connecting edge to be replaced. Once the face has been determined, the replacement process is performed in accordance with the following criteria:

- If edges that run parallel to two dissimilar directions of the trihedron converge to the vertices of the connecting edge, we simply extend the converging edges until they intercept each other (see Figure 7.a)
- If edges running parallel to a same direction in the xyz-axis converge to the vertices of the connecting edge, the direction running parallel to one axis xyz that does not converge to the connecting edge is used to determine the new vertex. Unless there are two possible valid configurations, the random choice of one of them does not affect the generality of the method (see Figure 7.b).
-

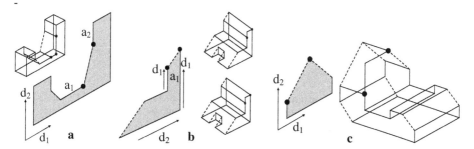

Fig. 7. Examples for the substitution of connecting edges

- If, at any of the vertices of the connecting edge, none of the edges running parallel to the directions of the dihedron converge, then an edge running parallel to the direction of the trihedron that does not exist in the other vertex of the connecting edge will be drawn in (see Figure 7.c).

The last step in the automatic auxiliary lines generation describe above is a simple check of the type of model, which is performed each time a connecting-edge is replaced by a pair of edges running parallel to some of the xyz-axis. After this check the following steps are taken: If the new model is connected, it is reconstructed, elsewhere the process is executed repeatedly for as long as there are still connecting-edges in the model.

4   Conclusions and Future Work

We have described an approach to input graphical normalons and quasi-normalon shapes using methods based on image processing. We plan to use this method as a foundation to shape input methods in current CAD systems. Instead of focusing on off-line algorithms, we aim at developing expeditious ways to construct geometric models through calligraphic interfaces. Our approach includes a three-dimensional reconstruction approach integrated in an interactive editor, using sketch input. This environment differs from previous approaches in that the speed of execution and timely feedback are more important than the ability to produce models from vectorized bitmaps in one step, as has been typical of previous efforts in computer vision. The cost for this is restricting the allowed shapes to a restricted set (quasi-normalons). However, using such shapes in conjunction with construction lines provides a sound basis for more sophisticated input techniques, including curves and surfaces. This will be approached in the future. Preliminary usability tests have shown encouraging results.

Acknowledgments. This work was supported in part by the Portuguese Science Foundation grant 34672/99, the European Commission project IST-2000-28169, the Spanish Generalidad Valenciana grant CTIDIB/2002/51 and Fundació Caixa Castelló-Bancaixa under the Universitat Jaume I program for Research Promotion (Project P1-1B2002-08).

References

1. Rubine, D.: Combining gestures and direct manipulation. Proceedings ACM CHI'92 Conference Human Factors in Computing Systems (1992) 659–660
2. Long, A.C., Landay, J.A., Rowe, L.A., Michiels, J.: Visual Similarity of Pen Gestures. Proceedings of Human Factors in Computer Systems (SIGCHI), (2000) 360–367
3. Fonseca, M., Jorge, J.: Experimental Evaluation of an On-Line Scribble Recognizer. Pattern Recognition Letters, **22** (12), (2001) 1311–1319
4. Zeleznik, R.C., Herndon, K.P., Hughes, J.F.: SKETCH: An interface for sketching 3D scenes. SIGGRAPH'96 Conference Proceedings (1996) 163–170
5. Eggli, L., Hsu, C., et al.: Inferring 3D Models from Freehand Sketches and Constraints. Computer-Aided Design, **29** (2), (1997) 101–112
6. Igarashi, T., Matsuoka, S., Tanaka, H.: Teddy: A Sketching Interface for 3D Freeform Design. ACM SIGGRAPH99 Conference Proc. (1999) 409–416
7. Pereira, J., Jorge, J., Branco, V., Nunes, F.: Towards calligraphic interfaces: sketching 3D scenes with gestures and context icons. WSCG'2000 Conference Proc. Skala V. Ed. (2000)
8. Huffman, D.A.: Impossible Objects as Nonsense Sentences. In: Meltzer B., Michie D. (eds.) Machine Intelligence, No. 6, Edimburgh UK. Edinburgh University Press (1971) 295–323
9. Clowes, M.B.: On Seeing Things. Artificial Intelligence, **2**, (1971) 79–116
10. Wang, W., Grinstein, G.: A Survey of 3D Solid Reconstruction from 2D Projection Line Drawing. Computer Graphics Forum, **12**(2), (1993) 137–158
11. Hoffman, D.: How we create what we see. Visual Intelligence, Norton Pub., **2**, (2000)
12. Marill, T.: Emulating the Human Interpretation of Line-Drawings as Three-Dimensional Objects. International Journal of Computer Vision, **6**(2), (1991) 147–161
13. Leclerc, Y., Fischler, M.: An Optimization-Based Approach to the Interpretation of Single Line Drawing as 3D Wire Frames. Int. Journal of Computer Vision, **9**(2), (1992) 113–136
14. Lipson, H., Shpitalni, M.: Optimization-Based Reconstruction of a 3D Object from a Single Freehand Line Drawing. Computer Aided Design, **28**(8), (1996) 651–663
15. Schweikardt, E., Gross, M.D.: Digital Clay: deriving digital models from freehand sketches. Automation in Construction, **9**, (2000) 107–115
16. Turner, A., Chapmann, D., and Penn, A.: Sketching space. Computers & Graphics, **24**, (2000) 869–-879
17. Oh, B.S., Kim, C.H.: Progressive 3D Reconstruction from a Sketch Drawing. In Proceedings of the 9th Pacific Conf. on Computer Graphics and Applications, (2001) 108–117

18. Igarashi, T., Matsuoka, S., Kawachiya, S., Tanaka, H.: Interactive Beautification: A Technique for Rapid Geometric Design, UIST'97, (1997) 105–114
19. Sugihara, K.: Interpretation of an axonometric projection of a polyhedron. Computers & Graphics, **8**(4), (1984) 391–400
20. Kanatani, K.: The Constraints on Images of Rectangular Polyhedra. IEEE Transactions on Pattern Analysis and Machine Intelligence, **8** (4), (1986) 456–463
21. Lamb, D., Bandopadhay, A.: Interpreting a 3D Object from a Rough 2D Line Drawing. Proceedings of Visualization´90, (1990) 59–66
22. Dori, D.: From Engineering Drawings to 3D CAD Models: Are We Ready Now?. Computer Aided Design, **27** (4), (1995) 243–254
23. Courter, S.M., Brewer J.A.: Automated Conversion of Curvilinear Wire-Frame Models to Surface Boundary Models. Comm. of ACM, **20**(4), (1986) 171–178

Intregated System and Methodology for Supporting Textile and Tile Pattern Design

José María Gomis, Margarita Valor, Francisco Albert, and Manuel Contero

DEGI, Universidad Politécnica de Valencia, Camino de Vera s/n,
46022 Valencia, Spain
{jmgomis, mvalor, fraalgil, mcontero}@degi.upv.es

Abstract. This paper presents a methodology for graphic pattern design and re-design applicable to tile and textile patterns. The methodology is based on a Design Information System integrated with two computer tools. One for the structural and morphologic analysis of graphic designs that uses as reference framework the scientific theory of symmetry groups, and a second interactive tool for the structural edition of patterns that exploits all the capabilities provided by the manipulation of the minimum region and fundamental parallelogram of pattern designs. We present some application examples to generate new designs as modifications from designs acquired from historic sources. The methodology and tools are oriented to bridge the gap between the historical and artistic production of graphic design and the tile and textile industries.

1   Graphic Design in the Textile and Tile Industries

In some industrial sectors, such as in the tile and textile industries, Graphic Design is an essential element, greatly contributing to product added value. Most companies have computer applications in their Design Departments able to create and edit decorative design patterns in raster and vector formats. In addition the Design Departments count with different sources of graphic information that help designers in their creative tasks. The data sources consist of ancient designs, catalogues and magazines and in some cases even available specialized databases.

On the other hand, an inherent aspect of the design activity is the reciprocity between pattern designs and the cultural environment in which the design activity is performed [1]. This particular aspect reflects the relationship between production and the social and cultural environment, as the image of a product in many cases is associated with the region, history and agents involved in its manufacture. Actually it would seem unreasonable not to take advantage and capitalize the rich artistic, crafts and industrial heritage present in many regions.

However, the relation between data sources and designers can be a difficult task. The great amount of information in design processes does not escape from the general situation of the general boom of information available. Added to this we have to men-

A. Butz et al. (Eds.): Smart Graphics 2003, LNCS 2733, pp. 69–78, 2003.

tion the great number of different formats used to present graphic information and the general lack of rigorous and objective classifications, a factor that is crucial for the fast and exhaustive access to relevant information. All these factors negatively affect the designer's data searching activity, which in the worst cases makes the designer abandon decorative images existing in design data sources, and in the best cases generates attitudes in the designers that are less keen on using data sources than desirable.

In our opinion, this situation arises as a consequence of the lack of integration of the data sources in the design environment and the lack of structural design tools for the exploration of data sources; this occurs because the designer's activity is not integrated in a unique Computer Aided Design and Manufacturing Environment.

2 Trends in Graphic Design in the Textile and Tile Industries

The future trends of graphic design systems will be marked by the development of computer assistants similar to those used in other computer applications. We believe that the work of graphic design specialists will improve the quality of the design activity, orienting their work to that of a creativity manager-planner. This possibility will depend on the availability of operational and efficient data sources and on the development of tools for database processing in the field of graphic pattern design. The influence of these potential tools on present graphic design techniques and methodologies will be significant. Summarizing, in our opinion some of the most remarkable factors that will define graphic design platforms in the future are the following:

1. Integration of the more conceptual stages of pattern design in integrated design and manufacturing systems. Integration involves two aspects: the use of specific and user-friendly peripheral devices and the development of interfaces that enable the use of the peripheral devices.

2. Creation and use of libraries at the different stages of the graphic design process. These libraries stored in databases should allow vertical (within the same decoration pattern design) and horizontal (considering a certain set of design patterns) data consultation through content retrieval tools. Using the analogy of literary creation, these libraries will provide the designer with the existing formal vocabulary in addition to the lexicon he himself can add to his own creations.

3. The development of advanced (structural) design tools for graphic design systems. Object and basic pattern design creation and edition tools are commercially available in the field of Computer Aided Graphic Design. However, there are no interactive computer tools for advanced pattern design at structural level. The development of design tools that allow acting on all hierarchical levels of pattern design will enhance the creative potential of designers who will be able to adapt their methodological approaches to textile and tile design activities.

3   Related Work

Many articles and books have been devoted to the study of ornamental patterns and tilings using the theoretical framework of the planar symmetry groups [1, 2, 3]. With the development of computer graphics, applications to design symmetric patterns have been developed. One of the first references is the system presented by Alexander at the 2nd annual SIGGRAPH conference, in 1975, for generating the 17 symmetry patterns in the plane [7]. Since then, many other research tools for automatic generation of symmetry patterns have been developed [8, 9, 10, 11, 12] mainly oriented to experiment with different algorithms for ornamental pattern creation.

Nowadays, we can find some graphic applications in the market that allow the edition of graphic designs using symmetries. Among them we can mention Terrazzo [16], available as a plug-in for Adobe Photoshop, and SymmetryWorks [17], available as a plug-in for Adobe Illustrator. Table 1 compares some of their main features. The major difference between these two tools comes mainly from the raster (Terrazo) or vector (SymmetryWorks) nature. Both select a determined minimum region for each plane symmetry group and directly apply the required isometries, but the edition process is restricted to the 17 symmetry groups without analyzing other parameters.

As a summary we can conclude that at this moment there is not any integrated graphic design application oriented to incorporate historical sources in the design cycle by means of ornamental design libraries that incorporate structural information.

4   Information System for Graphic Design

In the context, the authors of this work propose an Information System for Graphic Design (ISGD). This system uses the theory of symmetry groups to structure the information obtained from design databases, helping to develop a graphic design methodology for the textile and tile industries [15]. In the development of the system we have considered the simultaneous access to the same data source and that some modules can be used in other departments of the company. This concurrent operational system has been solved with a Client/Server architecture [14], which will be connected to Internet in the future. Figure 1 illustrates the modular architecture of ISGD that has two main modules:

-   The module DDMRS: Design Data Management and Retrieval System, consists mainly of two independent DB implemented with a Management System (SGBD). The Acquisition Database provides storage and management system of textile and tile images. The Pattern Design Database provides scientific-technical data storage and management system of industrial pattern designs.
-   The module DPAES: Design Pattern Analysis and Edition System, implements two individual applications. The Analysis Tool consists of a specific-purpose application for the analysis and cataloguing of pattern designs, and a set of transactions with the databases. It is fed by the acquisition databases and at the same time it feeds the design databases. This tool is explained in the following section of the paper. The Edition Tool provides specialiced query capabilityes to design

databases and edition functions to generate new design patterns from already existing designs. This tool follows the design process proposed in section 6.

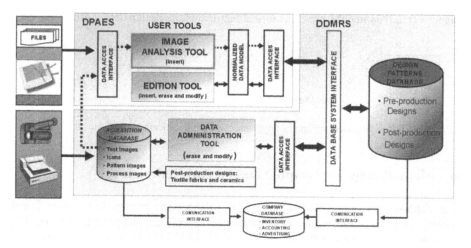

Fig. 1. Developed information system for graphic design

5   Analysis Tool for Textile and Tile Pattern Design

The analysis tool [13] consists of a set of operators each of which represents a stage in the graphic design process that gradually increases the level of the information processed [4]. The operators are organized in different spaces, illustrated in figure 2 with the analysis of a tiling design. This tool allows automatically extracting (see Fig. 3) the objects and groups together with the point symmetry group and the design structure (Fundamental Parallelogram). The design structure is obtained from the cataloguing resulting from the application of the scientific theory of plane symmetry groups [1, 2, 3, 5, 6]. It is important to note that this tool permits the theoretical reconstruction of the original decorative patterns, providing a way to make the most of the historical sources as seen in figures 8 and 9.

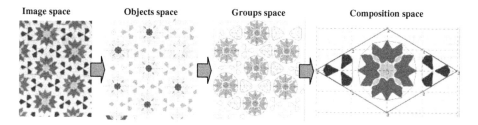

Fig. 2. Analysis tool: organization of the operators into spaces

The explotation of the syntactic and morphological understanding of design pattern requires to provide specific tools and methods. With this objective, we present a methodology for both design and redesign of ornamental patterns that empowers the designer's creativity and the use of historical textile and tile design data sources.

Fig. 3. Design understanding: image analysis output (objects, groups and structure)

6   Methodology for Graphic Design and Redesign

The methodology proposed here incorporates the aspects indicated in section 2 and having into account the graphic design structure described in the previous section. We propose a design method that works at three levels: objects, groups and structure, permanently fed by the creative sources as shown in figure 4. Object and basic group edition are available in commercial graphic design applications. However, the same does not happen with design composition structures.

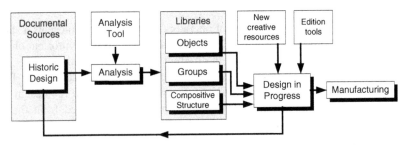

Fig. 4. Stages in the design and redesign method proposed by the authors

Our proposal for the structural edition of pattern designs is based on the fact that some plane regions are capable of generating different pattern designs depending on the isometries used. If each of these plane regions is considered as the tile or minimum region (MR) of a fundamental parallelogram (FP), which in our case is one of the results of the image analysis tool, the first problem to solve will be to obtain it from the FP and its plane symmetry group.

6.1   Principles

This method starts with the 93 types of tiles of an isohedral tiling [2]. Each one of the 93 tiles generates an isohedral tiling pattern with a given plane symmetry group. The tiles are defined by the combination of the following features: a) the shape or contour that delimits the tile; b) the isometries applied to the tile to generate a regular segmentation. In addition, we have taken into account that the geometry of the tile involves a number of geometrical constraints [8] to avoid gaps and overlapping when applying the isometries that generate the tiling pattern.

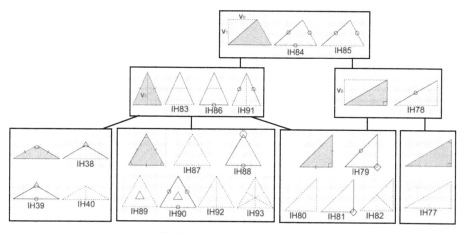

Fig. 5. Scheme of triangular tiles

The first task will be to relate the types of tiles given by [2] with the geometrical constraints presented by [8]; this allows to establish the geometry of the tile as the isometries applied to generate the tiling pattern. To do this, the 93 types of tiles were ordered according to the number of sides or vertices (3, 4, 5 or 6). Simultaneously, each of these four types was ordered depending on the geometrical constraints of the tile to generate a particular plane symmetry group. The ordering process is done from the tile with fewer geometrical constraints or less regular. The more regular a tile is, the more geometrical constraints it will involve. As the parameters are defined (angles and/or distances) in the less regular tile, more regular or with fewer constraint tiles are generated. The ordering process for a triangular tile is shown in figure 5; this figure illustrates the possible isohedral tiling patterns associated with the tile.

In addition to the associated tiling patterns, each tile can also generate other tile patterns associated with less regular tiles. This ordering process provides the starting point for the edition of the different design patterns of any tile or MR, for both already-existing and new design patterns.

6.2 Overall Scheme

The structural edition tool consists of a number of steps organized as shown in figure 6. Basically this edition system is developed from the parameters resulting from the definition of an MR and its associated isometries. The edition process varies depending on whether it starts with data obtained from the image analysis to create a redesign pattern or to create a new pattern design. In the first case, the MR is already specified, whereas in the second case it is defined by the designer. For the case of the edition of new pattern designs, the process follows the sequence shown on the left side of figure 6. Whereas in the case of pattern redesign, the edition permits any combination (regardless the order) of the steps shown on the right side of figure 6. In order to avoid gaps and overlapping, the system provides automatic constraints for side edition, object grouping and isometries edition.

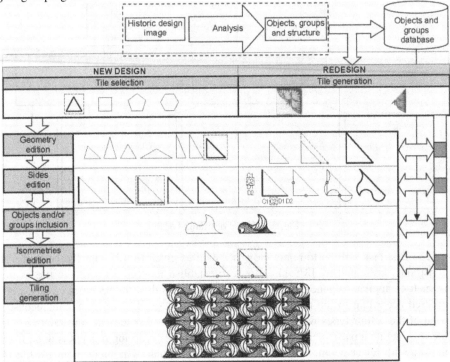

Fig. 6. Scheme of structural edition

7   Edition Tools

Our design methodology has been implemented by means of an Adobe Illustrator experimental plug-in. The design edition can be performed at two levels: group level and structure level. Design templates with the required isometries for the design generation are provided for both levels (see figure 7).

Group templates allow to create object grouping with a given point symmetry group. For structural design, there are two working procedures: through templates based on the fundamental parallelogram (FP) or on the minimum region (MR). In addition, the system permits to shift from one working mode to the other, combining the advantages of both methods: simplicity (FP) and generation of design variations (MR). In both cases, position, size and orientation can be changed as well as the free parameters of FP or MR geometry. With the FP (design template) the structure is defined by the FP, the isometries that define the Plane Symmetry group (PSG) and the location of the MR. In the illustration of the figure 7, the FP is presented in black, the symmetry axes with displacement are in red, the symmetry axes with no displacement are in green and the minimum region is in yellow. With the MR (tiling template) the structure is defined by the MR and the isometries to apply.

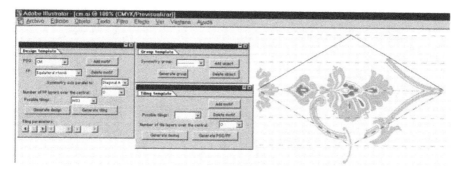

Fig. 7. Example screen of the experimental plug-in

Table 1 shows a detailed comparison among some of the most widespread commercial tools used in pattern design.

Table 1. Design tools comparison

Features of the edition tools			TERRAZO	SYMMETRY WORKS	OUR PLUG-IN
Group template	Symmetry: [C2,C12], [D1,D12]		NO	NO	YES
	One symmetry axis direction				
FP/PSG template	FP (fundamental parallelogram)	Geometry: square (S), rectangle (RE), rhomb (RH), equilateral rhomb (ERH), parallelogram (P)	NO	NO	YES
		Position			
		Size			
		Orientation			
		Parameters: S, ERH (0), RE, RH (1); P (2)			
	PSG (plane symmetry group)	PSG: P1, PM, PG, CM, P2 ...	YES	YES	YES
		One axis direction for PG, PM, CM and PMG	NO	NO	YES
	Design size		YES	YES	YES
Tile(MR) / IH template	Tile (MR. minimum region)	Geometry: 3, 4, 5 or 6 sides	NO	NO	YES
		Position	YES	YES	YES
		Size	YES	(but very difficult)	YES
		Orientation	NO		YES
		Parameters: 0,1,2,3,4,5 or 6	YES (but not all)	NO	YES
	IH (tiling)	Final IH and associated PSG	NO	NO	YES
		Different options from the same IH			
	Tiling size		NO	NO	YES
Obtaining Tile(MR)/IH template from FP/PSG template			NO	NO	YES
Obtaining FP/PSG template from Tile/IH template			NO	NO	YES

8   Results and Conclusions

This paper presents a new methodology for graphic pattern design and redesign applicable to tile and textile patterns. The methodology is based on a Design Information

System equipped with a computer tool for the structural and morphologic analysis of graphic designs and a tool for the structural edition of graphic designs. The methodology presented for pattern design combines the designer's creativity with the use of historical design data sources. The interactive design edition tool exploits the possibil-

Fig. 8. Textile pattern reconstruction (CM) and generation (P31M, P2, PMG)

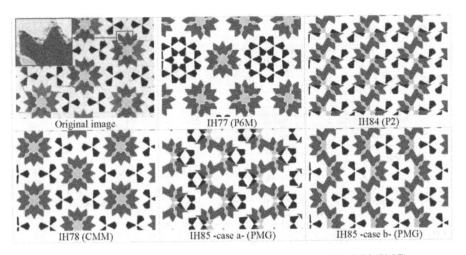

Fig. 9. Tite pattern reconstruction (CMM) and generation (P6M, P2, PMG)

ity of generating pattern designs using minimum regions and fundamental parallelograms. The results obtained allow applying this technique to the textile and tile industries, bridging the gap between the historical and artistic production of graphic design and the tile and textile industries. Figure 8, shows the generation of different textile pattern designs from a piece of a XVIII century cloth. The original image is a bitmap, where we have included a detail that shows the fabric texture. The other images show the theoretical reconstructed design and some redesigns in vectorial format.

Figure 9 illustrates the generation of some design patterns from an Islamic mosaic. Defects and deformation on mosaic pieces geometry that we can see in the detail of the original image (bitmap) are corrected by the analysis tool, as showed in the reconstructed image (vectorial).

Both figure 8 and 9 shows some of the features included in Table 1 such as isohedral tile design (IH) and plane symmetry group (PSG).

Acknowledgments. This work has been supported by the Spanish Science and Technology Ministry and the European Union (Project DPI2001-2713).

References

1. Washburn, D.K., Crowe, D.W.: Symmetries of Culture: Theory and Practice of Plane Pattern Analysis. University of Washington Press, Seattle (1988)
2. Grünbaum, B., Shephard, G.C.: Tilings and Patterns. W. H. Freeman, New York (1987)
3. Shubnikov, A.V., Koptsik, V.A.: Symmetry in Science and Art. Plenum Press, NY, (1974)
4. Valiente, J.M., Albert, F., Gomis, J.M.: Feature Extraction and Classification of Textile Images: Towards a Design Information System for the Textile Industry. 2nd Int. Workshop on Pattern Recognition in Information Systems, Alicante, Spain, (2002) 77–94
5. Martin, G.E.: Transformation Geometry. An Introduction to Symmetry. Springer-Verlag, New York (1982)
6. Schattschneider, D.: The Plane Symmetry Groups: Their Recognition and Notation. The American Mathematical Monthly **85** (1978) 439–450
7. Alexander, H.: The computer/ploter and the 17 ornamental design types. Proceedings of SIGGRAPH '75, (1975), 160–177.
8. Kaplan, C., Salesin, D.: Escherization. Proc. Of SIGGRAPH 2000, (2000) 499-510
9. Kaplan, C.: Computer Generated Islamic Star Patterns. Visual Mathematics **2** (3) (2000)
10. Field, M.: The Art and Science of Symmetric Design. Visual Mathematics **2** (3) (2000)
11. Ostromoukhov, V.: Mathematical Tools for Computer-Generated Ornamental Patterns. Lecture Notes in Computer Science 1375, (1998), 192–223
12. Akleman, E., Chen, J., and Meric, B.: Web-based intuitive and effective design of symmetric tiles. Proceedings of ACM Multimedia 2000 Workshops, (2000), 1–4.
13. Valor, M., Albert, F., Gomis, J.M., Contero, M.: Analysis Tool for Cataloguing Textile and Tile Pattern Designs. Procdings of the II International Workshop on Computer Graphics and Geometric Modeling CGGM'2003 Montreal, Canada, (2003)
14. Elbert, R.: Client-server Computing: Architecture, Applications, and Distributed Systems Management. .Boston, Artech House, (1994)
15. Valiente, J.M., Carretero, M.C., Gomis, J.M, Albert, F.: Image Processing Tool for the Purpose of Textile Fabric Modeling. Proceedings of the XII ADM International Conference on Design Tools and Methods in Industrial Engineering, Rimini, Italy, (2001) 56–64
16. Xaos Tools web site <http://www.xaostools.com/products/terrmain.html>
17. Artlandia web site <http://www.artlandia.com/products/symmetryworks>

Smart 3d Visualizations in Clinical Applications

Bernhard Preim[1] and Heinz-Otto Peitgen[2]

[1]Institute for Simulation and Graphics, Department for Computer Science
Otto-von-Guericke-University of Magdeburg, Universitaetsplatz 2, 39106 Magdeburg
`preim@isg.cs.uni-magdeburg.de`
[2]Center for Medical Diagnosic Systems and Visualization, Universitaetsallee 29,
28359 Bremen, `peitgen@mevis.de`

Abstract. We discuss techniques for the visualization of medical volume data dedicated for their clinical use. We describe the need for rapid dynamic interaction facilities with such visualizations and discuss emphasis techniques in more detail. Another crucial aspect of medical visualization is the integration of 2d and 3d visualizations. In order to organize this discussion, we introduce 6 „Golden" rules for medical visualizations.

1 Introduction

Many tasks in medical applications can be supported with appropriate visualizations. In addition to visualizations from textbooks, computer-generated and highly interactive 3d visualizations are employed in medical education. In anatomy education, for example, the VOXELMAN [9–11] is used to allow the exploration of medical volume data with advanced cut and clip functions. The volume data was enriched by a sophisticated knowledge representation about anatomical taxonomy ("intelligent" voxels). The pioneering work of the VOXELMAN has inspired some of the ideas presented here. Another long-term effort has been carried out in surgery simulation by KÜHNAPFEL et al. [1, 12]. They developed the KISMET system which simulates bleeding and smoke caused by surgical devices besides a variety of other interactions between surgical devices and human tissue.

"Idealized" and clinical data. The discussion of appropriate visualizations has to consider the quality of the underlying data which differs strongly between the above-mentioned educational applications and applications for the routine clinical use. For educational purposes, idealized data, such as the Visible Human dataset of the National Library of Medicine are employed. The use of a cadaver dataset has several advantages: high radiation can be applied and motion artifacts for example from breathing do not occur. These datasets are carefully prepared and enriched with additional information. Such a time-consuming approach is not feasible for medical diagnosis and treatment planning. The underlying data have less quality (because they are acquired from living patients). This paper is focused on clinical applications and dis-

A. Butz et al. (Eds.): Smart Graphics 2003, LNCS 2733, pp. 79–90, 2003.

cusses visualization and interaction techniques that are designed to support diagnostic processes and treatment decisions, such as operability of a patient.

This paper is organized as follows: In Sect. 2 visualization techniques currently used for medical diagnosis and treatment planning are described. This section is followed by the brief Sect. 3 which names six "golden rules" for smart medical visualizations which are discussed in the remainder of this paper.

2 3d Visualizations for clinical applications

3d visualizations in medicine are based on radiological image data. Primarily CT (computed tomography) data,and MRI (Magnetic Resonance Imaging) are used. The traditional – film-based or soft-copy – "reading" of radiological image data represents a slice-by-slice inspection. Due to the growing resolution of image scanners this is no longer feasible as the only inspection method. As an example, CT data of the human thorax acquired with multislice image devices produce some 500 slices. Therefore, 3d visualizations, such as direct volume rendering, isosurface rendering, and maximum-intensity-projections (MIP) are becoming more commonly used. MIP images depict the brightest voxel along each line of sight and thus do not require any user interaction with respect to opacity settings ([3] gives an excellent overview on these basic techniques). Direct volume rendering and isosurface rendering, on the other hand, strongly depend on user settings. Predefined transfer functions for certain visualization tasks, such as highlighting bony structures in CT data, are used to reduce the interaction effort. Unfortunately, such predefined settings are not reliable for MR data (which do not exhibit a standardized intensity scale and are less homogeneous) and for the visual delineation of structures with similar intensity values.

If the diagnosis is confirmed, radiologists demonstrate the images to the referring physician in order to discuss the therapy. Furthermore, if an intervention is considered radiologists and surgeons discuss the strategy. Still, it is common to use static images, either slices from the original data or rendered images for this discussion. If interactive 3d visualizations are used at all, it is the radiologist who operates the system in order to show what is important. In order to understand the 3d reality of a particular patient's organ, it is desirable that interactive 3d visualizations are used and that the surgeon is in control to explore the data in order to answer his or her questions.

3 The Six Golden Rules for the Design of Smart Medical Visualization

SHNEIDERMAN succeeded in convincing people of his 8 "golden rules" for user interface design [20]. Inspired by these we present 6 "golden rules" for the design of smart medical visualizations. "Smart" means that the visualizations are useful for clinical tasks which includes that they are recognizable and dedicated to a particular task. Moreover, smart medical visualizations are fast to generate and can be interactively explored. The following rules are based on our experience with the development and evaluation of clinical applications.

- Integrate 2d and 3d visualization with interaction facilities in both views
- Provide useful defaults for visualization parameters
- Provide dynamic interaction facilities
- Use model-based visualizations, for example for thin elongated structures
- Provide appropriate emphasis techniques
- Include anatomical context in the visualization of the relevant structures

The rest of the paper is devoted to the discussion of these 6 rules.

4 Integration of 2d and 3d Visualizations

On the first glance it seems that smart medical visualizations should be 3d exclusively. The human body is a three-dimensional system; therapy planning and surgery simulation based on 3d visualizations are therefore more realistic than visualizations based on 2d slice visualizations. 3d visualizations with appropriate depth-cues (first of all shading) are intuitively comprehensible and seem to be superior. Despite of these obvious advantages, clinically relevant therapy planning systems contain 2d and 3d visualizations and interactive manipulations are allowed in both often with some kind of synchronization between the views.

The question arises whether 2d visualizations are only needed for conservative medical doctors not accustomed to the great benefit of 3d visualizations, so-to-say to be upward compatible to slice-based reading. Researchers in the field agree on real benefits of and needs for 2d visualizations, too.

In general, 2d-visualizations better support precise interaction. Precision is required, for example when measurements are derived, implants are placed in the geometric model of the patient and drilling procedures are planned. 2d visualizations are useful for these tasks because selection tasks which are part of the discussed tasks can be accomplished more precisely. Each voxel can be selected if the appropriate slice is chosen for the 2d visualization. 3d visualizations provide an overview; the "big" picture of the data. They are used, for example, to decide which range of slices is displayed in the respective 2d view in more detail. As a consequence, 2d and 3d visualizations allow for interactions in both views.

While this general principle has been realized in several medical visualization systems, we have applied it consequently to all interactions frequently required for therapy planning ([16]). For example, 2d and 3d visualizations are employed for the placement of applicator devices used for minimally-invasive operations. The precise definition of the target point (the point where the applicator produces a maximum of energy to destroy the pathology around) is usually selected in 2d. The entry point (where the applicator penetrates the skin) might also be selected in a 2d visualization. Whether important structures are hurt by this access path, however, becomes more obvious in 3d visualizations (see Fig. 2). In a similar manner, 2d and 3d visualizations

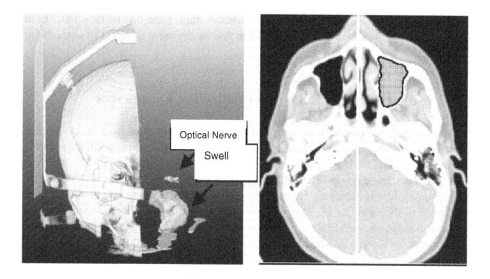

Fig. 1. The 3d visualization of a human head in CT data and the corresponding 2d visualization. The clipping plane is also included in the 2d visualization and can be manipulated in both views. The segmentation results are transparently overlaid to the original data in the 2d view. Radiological data kindly provided by University of Leipzig (Dr. Strauß).

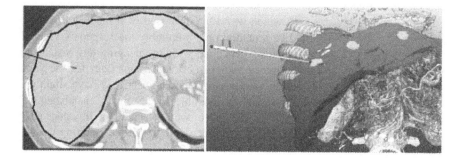

Fig. 2. Synchronized 2d and 3d visualizations of a CT liver data set with the segmented liver and three liver lesions (white). The visualization is used for the planning of a minimally-invasive therapy with a laser applicator. Radiological data kindly provided by the Technical University of Munich (Prof. Feussner)

are combined for measurements, such as distances and angles for the quantitative analysis of spatial relations. Another frequent task in therapy planning is the specification of resection areas (those parts of the body which should be removed later in surgery). Resection specification can be accomplished in 2d (by drawing into selected slices and interpolating between them) and in 3d by moving surgical tools through the data which virtually remove tissue. Again, it is crucial to evaluate the virtual resection in the other view. If the resection area was specified in 2d, the 3d view shows its general shape – which is important to assess whether this shape can be resected. On the other hand, if the resection was specified in 3d, the 2d view is useful to asses the affected regions.

5 Provide Useful Defaults for Visualization Parameters

Visualizations, such as these presented in Figs. 1-2 are controlled by a variety of parameters. These include object colors, transparency values, the viewing direction as well as smoothness and quality parameters. It is essential that these parameters are available via the graphical user interface. However, it is tedious if they have to be specified again and again for individual objects. Hence, meaningful default values which can be accepted in the majority of the cases are crucial for the usability of such a system. How can these be specified? First it is important to classify objects, because such a classification provides a useful base for the assignment of default values. Examples of object classes are organs, bony structures, vascular structures and tumors. Organs are large structures: usually it is desirable to see details of the organ interior. Therefore, by default they are rendered semitransparently whereas lesions and vascular structures are not. Note, that different transparency values are useful for 2d and 3d visualizations. In 2d visualizations (Fig. 2, left) the original data should be visible to some extent. Therefore, even lesions and vascular structures are not displayed fully opaque. Large compact structures such as organs can be displayed with lower resolution compared to thin elongated structures.

Finally, and that is an aspect which was often discussed with medical doctors: the initial viewing direction should be a natural one, preferably the surgeon's view. The two images in Fig. 2 for example are generated without changing any visualization parameter. All colors and transparency values, the transfer functions for the volume rendering correspond to the default values. An individual user may have slightly different preferences. Therefore, it should be possible to customize visualizations by storing personalized default values. The benefit of well-selected default values are not only time-savings but also better quality and reproducibility of the resulting visualization.

6 Dynamic Medical Visualizations

The understanding of the complex spatial phenomena inside the human body requires the interactive manipulation of images. Dynamic visualizations – interactive visualizations with rapid feedback after continuous interaction – are particularly useful for this understanding because changes between images can be observed and need not to be interpreted (see [21] for a discussion of active and dynamic visualizations).

There are several wide-spread interaction tasks in medical visualization which can be supported with dynamic interactions initiated with the pointing device on the image viewer (see Fig. 3). Clipping planes and clip boxes are translated and rotated in order

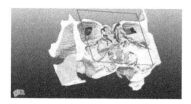

Fig. 3. Exploration of a CT data set of the human head. The continuous movement of the clipping plane is used to gain insight into the nasal cavities. The images were acquired to prepare surgery in this area. The spatial relations to critical structures, in particular the optical nerves, are essential. The cube in the lower left corner indicates the viewing direction. Radiological data kindly provided by University of Leipzig (Dr. Strauß).

to suppress parts of the underlying data. Radiologists are used to adapt brightness and contrast of volume rendered images by simply dragging the mouse (the x- and y-position of the mouse specify the parameters for the widely used ramp transfer functions). Again, the interaction can be initiated without moving the pointing device outside the visualization to some control element. Also, the traditional 2d slice view can be enhanced with dynamic interaction such that the displayed slice changes continuously as long as a certain combination of mouse buttons is pressed. This interaction is referred to as the cine-mode.

Another effective dynamic interaction facility is included in the VOXELMAN (recall [9-11]). It is based on a sorting process of the object's relation to the skin. With a continuous mouse movement objects are hidden starting from those closer to the skin giving sight to more distant ones. Compared to the traditional interaction required to hide objects (select them individually and press some button to hide them) this is much faster and again allows to concentrate on the visualization.

7 Integration of Anatomical Context

Medical visualizations for sophisticated treatment planning procedures are based on prior image analysis. Examples are planning processes for total hip replacements [2, 8], facial surgery [4], neurosurgery [6] and liver surgery [19]. In the image analysis stage, important anatomical and pathological structures are identified and delineated (segmented). The segmented objects are usually visualized by means of surface rendering. With appropriate smoothing and shading this often yields easy-to-interpret visualizations.

Segmented objects might be selectively displayed or hidden to customize the visualization to the questions related to the therapeutic process at hand. However, the mere visualization of important structures is often insufficient. The lack of surrounding tissue, in particular of skeletal structures makes it very difficult to understand the current view. Therefore, medical doctors appreciate the visual integration of bony structures (usually displayed by means of volume rendering) and structures which are in the focus (see Fig. 4).

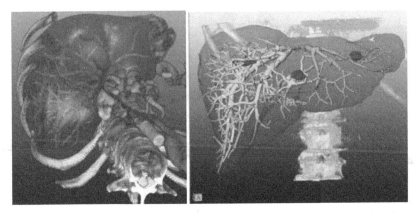

Fig. 4. Hybrid combination of the direct volume rendering of bony structures and surface rendering of intrahepatic structures (liver, vascular systems, tumors in the right view). The bony structures serve as anatomical context for the intrahepatic structures. Radiological data kindly provided by Medical School Hannover (Prof. Galanski).

8 Model-Based Visualizations

Medical visualizations for clinical use have two fulfil two requirements:
1. they should strictly adhere to the underlying radiological data and
2. they should be easy to interpret.

Let us discuss these requirements with respect to vascular structures. These structures are often very thin, for example in the periphery of vascular trees. Due to the limited spatial resolution of CT and MR scanners these thin structures are often represented by only one or two voxels per slice. A straightforward visualization that fulfils the first requirement usually results in noisy visualizations due to the limited spatial resolution of radiological data. For example, it is very difficult, to assess the topology of a vascular tree based on such visualizations. This, however, is often crucial for surgery planning where risks of a procedure have to judged. As an example of this risk analysis it is important to recognize which branches of a vascular tree would be affected if a certain branch is cut. To support those questions, more abstract visualizations serve better. Therefore, several attempts have been made to reconstruct vascular structures based on a prior vessel skeletonization [5, 17]. In the skeletonization process, the medial axis inside the vessel as well as the minimum and maximum diameter for each skeleton voxel is derived (see [19] for details). This information can be used to visualize vascular trees by means of graphics primitives fitted along the skeleton path. As an example, we used truncated concatenated cones as the underlying primitives [7]. Special care was taken to provide smooth transitions of surface normals at branchings. Fig. 4 and Fig. 5 show examples of this vessel visualization method. This method has been developed and refined in fruitful discussions with radiologists and obviously is a good comprise between the desire to have precise *and* easy-to-interpret visualizations.

The degree of correspondence to the radiological data is adjustable by the number of cones that are generated. Cones can be generated between two subsequent voxels (highest level of correspondence) or only between branchings of the vascular tree (lowest level of correspondence). Also, the vessel diameter can adhere strictly to the values measured in the skeletonization process or be smoothed in order to reduce the effect of rounding errors (see Fig. 6). In summary, the degree of realism is adjustable with such model-based visualizations.

This method is based on the assumption that the cross-section of vascular structures is circular. This assumption, of course, is a simplification. It is not appropriate when vascular diseases should be diagnosed. However, for many therapy planning tasks it is crucial to understand the spatial relation between pathologic structures and adjacent vascular structures. In such cases these model-based visualizations are very helpful.[1] Similar model-based visualizations are used in the VOXELMAN (recall [9-11]) where B-spline shapes are fitted to selected points which represent nerves in some slices. These structures are so small that they appear in some slices and disappear in others. Using the anatomical knowledge that the nerves are connected and using knowledge about their principal shape appropriate visualizations can be generated with the reconstruction process described in [14].

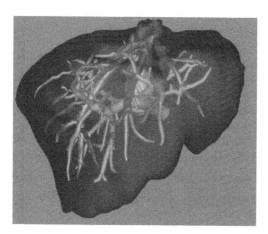

Fig. 5. High quality visualization of the intrahepatic vascular anatomy (hepatic and portal veins). Radiological data kindly provided by Medical School Hannover (Prof. Galanski).

9 Emphasis in Medical 3d Visualizations

In therapy planning applications as well as in software for medical education it is often necessary to highlight an anatomic or pathologic structure. As an example, the user of

---

[1] Some details of the described visualization are inspired by medical doctors. The visualization method is regularly used for liver surgery planning.

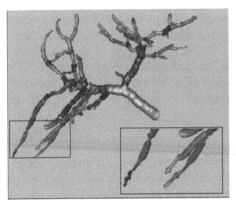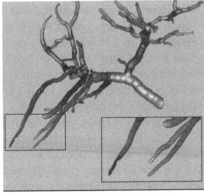

Fig. 6. Model-based vessel visualizations with different settings for the smoothing of the vessel diameter. The vessel diameter is color-coded. In the left image, no smoothing is applied which results in obvious discontinuities in the periphery. These discontinuities are due to the limited spatial resolution of the underlying data.

such a system selects an object in a list via its name and the system should provide feedback emphasizing this object. Another obvious reason for the need of 3d emphasis techniques is due to the integration of 2d and 3d views (recall Sect. 4). After an object is selected in a 2d view it should be highlighted in the 3d view to support the connection between the two visualizations.

The emphasis of objects in 3d visualizations is difficult by its very nature. From the current viewing position objects might be too small to be recognizable or they might be occluded by other objects. In medical visualizations these problems are prevalent: objects are often concave, are at least partly occluded by others. Therefore simple emphasis techniques such as the use of a special colour for highlighted objects or blinking do not work well. Emphasis techniques therefore should ensure the visibility of the involved objects (see [18]). In principle, two strategies are possible to achieve visibility:

- the camera position might be changed to make the desired object visible or
- visualization parameters of occluding objects might be adapted to allow to look through them.

The first strategy, in general, cannot be recommended. A radical change of the camera position, not initiated by the user, is often not comfortable because the user has to interpret this change and perhaps dislikes the chosen perspective. Unnatural viewing directions may result. The change of visualization parameters, the second strategy, can be implemented by using transparency: occluding objects are rendered semitransparently to reveal objects behind. This is a viable approach, however showing apparent drawbacks. If several objects are in front of the object to be emphasized all occluding objects must be strongly transparent with the result that they are almost unrecognizable (see Fig. 7). As an alternative, fast silhouette generation algorithms might be used to enhance the visualization of the transparently rendered objects. For the sake of brevity, emphasis techniques could only be touched here. There is a variety of emphasis techniques suitable for medical visualization, including those based on the shadow generation for selected objects (see [15] for a review on such techniques).

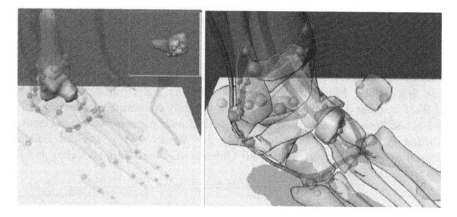

Fig. 7. Visualizations of bony structures and some muscles of the human foot as part of an educational system (the spheres represent docking positions to compose objects). A particular bone is emphasized using transparency of other objects (left). In the right view the shape of the transparent objects is emphasized with line drawing of their silhouette.

10 Concluding Remarks

Smart medical visualizations integrate 2d and 3d visualizations with a bi-directional link in order to synchronize changes between both. 3d visualizations of the relevant anatomic and pathologic structures are integrated with the anatomic context which provides a reference. Appropriate visualization parameters depend on the category of the respective object; vascular structures should be rendered with other parameters than organs or pathologic lesions per default. A comprehensible visualization of thin elongated branching structures requires other parameters as large compact structures. Smart medical visualizations include predefined parameters for different categories. In particular for vascular structures a model-based reconstruction is useful for the visualization. Finally, smart medical visualizations are highly interactive. They support dynamic changes which are initiated with the pointing device on an image view.

Future Work. So far, non realistic renderings [22] have not been integrated in medical visualizations used in the clinical routine. With their ability to emphasize shape and structures, these algorithms are promising for such applications. Another wide area for future work is the incorporation of uncertainty visualization techniques. The image acquisition and image analysis steps which are carried out prior to visualization may produce imprecise or unreliable results. At least some of these "errors" might be estimated. For example, tumor segmentation is often imprecise because the lesions have similar intensity values to the surrounding tissue and apparently no gradient at their borders. Special visualization techniques should be developed to encode this uncertainty (see for example [13]). Finally, the development of emphasis techniques dedicated to the complex shapes in medical visualizations is an area where further research is needed. In particular, the appropriate technique should be automatically selected by the visualization system (taking into account object visibility, size and shape).

Acknowledgements. We want to thank our collaborators at MeVis: Dr. Holger Bourquain, Horst Hahn, Milo Hindennach, Arne Littmann, Felix Ritter, Andrea Schenk, and Wolf Spindler. In particular, Horst Hahn carefully commented on the paper. The paper is also based on many discussions with our clinical partners: we want to thank in particular Prof. Hubertus Feussner (University Munich), Prof. Michael Galanski (Medical School Hannover), Prof. Karl Oldhafer (General Hospital Celle) and Dr. Gero Strauß (University Leipzig).

References

[1] HK Çakmak, U Kühnapfel (2000). "Animation and Simulation Techniques for VR-Training Systems in Endoscopic Surgery", *Eurographics Workshop on Animation and Simulation* (EGCAS '2000), Interlaken/Switzerland, pp. 173–185

[2] J Ehrhardt, H. Handels, T Malina, B Strathmann, W Plötz, SJ Pöppl (2001). "Atlas based Segmentation of Bone Structures to Support the Virtual Planning of Hip Operations", *International Journal of Medical Informatics*, Vol. 64, pp. 439–447

[3] TT Elvins (1992). "A Survey of Algorithms for Volume Visualization", *Computer Graphics*, Vol. 26 (3), pp. 194–201

[4] PC Everett, EB Seldin, M Troulis, LB Kaban, R Kikinis (2000). "A 3-D System for Planning and Simulating Minimally-Invasive Distraction Osteogenesis of the Facial Skeleton", *Proc. of MICCAI*, Springer, LNCS Vol. 1935, pp. 1029–1039

[5] G Gerig, T Koller, G Székely, C Brechbühler, O Kübler (1993). "Symbolic Description of 3d structures applied to cerebral vessel tree obtained from MR angiography volume data", *Proc. of Information Processing in Medical Imaging*, Springer, LNCS, Vol. 687: 94–111

[6] DT Gering, A Nabavi, R Kikinis et al. (1999). "An Integrated Visualization System for Surgical Planning and Guidance using Image Fusion and Interventional Imaging", *Proc. of MICCAI*, Springer, LNCS Vol. 1679, pp. 809–819

[7] HK Hahn, B Preim, D Selle, HO Peitgen (2001). "Visualization and Interaction Techniques for the Exploration of Vascular Structures", *IEEE Visualization* (San Diego, CA, Oct.), pp. 395–402

[8] H Handels, J Ehrhardt, B Strathmann, W Plötz, SJ Pöppl (2001). "An Orthopaedic Atlas for the 3D Operation Planning and the Virtual Construction of Endoprostheses", *Computer Assisted Radiology and Surgery* (CARS 2001, Berlin), Elsevier, pp. 312–317

[9] KH Höhne, B Pflesser, A Pommert, M Riemer, T Schiemann, R Schubert, U Tiede (1995). "A new representation of knowledge concerning human anatomy and function", *Nat. Med.*, Vol. 1 (6), pp. 506–511

[10] KH Höhne, B Pflesser, A Pommert et al. (2000). *VOXEL-MAN 3D Navigator: Inner Organs. Regional, Systemic and Radiological Anatomy*, Springer-Verlag Electronic Media, Heidelberg

[11] KH Höhne, A Petersik, B Pflesser et al. (2001). *VOXEL-MAN 3D Navigator: Brain and Skull. Regional, Functional and Radiological Anatomy*, Springer-Verlag Electronic Media, Heidelberg

[12] U Kühnapfel, HK Çakmak, H Maass (2000). "Endoscopic Surgery Training using Virtual Reality and deformable Tissue Simulation", *Computers & Graphics*, Vol. 24, pp. 671–682, Elsevier

[13] AC Pang, CM Wittenbrink, SK Lodha (1997). "Approaches to Uncertainty Visualization", *The Visual Computer*, Vol. 13 (8), pp. 370–390

[14] A Pommert, KH Höhne, B Pflesser et al. (2003). "Creating a high-resolution spatial/symbolic model of the inner organs based on the Visible Human". In: *Yearbook of Medical Informatics 2003: Quality of Health Care: The Role of Informatics*, Schattauer, Stuttgart, pp. 530–537

[15] B Preim, F Ritter (2002). "Techniken zur Hervorhebung von Objekten in medizinischen 3d-Visualisierungen", *Proc. of Simulation and Visualization 2002*, SCS, pp. 187–200

[16] B Preim, M Hindennach, W Spindler, A Schenk, A Littmann, HO Peitgen (2003). "Visualisierungs- und Interaktionstechniken für die Planung lokaler Therapien", *Proc. of Simulation and Visualization 2003*, SCS, pp. 237–248

[17] A Puig, D Tost and I Navazo (1997). "An Interactive Cerebral Blood Vessel Exploration System", *IEEE Visualization* (Phoenix, Arizona, October), pp. 433–436

[18] T Rist, E André (1992). "Incorporating Graphics Design and Realization into the Multimodal Presentation System WIP", *Advanced Visual Interfaces (Proceedings of AVI '92, Rome, Italy)*, World Scientific Press, Singapore, pp. 193–207

[19] D Selle, B Preim, A Schenk, HO Peitgen (2002). "Analysis of Vasculature for Liver Surgery Planning ", *IEEE Transactions on Medical Imaging*, Vol. 21 (11), pp. 1344–1357

[20] B Shneiderman (1997). *Designing the User Interface*, Addison Wesley

[21] R Spence (2001). *Information Visualization*, Addison Wesley

[22] T Strothotte, S Schlechtweg (2002). *Non-Photorealistic Computer Graphics: Modeling, Rendering, and Animation*, Morgan Kaufmann, San Francisco

Shadows with a Message

Wallace Chigona, Henry Sonnet, Felix Ritter, and Thomas Strothotte

Department of Simulation and Graphics,
University of Magdeburg,
Universitaetsplatz 2, D-39106 Magdeburg, Germany
{chigona|sonnet|fritter|tstr}@isg.cs.uni-magdeburg.de

Abstract. Providing textual annotations for 3D visualizations poses a number of interesting challenges: It is difficult to find a suitable position for the text such that the image-text co-referential connection is obvious for the user and, at the same time, the text does not occlude the 3D model. In this paper we address this problem by using cast shadows as text containers. This approach leverages the existing benefits of the shadow metaphor in visualizations. Problems which arise in this context are also discussed.

1 Introduction

We introduce a novel technique for providing textual annotations for 3D geometrical models without occluding the models and without coming in the way of users' interaction with the model. In addition, our technique provides obvious co-referential links between corresponding image and text, thereby reducing cognitive burden which is involved in linking multiple presentations [8,9].

The benefits of providing textual annotations for images are long known. For instance, MAYER [8] states that textual annotations enhance users' comprehension of images. It has also been shown that interactive 3D presentations of visualizations help users perceive spatial as well as functional relationships among objects [11]. Providing text explanations for interactive 3D illustrations, however, raises a number of interesting challenges: There is a need to present the text such that referential connections between corresponding textual and pictorial representations are obvious and, at the same time, the text should neither occlude nor come in the way of users' interaction with the 3D model. Unfortunately, this is not possible using existing techniques.

We address the above stated problem by positioning text within cast shadows of corresponding objects. Cast shadows, as used in [5,12], are 2D abstractions of objects in a 3D scene. Shadows provide important information about spatial relationships among objects [6,14]. Therefore, by placing text in a shadow we leverage an integral feature of a 3D visualization. Alternatively, if provided primarily to cater for textual annotations, shadows also offer the above mentioned benefits to the visualization.

The benefits of providing textual annotations in a shadow of a corresponding object in the model include the following:

A. Butz et al. (Eds.): Smart Graphics 2003, LNCS 2733, pp. 91–101, 2003.

1. The co-referential link between the shadow and the corresponding object is natural Since the shadow and the text are intimately linked, this means the text-image co-referential connection is also natural
2. Since text is provided within a secondary object, it does not occlude or come in the way of users' interaction with the 3D model.

In overview: After providing background information in Section 2, we discuss the concept which we are developing in this paper in Section 3. User interaction details are presented in Section 4, after which, we discuss implementation details in Section 5. Section 6 presents application areas for the technique developed in this paper. Related work is analyzed in Section 7 and Section 8 draws conclusions to this paper.

2 Background

The concept which we are developing is based on the concepts of DUAL-USE OF IMAGE SPACE (DUIS) [3] and ILLUSTRATIVE SHADOWS [12]. In this section we present summaries of both systems.

2.1 Dual-Use of Image Space

In DUIS text corresponding to images is presented within the image space. From a technical point of view, the pixels in the image space represent both readable text and, at the same time, shading information for the images. Weight and width of character glyphs are varied to achieve desired shading of graphical objects. Users find text with weight and width variations irritating and difficult to read. To address this problem DUIS has an option of presenting text in a mode which enhances readability (the reading mode).

Unfortunately no 3D provision: DUIS is designed for 2D. Applying it on 3D models poses readability problems due to occlusion and perspective distortion.

2.2 Illustrative Shadows

ILLUSTRATIVE SHADOWS [12] is a concept which allows users to interactively explore a detail-rendered 3D model; to avoid interference with the interactions as well as the view of the model, contextual information is displayed in the background. The concept uses the shadow metaphor: Object shadows projected onto a plane, serving as a 2D information display, are a secondary abstract representation of the 3D model. The shadow projection has two significant effects on the visualization:

1. It facilitates the visual understanding due to additional depth cues.
2. It leaves out details which are not relevant and, at the same time, emphasizes relevant elements. This helps to guide users' focus.

Textual information (in annotation boxes) for objects in the 3D model are connected to respective shadows using referential lines. This indirect connection between the corresponding image and text leads to problems in establishing co-referential links between the image and the corresponding text.

Text positioning problem: ILLUSTRATIVE SHADOWS faces the problem of identifying suitable text positions. It is difficult to find a position for the text near the corresponding object where textual information does not occlude the model. The text positioning problem is more complex in interactive environments: Here a once-correct text position may become invalid due to changes in the 3D model. Further on, interaction may produce undesirable effects such as referential lines crossing each other or crossing the scene.

We are proposing positioning text in shadows of corresponding objects using DUIS techniques. Our approach inherits ILLUSTRATIVE SHADOWS benefits while, at the same time, overcoming the above mentioned problems.

Note that we are dealing only with cast shadows. Object cast shadows on a shadow plane and never on other other objects. The shadow is cast along a specific vector (usually in the direction of the plane normal) independent of light sources by multiplying the 3D model with a projection matrix [2].

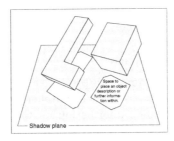

Fig. 1. Shadows with a message: Textual annotations are placed in corresponding shadows.

3   Text in Shadows

To explain our concept let us assume a scenario where a user is interacting with a 3D model. Since the main object of interaction is the 3D model, the shadow is positioned behind the 3D model so that it does not occlude the 3D model. When an individual object is selected the following things happen (See Figure 1 and Figure 2-1):

1. The selected object is emphasized, for example, by using color (see Figure 2).
2. The shadow cast by the selected object is emphasized: Its silhouette is rendered using thicker lines.
3. Corresponding textual information appears in the shadow of the selected object.

Positioning text in object shadows in a 3D scene raises a number of new interesting challenges. The following are the main challenges:

1. The shadow may not be accessible to users due to occlusions, i.e. it could be totally or partially occluded by the 3D model or shadows of other objects.
2. The shape of the shadow may not be conducive to reading.
3. The area of the shadow could be too small for the available text.

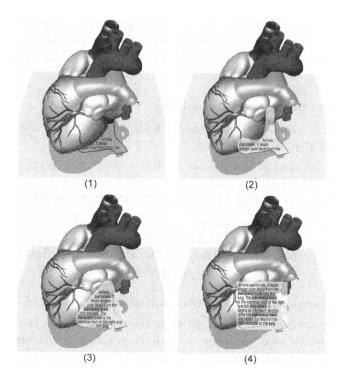

Fig. 2. Text in shadows: The selected object (the one rendered in light-blue) is empha-sized. (1) A shadow (and therefore the text) may be partially or totally occluded. (2) To ensure accessibility, the shadow is brought in the foreground. (3 & 4) If the shape of the shadow is not conducive to reading, it can be morphed into its convex-hull or into a rectangle.

3.1   Accessibility of the Shadow

Occlusion by 3D model: See Figure 2-1 or the shadow of the L-shaped object in Figure 1. Consequently users cannot access or interact with the text. Solution: When users click a visible portion of the shadow, the shadow moves to the foreground as illustrated in Figure 2-2. The same effect can be achieved by double-clicking the object; this option is particularly necessary when a shadow is totally occluded by the 3D model.

When presented in the foreground, the textual background is semi-transparent so that 3D model in the background remains visible (see Figure 2). This preserves the context.

Occlusion by other shadows: e.g. Figure 4. Since we assume readers would be interested in reading text for the last selected object, we display the shadow layers in chronological order of selection. That is, the shadow of the object which has been selected last is positioned on top. An occluded shadow may be brought in the foreground by either selecting it (if it is partially visible) or selecting the corresponding object.

To ensure readability and legibility of text, only the text for the topmost object is displayed and the shadows of the other selected objects are only high-lighted. Displaying text for more than one shadow impedes readability as shown in Figure 4.

3.2   Object Shapes and Readability

The shapes of shadow silhouettes are usually irregular. This poses readability problems for the following reasons:

1. Lack of familiarity: Humans are used to reading from rectangular surfaces.
2. Text lines presented in concave objects are interrupted by the object shape. These interruptions have negative effects on the reading process [3].

To address these problems, the shape of the shadow morphs into the object's convex-hull or into a rectangle (see Figure 2-3 and 2-4). To ensure that users maintain the relationship between the original and the distorted object the distortion is achieved in a smooth continuous animation.

3.3   Discrepancies between Object Size and Amount of Text

When there is more text than could fit on the available space, the text is broken into pages which users can page through. However, a special case arises when the space is too small for reasonable amount of text. Here, readers zoom-in to increase the available space. Shape distortion also offers solutions to this problem since in most cases the convex-hull or a rectangle formed from an object has more space than the original.

4   Text-Driven Model Exploration

While reading shadow messages, users frequently wish to look up referenced structures in the 3D model. The visibility of the referenced structure is not guaranteed: objects may be partially or totally occluded by other structures. In such cases it is necessary for users to interact with the model to make the desired structures accessible. However, modifications in the viewpoint or the spatial arrangement of the model result in changes in the shadow projection. This poses a usability challenge when users want to resume reading text for a particular object: Users must relocate their previous reading spot. This is an extraneous cognitive burden to the reading process. The following solutions have been adopted to avoid or attenuate the negative effects:

1. The system provides features to aid users relocating their previous reading spot.
2. Allow users to freeze the shadow so that it does not change when users look up structures in the 3D model.

Our informal tests have shown a positive correlation between the looking up of structures and the encounter of the structure's textual reference (often the name of the structure). In other words, users are likely to look up a structure after encountering its textual reference. This is consistent with the findings of HEGARTY et al. [4] on the eye movement pattern when users are reading textual annotations for illustrations. HEGARTY et al. observed that after reading a sentence or two, readers look up the part of the illustration which was mentioned in the text. We take advantage of this reading behavior to set landmarks in the text body which aid users in relocating their reading positions. Names of the 3D model segmented structures which appear within the text body are highlighted (see Figure 2). A user returning to a page can quickly scan through the landmarks to locate the previous reading position.

Highlighted terms in the text do not only provide landmarks for relocating reading positions, they also serve as means of interaction with the 3D model. When a textual reference of a structure is clicked, the structure is emphasized in the 3D model. Currently visible structures are locally emphasized (we use color and outline to emphasize structures), in contrast, hidden ones require global modifications. We are currently experimenting with exploding the model (adapted from technical illustrations [11]) to reveal otherwise occluded structures. To bring the model to its normal state, the user clicks on the name of the structure again. The shadow and the text, however, is frozen, i.e. they do not change along with the 3D model.

5   Implementation Details

The OPEN INVENTOR library is extended by several nodes for rendering the scene and its shadow projection. Other nodes, which are also part of the scenegraph, are responsible for computing objects' outline, for placing textual information inside shadows and for the smooth distortion of the shadow objects.

5.1   The Shadow

The scene is rendered in two steps: First, the illustration plane and the projected model (the shadow). Afterwards the illuminated model is rendered in detail in accordance to its 3D coordinates and material properties. The implication of this rendering order is that the shadow is positioned behind the 3D model so that the model is not occluded. The shadows are managed as layers: The shadow for a selected object is placed at the top and can, therefore, easily be selected. (For details see [12].)

5.2   Positioning Text Inside a Shadow Polygon

We require an algorithm which ensures legibility and readability of text as well as permits interaction with the text. The scanning algorithm which we are using meets these requirements. One alternative is to use textures with the textual information which can be mapped onto the shadow polygon. Although this approach might be more efficient (it is hardware-based), it does not permit interacting with elements of the text.

The problem of positioning text in a shadow polygon can be phrased as follows: Given a polygon, find connected rectangle blocks where the text can be positioned. The height of the rectangle blocks should be equal to the font height.

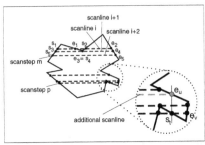 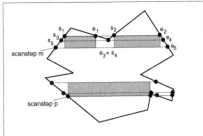

Fig. 3. Left: Polygon scanning; two scansteps (m and p) and the respective scanlines are illustrated. s_i and e_i are starting or ending intersections of respective scanlines. Right: The resulting blocks where text can be placed.

OPENGL GLU library tesselation methods are used to compute the outline (the polygons) of the shadows. To optimize readability we use bitmap fonts. For this reason it is necessary to project shadow polygon coordinates into screen coordinates.

Our scanning algorithm works as follows:

1. Sort (in ascending order) line segments according to their maximum Y coordinate.
2. $maxY :=$ polygon's max Y coordinate;
   $minY :=$ polygon's min Y coordinate;
   $scanIncrement :=$ difference between two sequent scansteps;
   $currentScanBase := maxY - scanIncrement$;
   $scans :=$ list of Y positions to be scanned;
   $finalIntersections :=$ list of final coordinates of current scanstep intersections;
   while $currentScanBase \geq minY$ **do**
      $currentPolyLines :=$ list of active line segments;
      sort $currentPolyLines$ in X order;
      clear $scans$ and add new scan positions;
      $startIntersections :=$ list of intersections of scan line with $currentPolyLines$;
      $endIntersections :=$ list of intersections of scan line with $currentPolyLines$;
      for each element of $scans$ **do**
         $next :=$ next element of $scans$;
         $intersections :=$ list of scan line intersections with $currentPolyLines$ at $next$;
         add $intersections$ to $startIntersections$ and $endIntersections$ alternately;
      od
      $finalIntersections :=$ merge($startIntersections$, $endIntersections$);
      place text within pairs of $finalIntersections$ coordinates;
      $currentScanBase := currentScanBase - scanIncrement$;
   od

Figure 3-left illustrates the scanning algorithm: m and p are two non-consecutive scan steps. Figure 3-right shows the blocks resulting from the scan algorithm.

Scanstep m: Based on the current scan base, three scan lines are computed as follows:

1. The lower line: The line on the base (this has intersections $\{s_5, e_5\}$).
2. The upper line: The line formed by adding the font height on the base. This forms the following intersections $\{s_1, e_1, s_2, e_2\}$.
3. The line between the lower and upper lines is formed due to an edge which is within the scan step (intersections $\{s_3, e_3, s_4, e_4\}$).

Two lists ($startIntersections$ and $endIntersections$) are created from the intersections of the three scan lines: The lists are sorted in an ascending order according to the X coordinate. The two lists are then merged to form a new list ($finalIntersections$) with intersection pairs. Below is a summary of the lists: $startIntersections = \{s_5, s_3, s_1, s_4, s_2\}$, $endIntersections = \{e_1, e_3, e_2, e_4, e_5\}$, $finalIntersections = \{s_1, e_1, s_2, e_2\}$.

The lists merging function searches for connected rectangular blocks within a scan step: Beginning with the first element of startIntersections, the X coordinates of startIntersections and endIntersections elements are compared stepwise. At each step the function searches for the last startIntersections element which is smaller or equal to the current element of endIntersections (e.g. s_1 and e_1). This pair forms a connected rectangular block.

For the next connected block on the same scan line, the function considers the next startIntersections element (s_k); In endIntersections Move to first element which is greater than s_k. The merging function stops when the last startIntersections element has been reached and the corresponding endIntersections element is found.

Scanstep p: Using the process described above the final segment on the scan step would be $\{s_t, e_v\}$. However, text placed in this segment would overlap the polygonal outline since the height of this segment is less than the font height. To overcome this problem the process has to be forced to stop at s_t by adding a new $endIntersection$ (e_u). This is achieved by adding to the list of scanline positions a new scanline such that the new scanline intersects the polygon at (e_u). Intersection e_u is a point at which a line starting from s_t and perpendicular to the scan lines intersects the polygon.

6   Applications

The techniques developed here have application in interactive exploratory learning environments. It is widely recognized that interactivity enhances learning [10]. In our system, users interact with 3D models without interference from secondary information.

Fig. 4. Two engine elements are selected in the 3D model as well as within the illustration plane. When shadows overlap, the shadow of the object selected last is laid on top. Text is displayed only on the topmost shadow. RIGHT: Displaying text on more than one shadow impedes readability.

Figure 4 illustrates a potential learning scenario during an apprenticeship. In this case students are learning the spatial composition and functionality of an engine. As they interact with the 3D model textual information is displayed within the shadow. Since the text is displayed in the background and comes in the foreground only upon users' explicit request, it does not interfere with the users' explorative interactions.

7   Related Work

Providing textual information close to corresponding images is a well known problem in the area of label placement in cartography. Area features labeling techniques typically attempt to position labels within features; when the space inside a feature is not sufficient for the label, another position outside the feature is sought. For a detailed list on label placement research refer to the Map Labeling Bibliography [15]. BELL et al. [1] extended the map labeling to cater for augmented reality scenes. The text labels are positioned on projected images of the scene on a head-worn display. Both approaches, however, deal with short text usually just the name of the feature; Long text, as is the case in our approach, lead to the following problems:

1. The text occludes the pictorial information and hinders interactions with the model.
2. Text displayed on a such "textured" background may be difficult to read due to lack of clear contrast between the text and its background [13].

Popup windows may also be used to position textual information close to corresponding images. To avoid the textual information occluding the image, transparent windows may be used [7]. Even though the user may see the image, the text windows hinder interaction with the model.

Another system closely related to our work is the INTERACTIVE SHADOWS [5]. In this approach, in addition to serving as a secondary representation, the shadow is used as an interaction tool for the 3D model. However, the focus is not on integration of textual explanations in visualizations; instead, text is used only to label the shadows.

8   Conclusion

Using the shadow metaphor, ILLUSTRATIVE SHADOWS addressed an interesting interaction problem: Given a 3D model, present corresponding secondary information such that it does not interfere with the rendering as well as the interaction of the 3D model. Here the secondary information is presented as a shadow projected on a plane. The shadow also enhances users' comprehension of the 3D model.

In this paper we use the shadow metaphor to address another critical problem in 3D illustrations: The problem of providing text explanations for the 3D illustrations. We present text corresponding to objects in respective shadows. The techniques for positioning text in the shadow are adapted from DUIS. The paper has demonstrated problems and corresponding solutions of positioning text in shadows.

Future W ork: The problem of occlusion (both 3D model occluding the shadow, or shadow occluding shadow) may be addressed by introducing multiple projection planes and multiple light sources. This option, which was employed in INTERACTIVE SHADOWS [5], would provide more positions where the shadow can be projected. It would also be possible to view text for different objects simultaneously.

For more details about the work (including a video) please refer to: http://wwwisg.cs.uni-magdeburg.de/research/ts.

References

1. B. Bell, S. Feiner, and T. Hö llerer. View Management for Virtual and Augmented Reality. In *Proc of ACM UIST*, pages 101–110, November 2001.
2. J. Blinn. Me and My (Fake) Shadows. *IEEE Computer Graphics & Applications*, 8(1):82–86, Jan. 1988.
3. W. Chigona and T. Strothotte. Improving Readability of Contextualized Text Explanations. In *Proc. of AFRIGRAPH 2003*, pages 141–149. AFRIGRAPH, Feb., 03–05 2003.
4. M. Hegarty, P. Carpenter, and M. Just. Diagrams in the Comprehension of Scientific Texts. In R. Barr, P. M. M.L. Kamil, and P. Pearson, editors, *Handbook of Reading Research. Volume II*, pages 641–668. Mahwah, NJ: Erlbaum, 1996.
5. K. P. Herndon, R. C. Zeleznik, D. C. Robbins, D. B. Conner, S. S. Snibbe, and A. van Dam. Interactive Shadows. In *Proc. of the 5th Annual Symposium on User Interface Software and Technology (UIST'92)*, pages 1–6, Monterey, CA, 1992.

6. G. S. Hubona, P. Wheeler, G. Shirah, and M. Brandt. The Role of Object Shadows in Promoting 3D Visualization. *ACM Transactions on Human Computer Interaction Journal*, 6(3):214–242, Sept. 1999.
7. S. Hudson, R. Rodenstein, and I. Smith. Debugging Lenses: A New Class of Transparent Tools For User Interface Debugging. In *Proc of the 10th ACM UIST*, pages 179–187, 1997.
8. R. Mayer. *Multimedia Learning*. Cambridge Press, Cambridge, UK, 2001.
9. R. Mayer and V. Sims. For Whom is a Picture Worth a Thousand Words? Extensions of Dual-Coding Theory of Multimedia Learning. *Journal of Educational Psychology*, 86:389–401, 1994.
10. D. Mesher. Designing Interactivities for Internent Learning. *Syllabus*, 12(7), 1999.
11. F. Ritter, O. Deussen, B. Preim, and T. Strothotte. Virtual 3D Puzzles: A New Method for Exploring Geometric Models in VR. *IEEE Computer Graphics & Applications*, 21(5):11–13, Sept./Oct. 2001.
12. F. Ritter, H. Sonnet, K. Hartmann, and T. Strothotte. Illustrative Shadows: Integrating 3D and 2D Information Displays. In *Proc. of ACM Conference on Intelligent User Interfaces (Miami, Florida, Jan. 2003)*, pages 166–173. ACM Press, New York, 2003.
13. L. Scharff, A. Hill, and A. Ahumada. Discriminability Measures for Predicting Readability of Text on Textured Backgrounds. *Optics Express: The International Journal of Optics*, 6(4):81–91, 2000.
14. L. R. Wanger. The Effect of Shadow Quality on the Perception of Spatial Relationships in Computer Generated Imagery. In *Proceedings of Conference on Computer Graphics*, pages 39–42. ACM SIGGRAPH, 1992.
15. A. Wolff and T. Strijk. The Map-Labeling Bibliography. `www.math-inf.uni-greifswald.de/map-labeling/bibliography`, 1996.

Dynamic Glyphs – Depicting Dynamics in Images of 3D Scenes

Marc Nienhaus and Jürgen Döllner

Hasso-Plattner-Institute
at the University of Potsdam,
Department for Computer Graphics Systems,
Prof.-Dr.-Helmert-Str. 2-3,
14482 Potsdam, Germany
{nienhaus, doellner}@hpi.uni-potsdam.de
http://www.hpi.uni-potsdam.de/deu/forschung/cgs

Abstract. Depicting dynamics offers manifold ways to visualize dynamics in static media, to understand dynamics in the whole, and to relate dynamics of the past and the future with the current state of a 3D scene. The depiction strategy we propose is based on visual elements, called dynamic glyphs, which are integrated in the 3D scene as additional 2D and 3D geometric objects. They are derived from a formal specification of dynamics based on acyclic, directed graphs, called behavior graphs. Different types of dynamics and corresponding mappings to dynamic glyphs can be identified, for instance, scene events at a discrete point in time, transformation processes of scene objects, and activities of scene actors. The designer or the application can control the visual mapping of dynamics to dynamic glyphs, and, thereby, create own styles of dynamic depiction. Applications of dynamic glyphs include the automated production of instruction manuals, illustrations, and storyboards.

1 Introduction

Depicting dynamics represents a challenging task for smart graphics: It is a powerful tool, deployed in arts and science yet for a long time as technique to illustrate dynamics of actors, objects, and processes in static media. As underlying principle, illustrations encode in images more than 3D scenery – abstract elements, for instance, arrows indicating a direction of movement, rays symbolizing an extraordinary event, or clouds containing descriptions of thoughts of an actor. This way, depictions of dynamics in images enable observers to understand dynamics of 3D scenery even in static images, to relate dynamics of the past and the future with the current state of a 3D scene, and to communicate all kinds of non-geometric information such as tension, danger, and feelings.

3D computer graphics provides a wealth of modeling and rendering techniques, which represent the technical basis upon which smart graphics technology can be built. In that direction, we propose a concept for augmenting images of 3D scenes by

A. Butz et al. (Eds.): Smart Graphics 2003, LNCS 2733, pp. 102–111, 2003.

visual elements that abstract and symbolize dynamics (s. Fig 1). It is (1) based on the formal hierarchical specification of dynamics by *behavior graphs*; (2) performs the visual mapping of behavior graphs to *dynamic glyphs* for a given point in time or time interval; and (3) uses *non-photorealistic rendering* as an appropriate rendering style to produce illustrations of 3D scenes and their dynamics.

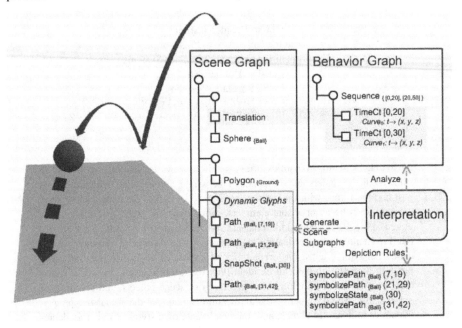

Fig. 1. Screen aligned arrows as dynamic glyphs depict the animation of a ball bouncing on the ground (left). The conceptual structure to generate dynamic glyphs is given in a diagram (right). After analyzing the behavior graph, depiction rules build scene subgraphs that represent dynamic glyphs.

The concept of depicting dynamics in images of 3D scenes can be applied to many application areas. For instance, it can be used to implement a system for digital 3D storyboards generating a collection of representative images of 3D scenes with visually encoded dynamics summarizing part of a story. Another application area includes systems for producing illustrations of instruction manuals in an automated way. Furthermore, the concept can be applied to generate visual indices of linear media such as movies.

2 Specifying Dynamics

To specify dynamics of a 3D scene in a formal way, we construct behavior graphs. A behavior graph is a directed acyclic graph (DAG) that specifies time-dependent and event-dependent behavior of scene objects. A scene graph, in contrast, formally specifies geometry and appearance of scene objects [1].

Nodes of behavior graphs manage time layouts, calculate lifetimes, and control time assigned to child nodes. In addition, they maintain time-dependent constraints for elements of associated scene graphs.

Of course, both scene graphs and behavior graphs are tightly related: Scene graph elements define visual aspects of scene objects, whereas behavior graph elements define dynamic aspects of scene objects. In general, a single scene graph may have a number of behavior graphs associated with it.

2.1 Time Moments and Time Requirements

We define the following temporal abstract data types to manage the time flow in behavior graphs:

- **Moments.** A *moment* $M = (t_0, t_1, t)$ represents a point t in a time interval $[t_0, t_1]$. A moment assigned to a behavior node determines the node's lifetime interval and the current point in time within this interval. Moments are essential for behavior nodes that specify processes. Based on the knowledge about their lifetime, behavior nodes can plan their activity. The point in time t contained in a moment M communicates the current time to behavior nodes.

- **Time Requirements.** A *time requirement* $R = (T_{natural}, T_{max}, T_{min}, A)$ describes the time demand of a behavior node. It consists of the natural (i.e. desired, optimal) duration $T_{natural}$, the minimal duration T_{min}, and the maximal duration T_{min}. A time requirement can also specify that the natural duration is infinite. Furthermore, it defines a time alignment A, which determines how to position a shorter moment within a longer moment. With $A = 0.0$, the shorter moment starts at the same time as the longer moment; $A = 1.0$ causes both moments to end at the same time; and $A = 0.5$ centers the shorter moment within the longer moment.

Behavior nodes do not include time requirements by default. We add these requirements by a special kind of behavior nodes in the behavior graph, called *time setters*, or calculate them implicitly through *behavior groups*.

2.2 Managing Lifetimes

One of its fundamental tasks of a behavior graph is to define lifetimes of activities and point in times of events. To organize the overall structure of the time flow, we set up time groups, whereas the local time flow can be modified by time modifiers. We are going to explain both types of behavior nodes in the following.

2.2.1 Time Groups

Time groups represent a major category of nodes that constitute a behavior graph. A time group node calculates the individual lifetimes of its child nodes based on the children's time requirements and its own time-layout strategy. If a time group node receives a time event, it checks which child nodes to activate or deactivate. It synchronizes all active child nodes to the new time, and assigns new moments to them.

A number of time group nodes implement specific time layouting strategies. Examples for those classes include:

- **Time Sequence.** Defines the total time requirements as sum of the time requirements of its child nodes. It distributes a received moment proportionally to the child nodes. The moments assigned to the child nodes are sequential and disjoint. Only one child node is alive at any given time during the lifetime of the sequence.
- **Time Simultaneity.** Defines the total time requirement as the maximum of the time requirements of the child nodes. It distributes a received moment to the child nodes if their natural duration is equal to the duration of the moment. If not, the simultaneity layout tries to shrink or stretch the time requirements of the child nodes to fit the duration. If they still do not match it aligns the lifetime of the child nodes within the moment.
- **Time Table.** Defines for each child node an explicit time requirement. It manages activation and deactivation of child nodes according to it own lifetime.

Since time groups automate distribution and alignment of time intervals, designers are relieved from calculating absolute times in specifications of dynamics. Time groups also take care of the discrete nature of points in time. If a new point in time is reached, they take care not to forget discrete events being scheduled for the past time interval. As main feature, time groups facilitate hierarchical specifications of activities and events at a high level of abstraction similar to specifications in storybooks.

Fig. 2 shows how time groups can compose activities, and how time requirements get evaluated. The behavior nodes A_1, A_2, and S_1 are processed sequentially. Behavior node S_1 consists of two simultaneous behavior nodes, A_{3a} and A_{3b}. D_1, D_2, and D_3 define infinitely stretchable time requirements of 1, 2, and 1 seconds; they are not shrinkable. The sequence S_e is prefixed with a duration D of 100 seconds. If S_e actually gets from its parent 100 seconds, it distributes this moment proportionally to its child nodes, i.e. A_1 and S_1 get 25 seconds each, and A_2 50 seconds. Since A_{3a} can last at most $(1+14) = 15$ seconds, S_1 centers the lifetime of A_{3a} within the 25 seconds. S_e activates in turn A_1, A_2 and S_1, A_{3a} and A_{3b} are activated by S_1.

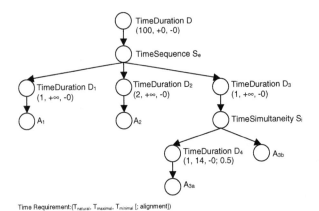

Time Requirement:$(T_{natural}, T_{maximal}, T_{minimal}$ [; alignment])

Fig. 2. Example of a behavior graph.

2.3 Activities and Events

Constraint nodes represent activity and events as core elements of dynamic specifications. A generic class takes care of most variants of constraints:

- **TimeCt.** Associates a time-to-value mapping with a property of a scene object. For example, a time-constraint can constrain the position of an object associating a time-to-vector mapping with the object's midpoint.

Technically, constraint nodes control time-varying parameters of objects contained in scene graphs, for instance, position, direction, color, or size of a scene object. For each of the time-varying parameters, constraint nodes require a time-to-parameter mapping. Whenever a constraint node receives a new moment, it calculates new parameter values, and assigns these values to its constrained scene objects. A number of classes implement specific time-to-parameter mappings. Examples for those classes include:

- **Constant Map.** Assigns a constant value to constrained objects.
- **Linear Map.** Assigns a value that results from linear interpolation of specified values.
- **Curve Map.** Assigns a value that results from calculating a point of a parameterized curve by interpreting time as curve parameter.
- **Method Map.** Assigns a value that results from a method call.
- **Function Map.** Assigns a value that results from a function call.

2.3.1 Modifying Local Time Flows

As additional building blocks to specify dynamics, we define a number of time modifier nodes, which transform local time received by child nodes. Mathematically, these nodes define a time-to-time mapping that is applied to all moments passed through the node. Among the kinds of transformations (s. Fig. 3) are:

- **Constant Transformation.** It assigns a constant time to its child nodes regardless of the time progress communicated to the time modifier node.
- **Discrete Transformation.** It defines a conceptually discontinuous time progress. The available lifetime interval is decomposed in piecewise constant time intervals. Using this kind of time modifier, for instance, jerky movements can be modeled.
- **Repeat Transformation.** It maps a moment modulo a time interval, and passes the resulting moment to its child nodes. For example, to model an activity that lasts 5 seconds and that should be repeated permanently, we specify an infinite duration followed by a time repeater with the modulo moment [0, 5sec].
- **Reverse Transformation.** It inverts the direction of the time progress for the child nodes. Time reversal nodes are useful to model invert activities (provided that the underlying time constraints are invertible).
- **Creep Transformation.** It defines a creeping time progress, i.e., the time progress is slow in the beginning and speeds up at the end of a time interval. Alternatively, the time progress can be speed up in the beginning and slow down at the end.

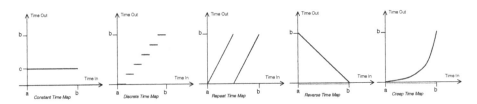

Fig- 3. Examples of time-modifier functions.

3 Dynamic Glyphs

Dynamic glyphs are visual elements that symbolize dynamics in images of 3D scenes. They do not represent original scene elements, and hence are not modeled as part of the scene by the scene designer. Instead, dynamic glyphs result from analyzing and interpreting behavior graphs for a specified time interval, and the subsequent visual mapping of the results to graphical elements. These elements are inserted as part of the scene graph automatically in order to augment the image by the abstract representation of dynamics found in the behavior graph.

For analysis, we traverse the behavior graph searching for behavior nodes that are active in the specified time interval. Behavior nodes that do not become active in the specified time interval are ignored in the following. The remaining nodes can be interpreted at different levels of abstraction.

Low-Level Depiction Rules. At the lowest level of abstraction, we can interpret each single node for itself, and we can at least determine for each node the set of geometries in the scene graph that are modified by the node's activities.

For example, if an active time-constraint node is encountered that specifies a time-dependent function applied to a translation object in the scene graph, we can conclude that all geometries affected by the translation will be moved. For them, we can depict the path they will follow by creating an additional visual element, called path. A path has the shape of a flexible 3D arrow, represented graphically as quad-strip, and oriented towards the viewer to ensure full visibility (s. Fig. 1). If the time-to-vector function of the constraint node is based on a parameterized curve, for example, the path will resemble the shape of the curve (while the curve will never be visualized because it is used only to calculate object positions). The path type represents a prototypic dynamic glyph: It is a 3D shape whose configuration, appearance, and position is set up automatically based on the kind of constraint and its time-to-value mapping. It also becomes part of the scene graph without being a scene object.

The way encountered constraint nodes are interpreted can be graphically designed arbitrarily. The aforementioned time constraint associated with a time-dependent function and a translation object could also be visualized by indicating the followed path using 3D points. Technically, a dynamic glyph is encoded by a scene subgraph, which can take advantage of all defined shapes, graphics attributes, and containers like the main scene graph can do.

A formal definition of the general visual mapping of time constraints at the lowest level of interpretation can be given at this point. It maps the triple consisting of time constraint, its time map, and its constrained scene objects to a dynamic glyph.

Higher-Level Depiction Rules. We can also detect patterns in encountered behavior nodes that indicate dynamics at a higher level of abstraction. Mappings based on detecting patterns are applied prior to lower-level mappings. They aim at symbolizing complex dynamics.

For example, if a scene object is animated by a tailspin, a simultaneity group having two child nodes, one for constraining its position and one for constraining its rotation angle, encodes this kind of dynamics in a behavior graph. It is symbolized by a single dynamic glyph, a twisted path.

Integrating Dynamic Glyphs and Scene Graphs. After analyzing behavior graphs and applying higher-level and lower-level interpretations, we can add the resulting scene subgraphs to the main scene graph. For different time intervals being considered for analysis, dynamic glyphs are added to or removed from the scene graph, respectively for image rendering. We assume that interpretation of behavior nodes as well as scene subgraphs representing dynamic glyphs are subject to a user-controlled design process in order to fine-tune the visual appearance. Of course, these processes can also be automated as well if interpretation schema and dynamic glyph designs are fixed for a given category of scene objects and related dynamics, for example, instructions for assembling furniture parts.

4   Rendering Scenes with Dynamic Glyphs

In general the images we are interested in outline and sketch complex scenarios and their related dynamics. Therefore, to achieve abstraction is essential for images of high perceptual and cognitive quality. We found as most appropriate the styles of hand drawn illustrations [8], storyboards [3], and comic strips [5]. The concept allows us to adopt the creation of dynamic glyphs from guidelines used for classic media, which have been successfully approved over decades. With respect to arrows, for example, we generate a 3-dimensional visual element that appears to be mostly parallel to the view plane.

To render dynamic glyphs in a non-photorealistic fashion we particularly deploy artistic strokes [7]. Artistic strokes are well suited to place lines and curves into 3D scenery, for instance, to visualize a motion path (see Fig. 4). Using variations in style leads to individual strokes and thus emphasize hand drawn creation.

Speedlines depict dynamics of scene objects [4]; as dynamic glyphs they symbolize direction and velocity of animated scene objects for a given point in time. Additionally, speedlines relate the past since they picture where the scene object has been before. Furthermore, they also relate the future since the position where the scene object will be soon can be estimated by deriving the future direction of flight from speedlines. To render speedlines, we extract extreme or artistically chosen points of polygonal geometry and, then, process their positions in 3-dimensional space with respect to a given time interval. Based on these, we form an appropriate artistic stroke that symbolizes motion (see Fig. 5).

We also apply non-photorealistic rendering to the main 3D scene to achieve a consistent graphics style. For example, 3D scene objects can be rendered with enhanced edges [6] and NPR illumination models [2]. Real-time NPR techniques allow us to integrate dynamic glyphs in interactive graphics applications. The snapshots shown in this paper are actually derived from our interactive prototypic implementation.

5 Examples

Flight of a Paper Plane. We consider the following scenario: A paper plane flies beside a wall. It collides with the wall twice. Each collision alters the direction of flight. Finally, the paper plane descends smoothly nearly the camera.

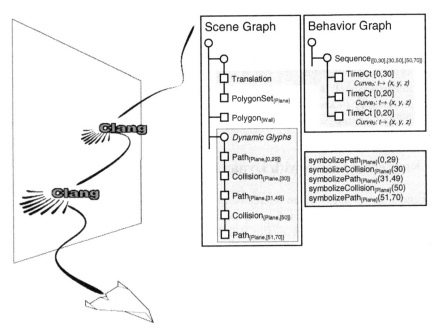

Fig. 4. Dynamic glyphs depicting the flight and collisions of a paper plane (left). The diagram shows scene and behavior graph and depiction rules needed to construct dynamics glyphs (right).

The initial scene graph for the animation consists of a translation node that specifies the position of the paper plane, a set of polygons representing the geometry of the paper plane, and a single polygon representing the wall. Since the trajectory of the flight gets interrupted twice, the whole animation of the flight specified in the behavior graph consists of three curves that are processed in sequential order. The three curve-map based constraint nodes, shown in Fig. 4, map a point in time to a 3-

dimensional vector derived from the given curve. Then, the constraint nodes manipulate the translation in the scene graph and, thus, position the paper plane in 3D scenery. The time-sequence behavior node activates and deactivates, respectively, the constraint nodes in sequential order due to their time requirements.

To visually communicate the animation of the flight, we symbolize each curve in a chosen time interval and both collisions at that points in time, when the events take place, by the use of dynamic glyphs.

Therefore, we specify what to depict for a certain scene object in either a time interval or at a point in time in depiction rules. The collection of depiction rules specifies the symbolization of dynamics; they can be given in any order since they do not influence each other.

If both, the behavior graph and a collection of depiction rules, are provided we analyze the behavior graph to extract information related to scene objects used for interpreting the rules to, finally, generate dynamic glyphs. To symbolize the path of the paper plane's flight, we choose long artistic strokes placed along each curve according to the specified time interval. As dynamic glyphs depicting the collision at a discrete point in time, we place short artistic strokes starting around the point of collision and following the direction of flight to visualize the impulse. Furthermore, we add a notation at or nearby the point of collision to symbolize the noise that arises. These dynamic glyphs will then be inserted into the scene graph. Fig. 4 illustrates the whole flight of the paper plane.

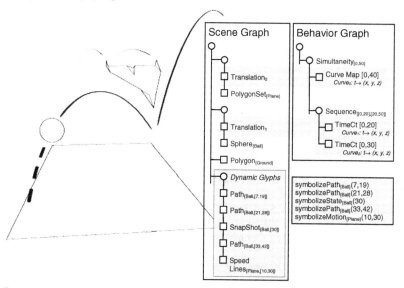

Fig. 5. Dynamic glyphs depicting the simultaneous animation of a bouncing ball and a flying paper plane (left). The diagram shows scene and behavior graph and depiction rules needed to construct dynamics glyphs (right).

Bouncing Ball and Flying Paper Plane. We consider the following scenario: A ball bounces on the ground. It has hit the ground once, has lifted up, and falls down following a parabolic curve. Simultaneously, a paper plane is flying around.

As before, the scene graph contains a translation node that controls the position of the paper plane. Additionally, it contains a translation node and a spherical shape to position and visualize the ball. Since the bouncing ball and the flying plane are animated simultaneously the behavior graph contains a simultaneity behavior node that starts the animations of both scene objects at the same time. One curve-map based constraint node describes the trajectory of the plane. Again, the path of the ball is divided into two curves. The corresponding constraint nodes are assembled in a sequence behavior node to be processed one after another.

For depicting this scenario, speedlines gradually fade off in the past like condensation trails disappear behind a plane. In analogy, we can conceive speedlines like turbulences behind a moving object invoked by its velocity and its striking surface. Fig. 5 shows the resulting image of the 3D scene with integrated dynamic glyphs.

5 Conclusions

The presented concept formally specifies dynamics and derives dynamic glyphs that visually encode events and activities in images of 3D scenes; it extends the well-known scene graph by a complementary behavior graph. Dynamic glyphs offer a rich vocabulary to designers for expressing different kinds of dynamics; depiction rules can be designed on different levels of abstraction.

We see a large potential of application for the automated production of technical and instructive illustrations as well as for visual summaries of linear media contents. Our future research concentrates on identifying and categorizing dynamic glyphs, depiction rules, and appropriate rendering techniques. We also would like to apply the presented technique to concrete application domains such as authoring tools.

References

1. Döllner, J., Hinrichs, K.: Object-oriented 3D Modeling, Animation and Interaction. In: The Journal of Visualization and Computer Animation (JVCA), 8(1) (1997) 33–64
2. Gooch, B., Gooch, A.: Non-Photorealistic Rendering. A.K. Peters (2001)
3. Katz, S.D.: Film Directing Shot by Shot: Visualizing from Concept to Screen. Focal Press (1991)
4. Masuch, M., Schlechtweg, S., Schulz, R.: Speedlines – Depicting Motion in Motionless Pictures. In: ACM SIGGRAPH'99 Sketch and Applications (1999) 277
5. McCloud, S.: Understanding Comics – The Invisible Art. HarperPerennial, New York (1994)
6. Nienhaus, M., Döllner, J.: Edge-Enhancement – An Algorithm For Real-Time Non-Photorealistic Rendering. In: Journal of WSCG'03, 11(2) (2003) 346–353
7. Northrup, J.D., Markosian, L.: Artistic Silhouettes: A Hybrid Approach. In: Proceedings of NPAR 2000 (2000) 31–38
8. Strothotte, T., Schlechtweg, S.: Non-Photorealistic Computer Graphics: Modeling, Rendering and Animation. Morgan Kaufman, San Francisco, CA (2002)

A New Approach to the Interactive Resolution of Configuration Problems in Virtual Environments

Carlos Calderon[1], Marc Cavazza[1], and Daniel Diaz[2]

[1] School of Computing and Mathematics, University of Teesside,
UK-TS1 3BA, Middlesbrough, United Kingdom
{c.p.calderon, m.o.cavazza}@tees.ac.uk
[2] University of Paris 1
90 rue de Tolbiac, CRI bureau C1405 Paris, 75013, France
Daniel.diaz@univ-paris1.fr

Abstract. Intelligent Virtual Environments integrate AI techniques with 3D real-time environments. As such, they can support interactive problem solving, provided the underlying AI techniques can produce solutions within a time frame matching that of user interaction. In this paper, we describe an intelligent virtual environment based on Constraint Logic Programming (CLP), integrated in a real-time 3D graphic environment. We have developed an event-based approach through which user interaction can be converted in real-time into appropriate solver queries which are then translated back into automatic reconfigurations of the Virtual Environment (VE). Additionally, this framework supports the interactive exploration of the solution space in which alternative solutions (configurations) can be found. We demonstrate the system behaviour on a configuration example. This example illustrates how solutions can be interactively refined by the user through direct manipulation of objects in the VE and how the interactive search of alternative solutions in the VE is supported by these type of systems.

1 Introduction

Virtual Environments (VE) can be used to represent complex situations. It is thus a logical evolution to extend them to carry out problem solving tasks as well. In these systems, called Intelligent Virtual Environments [1] the visual space is directly interfaced to a problem solver. Interacting with objects in the VE serves as input to the problem solver, which outputs new solutions directly as, in this instance, object configurations. This kind of system has many potential applications in design, configuration, situation assessment, etc.

This research aims at the integration of interactive visualisation with interactive problem solving in virtual worlds. A central argument to this paper is to reach a high-level of integration between the visualisation component and the problem-solving component. This can be achieved by selecting a problem solving technique compatible

A. Butz et al. (Eds.): Smart Graphics 2003, LNCS 2733, pp. 112–122, 2003.

with the nature of user interaction in Virtual Reality (VR) (including its timescales) and integrating them using an interaction model.

Our problem-solving component is based on Constraint Logic Programming (CLP). Generally speaking, constraint programming is an optimisation technique that provides solutions in terms of relations between domain variables. The solving mechanisms of many constraint systems can be triggered by any modification of variable values. More specifically, physical interaction with the virtual world objects can be translated into real-time input to the CLP solver by selecting the variables whose values have been altered by the interaction. This supports data-driven changes, and provides a strong basis for its integration in an interactive VR system. For instance, when visualising a configuration, the user can alter the position of certain objects which modifies the constraints involving these objects. This triggers the solver on a new set of variables. The solver in turn outputs resulting solutions in the form of new object configurations within the environment, thus seamlessly integrating the solving process in the VR interaction loop.

Previous work using constraint logic programming in 3D environment has essentially been dedicated to the behaviour of individual objects or autonomous agents within the environment. For instance, Codognet [2] has included a concurrent constraint programming system into VRML (VRCC) to specify the behaviour of artificial actors in dynamic environments. Axling et al. [3] have incorporated OZ [4], a high-level programming language supporting constraints, into the DIVE [5] distributed VR environment. Both Axling and Codognet have put emphasis on the behaviour of individual objects in the virtual world and did not address user interaction or interactive problem solving. However, CLP naturally provides solutions for combined behaviours, in this instance, for sets of objects. This is the property we use to implement behaviours for the virtual environment as a whole.

As demonstrated by Honda [6] and Pfefferkorn [7], CLP techniques are particularly appropriate for the resolution of configuration problems. Both have demonstrated the suitability of CLP as an approach based on: the declarative nature of the formalism, which facilitates the description of the problem, and its efficiency for avoiding combinatorial explosion. Our approach extends Honda and Pfefferkorn into the realm of 3D real-time environments and demonstrates that CLP techniques can produce solutions within a time frame matching that of user interaction. Consequently, seen from the user's perspective, the VE reacts to the user's interaction by reconfiguring itself. Furthermore, once an initial solution has been found, the framework we propose in this paper enables the user to interactively search for alternative solutions in the VE.

2 System Overview

The system is an interactive 3D environment, developed using the Unreal Tournament^{TM} (UT) game engine, in which the user can freely navigate and interact with the world objects. That is, the system initially proposes a first solution (in the form of a configuration of objects) which serves as a starting point for user's exploration of possible configurations. Once the user has explored this configuration, he can interact with it by displacing the constituent objects. The correct allocation of an object instantly triggers new solutions (configurations) from the solver which, in turn, are displayed in the virtual environment (see Figure 1).

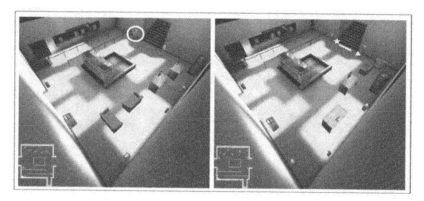

Fig. 1. The user refines a given configuration by reallocating an object. As a result of this, the environment reconfigures itself.

The intelligent configuration module (the solver) is based on Constraint Logic Programming (CLP). We have used GNU Prolog [8] as a programming environment, which contains an efficient constraint solver over Finite Domains (FD). This allows the implementation of many different types of constraints which can be represented over a finite domain, i.e. an ordered list of properties. This makes possible to represent "semantic" constraints, i.e. constraints involving object properties such as materials, friction coefficient, resistance to fire, etc. In the following sections, we give a more detailed insight into the implementation considering the specific techniques used.

3   The Interaction Model

The aim of the interaction model is to relate the user interactions which are taking place in the virtual environment to the I/O of the solver, within an interaction rate which is that of the user. The solver works with a specific logic, according to which it is triggered by the addition of new clauses and its results are produced as sets of variable allocations. The interaction model should bridge the gap between these two different logics, from the dynamic perspective of the user's intervention. We thus discuss two aspects: firstly how the solver is made to react to user input, secondly how results produced from the solver should interactively modify the virtual environment.

Unreal tournament supports the real-time generation of events, i.e. those generated by the user's transformation of a configuration displayed in the virtual environment. These events (see Figure 2) are used to generate new "queries" to the solver (using the term query in its Prolog sense). Consider the following example, where from a deployed configuration the user displaces an object, e.g ATM, to a new position. The

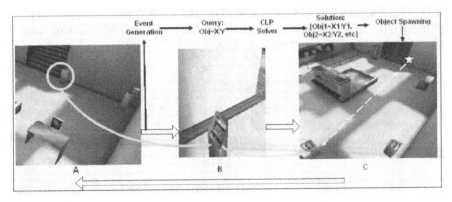

Fig. 2. Interaction model.

event is automatically generated from the user's physical interaction. In this case, when the user drops an object using the low-level interaction features implemented in the game engine, this triggers the corresponding event. From this event, a new query is passed to the solver which takes the form of a new Prolog fact about the altered object (this would replace older facts about that same object). This new fact is passed as a structured message via a TCP/IP socket.

The solver is triggered by the reception of the new query via the socket: a listening mechanism, a server embedded in the solver, translates the received message into an actual query, that is able to trigger a new solution. The solving mechanism produces solutions one by one, but the search is interrupted after the production of the first solution, as solutions have to be proposed interactively A solution is a set of object positions, whose variables are the targets of the constraint solver.

The set of new object positions is passed as another message via the same TCP socket. In the virtual environment, the reception of this message triggers the corresponding series of low level events specifically implemented in the engine. The end result of these events is the transformation of the accepted message into a new configuration in the virtual environment.

It must be noted that, according to our results, the communication time for the overall cycle is on average less than 20ms, which is fully compatible with the user interaction (as the user is not navigating when interacting with objects).

4 Example

An intelligent configuration system is used as an application example. The data used in this configuration scenario is derived from a simple yet realistic example which uses real-world design knowledge in terms of building interior design for offices (a bank agency in our case). More specifically, the data used for both objects and constraints was drawn from real specifications [9].

In our intelligent configuration system, the spatial relationships between the objects in a layout configuration are all known and the constraints whose formulation depends on these relations reflect those specific spatial relations. Moreover, the objects involved in the configuration have been divided into non-movable objects (e.g. ventilation ducts, sources of heat, etc) and movable objects (e.g furniture: sofas, desks, etc). This is a purely semantic distinction which can be easily reversed. In our case, this means that whilst all objects take part in constraints specifying the design requirements, the user will only interact with the movable objects: the furniture. Consequently, when the user decides to reallocate a movable object, this, in turn, disrupts the imposed constraints in the configuration and forces the system to re-allocate the remaining movable objects to generate a solution compatible with all the design requirements.

In our case, the movable objects are: one vending machine, two desks (which represent the customer attention area), two sofas (waiting attention area), two automatic teller machines (ATMs), three fire extinguishers and four bins. This constitutes a subset of 14 objects: considering the size of the environment and that the overall size of the available set of constraints for each object is eleven, the corresponding search space (abstract problem space) is substantial and indeed impossible to search systematically, even less so in real-time.

4.1   Problem Representation in CLP

The problem knowledge (design requirements in our case) is expressed in the topological description of the 3D environment (non-movable objects or building elements) and in a set of constraints on the objects' attributes (movable objects or furniture, see Figure 3). There are two types of constraints on the movable objects: *local* and *global* constraints. Both types incorporate geometrical as well as more "semantic" attributes such as lighting and temperature levels. That is, those constraints without a geometrical component.

The *topological constraints* are inherited from the 3D environment and are transformed into Prolog facts which describe room's topological characteristics. Consequently, from the user's perspective, there is a perfect matching between the topological characteristics of the 3D environment and the Prolog facts implemented in the solver. For instance, sources of heat or radiators and different lighting levels are visually apparent to the user in the 3D environment. Therefore, both characteristics have been formalised as Prolog facts:

```
source_of_heat([X_0/Y_0,X_1/Y_1,X_2/Y_2])
luminosity(  [lightingvalue  =  Area_0,  lightingvalue  =
Area_1, lightingvalue = Area_2,])
```

These facts define the coordinates of the sources of heat (a list of points X/Y in the search space) and the regions where the lighting level is less than 200 lux (a list whose each element defines a lighting value and an associated rectangle $-Area_i-$ in the search space).

In the example, there are also definitions for the location in the 3D environment of the following elements: power points, ventilation ducts, special features (e.g. the central fountain), queuing area, counters, walls, luminosity and temperature levels.

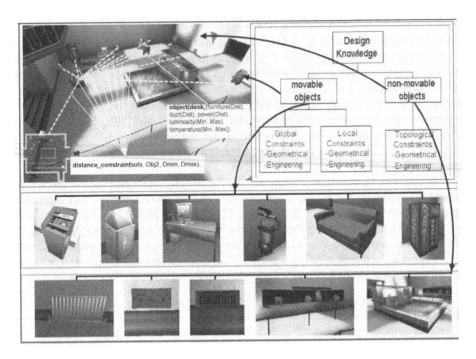

Fig. 3. CLP formalisms enable the transformation of design knowledge into a set of constraints between objects.

Local constraints are constraints on the attributes of a single object and specify how the object relates to the topological characteristics of the virtual environment. For instance, let us imagine that the user wanted to reallocate the object desk. The new object location would be constrained by the object's attributes (or design requirements) expressed in the corresponding Prolog clause: object(desk, [features_min(6), duct_min(3), power_max(3), luminosity (300 ..500), temperature(19..24)]. This clause reads as follows: a desk should be placed at a minimum distance of 6 units from any special feature (e.g. the central fountain), at a minimum distance of from any ventilation duct, at a maximum distance of 4 from a power point, inside a region whose luminosity is between 300 and 500 flux and whose temperature is between 19° and 24°.

Global constraints are constraints whose formulation involves more than one object and therefore, are imposed on the configuration. These constraints relate, for example, objects of each kind, objects of two different types, all the objects and so on. Consequently and following with the reallocation of a desk object, this not only disrupts its local properties but also the properties that link that object to the rest of the configuration. For example, the following constraint: distance_constraint (desk,atm,6,12) enforces the minimum and maximum distance between 2 objects: a desk and an atm in this case. Hence, if the new allocation is nearer than six units or further than 12 it will force the atm to be reallocated which, in turn, will force any other object linked to the atm to behave in the same fashion. In this case, constraint propagation serves as the basics for interactive problem solving, as it solves the configuration problem created by the user by displacing an object.

Global constraints are particularly relevant to express design requirements which involve group of objects. For instance, the following requirement: fire extinguishers and bins need to be distributed in the room to comply with health and safety regulations has been implemented in a similar fashion.

4.2 Sample Run

In this section, we give a step-by-step description of a system's run on an example, and for the sake of clarity we will only detail the internal mechanisms on a sub-configuration extracted from the full application.

First running the system results in the solver producing a set of variable allocations satisfying all the design constraints (see left side of Figure 1). These variables are translated in the virtual environment in terms of object types and positions, which spawns all furniture objects at their respective locations, thus constituting a first design solution.

Once the initial configuration has been deployed, the user can explore this first solution by navigating in the virtual environment and test variants of the configuration by changing objects' positions.

For instance, let us image that the user is not satisfied with the initial allocation of an object (e.g ATM is too close to the stairs). Consequently, the user seizes the ATM object and proceeds to reallocate it while he explores the 3D environment. Once, a suitable location has been found the user will drop the object. In our implementation, the user's actions trigger the corresponding Unreal events. For instance, when the object is dropped an unreal event is triggered which sends the object's location to the solver in the appropriate query format (e.g atm=34/9.).

The solver has an embedded server which deals with all the incoming queries. In other words, the server detects the incoming unreal events and transforms their content into logical terms which, in turn, prompt the main clause in the solver and triggers a new solution search. Consequently and continuing with the example, when the user seizes the ATM object he is disturbing both the local and the global constraints attached to it. As shown in figure 4, an ATM object, can only be allocated away from a source of heat (`heat(Dist)`) and, similarly, it needs to be away from any other object of the configuration a specified distance (`distance_constraint(Obj1, Obj2, DMin, DMax)`).

As a consequence, when the user decides to reallocate the object to a new position, this in turn disrupts the imposed constraints in the configuration and forces the system to "propagate" all the constraints and to generate a solution compatible with the design requirements. This propagation and a non-deterministic search are the basic mechanisms for interactive problem-solving. Thus, since the resolution process is invisible to

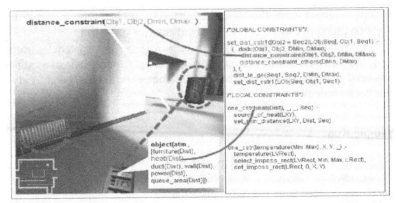

Fig. 4. The solver uses generic constraints that can be instantiated on the VE's objects

the user, seen from his or her perspective, the 3D environment automatically reconfigures itself as a consequence of his/her interactions (see right side of Figure 1).

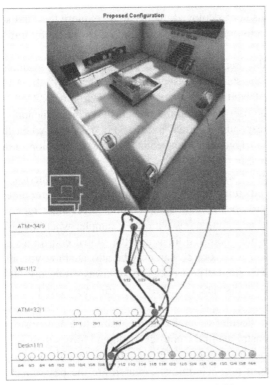

Fig. 5. The systems instantiates the variables to propose a solution to the user: labeling stage.

Let us now describe the resolution phase as seen from the variables standpoint. The resolution phase is divided into three stages: the Finite Domains (FD) of variables are defined, then the constraints are imposed *(constraint propagation)*, and finally the labeling stage *(search)* finds concrete solution(s).

For instance, let us think of a specific object: a vending machine (vm). Initially the finite domain of its spatial variables is: vm=_#[0..35/0..35]. Then, the constraints are imposed on the FD variables till no further domain reduction (due to constraint propagation) is possible: vm = _#3(1..3 :11..13 :16..18 :24..25 :27..28) / _#25(1..2 :10..12 :23..25). This example illustrates the power of constraint propagation and its importance to support the integration of the solving process in the VR interaction loop.

Consequently, when no further reduction is possible, the system must explicitly instantiate the variables to reach or "search" a solution: enumeration or labeling stage (see Figure 5). In this case, the choice of heuristics for labeling stage is: first-fail –the variable with the smallest number of elements in its FD is selected- for the choice of variable and "random" for selection of value (which gives us good execution times and offers a good visual aspect). Thus, this means that the CLP Solver outputs a list of predicates which contains the objects' types and spatial coordinates: [Obj1=X1/Y1, Obj2=X2/Y2, ...]. This list is sent to the 3D engine where a series of low-level system events transform this incoming symbolic list into the configuration of objects displayed in the virtual environment. In our example, a possible solution would be the following: [vm=1/12, atm=34/9, atm=32/1,desk=11/1] which corresponds to the configuration displayed to the user in the virtual environment (see Figure 5).

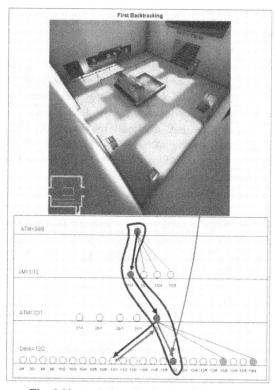

Fig. 6. Next solution: first backtracking.

Once the proposed configuration has been displayed, the user can explore all the feasible alternatives. In our case, in order to enable the user to explore the solution space a specific interaction mechanism has been implemented: when the user presses a specified key, an implemented low-level event is generated by the visualization engine which, in turn, produces a new "query" for the solver. Consequently and following the implemented interaction model previously explained, this new query triggers the deployment in the virtual environment of the next solution (see Figure 6). The concept of next solution is intimately related to the heuristics used to explore the search space. In other words, the heuristics used in the enumeration (search) stage determined how the next solution is found. For instance and continuing with the example, once a solution is proposed: [vm=1/12, atm=34/9, atm=32/1,desk=11/1]. The user could request the next one which, according to the selected heuristic, is the following: [vm=1/12, atm=34/9, atm=32/1,*desk=12/2*].

5 Conclusions

We have presented a novel framework for the use of virtual environments in interactive problem solving. This framework extends visualisation to serve as a natural interface for the exploration of configuration spaces and enables the implementation of reactive virtual environments.

This implementation is based on a fully interactive solution, where both visualisation and the generation of a new solution are under the control of user. In other words, our approach extends VR towards fully interactive environments by introducing the concept of reactive environments which react to the user's interaction whilst preserving the user-centred aspects of VR: exploration and interaction in a 3D real-time environment. Additionally, our approach supports the interactive exploration of the solution space in which alternative solutions can be found.

The system has potential for extension in different directions. For instance, in terms of mechanisms of user interaction, we envisage offering yet more interactivity to the user for more efficient object manipulation [10][11][12]. For instance, it is fairly simple to "lock" some objects in the virtual environment which would ensure that an object will remain at the some location after the user has interacted with the configuration. That is, the user could select a rectangle (an X and Y coordinates) where he wants a given object to be located and the object will remain there. It is also easy to dynamically redefine parameter for the objects, e.g. minimum/maximum distances amongst objects. As well, taking advantage of the incremental capabilities of the solver, we could give the user the possibility of adding objects on-the-fly and to choose the constraints for that objects from a set of predefined constraints.

In its current form, the system is still faced with a number of limitations, the most important being the absence of an explanatory module that would provide the user for justifications for the proposed solutions. Such a module is even more important to explain why there exist no acceptable solutions for some object positions proposed by the user. Further work will be dedicated to providing more feedback from the configuration system.

References

1. Aylett, R. and Cavazza, M.: Intelligent Virtual Environments – A State-of-the-art Report. Eurographics (2001).
2. Codognet, P.: Animating Autonomous Agents in Shared Virtual Worlds. Proceedings DMS'99, IEEE International Conference on Distributed Multimedia Systems, Aizu, Japan, IEEE Press (1999).
3. Axling, T., Haridi, S, and Fahlen, L.: Virtual reality programming in Oz. In Proceedings of the 3rd EUROGRAPHICS Workshop on Virtual Environments, Monte Carlo, February (1996).
4. Smolka, G, Henz, M and Wurtz, J.: Object-Oriented Concurrent Constraint Programming in Oz. Research Report RR-93-16, Deutsches Forschungszentrum fur Kunstliche Intelligenz, Stuhlsatzenhausweg 3, 66123 Saarbrucken, Germany, April (1993).

5. Andersson, M. Carlsoon, C. Hagsand, O, and Stahl, Olov.: DIVE – The Distributed Inter-active Virtual Environment, Tutorials and Installation Guide. Swedish Institute of Computer Science, March (1993).
6. Honda, K. and Mizoguchi, F.: Constraint-based Approach for Automatic Spatial Layout planning. Conference on Artificial Intelligence for Applications, IEEE Press (1995).
7. Pfefferkorn, C.: A heuristic problem solving design system for equipment or furniture layouts. Communications of the ACM, 18(5):286–297. (1975).
8. Diaz, D. and Codognet, P.: Design and Implementation of the GNU Prolog System. *Journal of Functional and Logic Programming*, Vol. 2001, No. 6. (2001).
9. British Educational Communications and Technology agency . Health and Safety: planning the safe installation of ICT in schools. http://www.becta.org.uk / technology / infosheets / html / safeuse.html (last visited 4/06/2002). (2002).
10. Bukowski, W. R. and Séquin, H. C. Object Associations. ACM Symp. On Interactive 3D Graphics, Monterey, CA, USA, (1995).
11. Kallman, M. and Thalmann, D. Direct 3D Interaction with Smart Objects. *ACM International Symposium on Virtual Reality Software and Technology, VRST 99*, London. UK, December, (1999).
12. Stuerzlinger, W. and Smith, G. Efficient Manipulation of Object Groups in Virtual Environments. *Proceedings of the IEEE VR 2002, March 24–28, Orlando, Florida.* (2002).

Building Smart Embodied Virtual Characters

Thomas Rist[1] and Elisabeth André[2]

[1]DFKI GmbH, Stuhlsatzenhausweg 3, Saarbrücken Germany
rist@dfki.de
[2]Laboratory for Multimedia Concepts and Applications, Universität Augsburg, Germany
andre@informatik.uni-augsburg.de

Abstract. Embodied conversational characters are autonomous, graphically embodied virtual creatures that live in a 2D or 3D virtual environment. They are able to interact intelligently with human users, other characters, and their digital environment. While for decades research has concentrated on geometric body modelling and the development of animation and rendering techniques for virtual characters, other qualities have now come in focus as well, including the provision of conversational skills as well as the simulation of believable behavior including affect and peculiarities induced by individual personality traits. As a consequence, the domain of virtual characters has become much more diverse and now encompasses a wide range of disciplines, from computer graphics and animation to AI and more recently also psychology, sociology as well as design and arts. The current paper discusses a number of design issues that arise when building an application with one or more embodied characters. By means of selected sample applications we also illustrate a yet ongoing development of animated presentation agents starting with TV-style information presenters to highly interactive multi-character scenarios in which information is conveyed to the user in the form of multi-party conversations.

1   Introduction

The creation of virtual humans is an old dream of mankind – indeed much older than computer science, AI, computer graphics and animation. With the advent of powerful but nonetheless affordable multimedia workstations, in the early nineties some groups have started research on animated virtual characters in order to deploy them in information presentation tasks, and in some cases, to promote them even as a general and ultimate metaphor for human-user interaction. Work in this area is motivated by a number of supporting arguments including the fact that such characters allow for communication styles common in human-human dialogue and thus can release the user from the burden to learn and familiarize with less native interaction techniques. Furthermore, well designed characters show great potential for making interfacing with a computer system more enjoyable.

The development of a presentation agent or a user interface with conversational embodied characters requires a number of design decisions and implementation tasks.

A. Butz et al. (Eds.): Smart Graphics 2003, LNCS 2733, pp. 123–130, 2003.

2   Character Embodiment

One aspect when designing a character is to find a suitable visual and audible appearance. In fact, there is now a broad spectrum of characters that rely on either cartoon drawings, recorded (and possibly modified) video images of persons, or geometric 3D body models for their visual realization while recorded voices or synthesized speech and sound determine their audible appearance. In our own projects we have also experimented with a wide range of different character types and different graphical realizations. Fig. 1 shows sample characters arranged in a two-dimensional design space. So-called video-agents or video actors are located in the lower left-hand corner. Their production usually requires a human actor that performs gestures which are recorded and stored in a library of video clips. By concatenating these clips, complex behaviors can be assembled and played back.

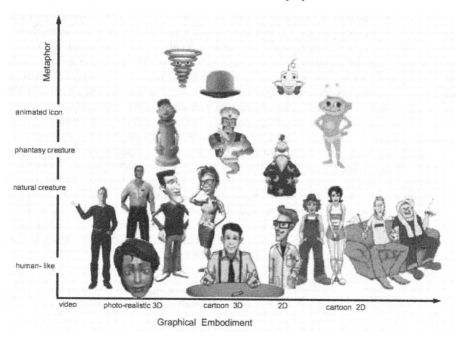

Fig. 1. Different kinds of characters[1] and different forms of graphical embodiment.

Audio-visual attractiveness, however, does not make characters smart. Rather, the success of an animated character in terms of user acceptance and interface efficiency very much depends on the character's communication skills and the impression of its overall behavior. Moreover, empirical studies show that there are dependencies between a character's appearance on the one hand and its skills on the other hand

---

[1] Characters shown in this diagram have been designed by Peter Rist except the Microsoft characters Genie and Merlin, the 3D talking head Greta which is a courtesy of Catherine Pelachaud, and the "video avatar" which is based on video recordings of Andreas Butz.

[5,9]. One extreme are photo-realistic humans (video or animated 3D models). In this case, humans who interact with such characters often have high expectations in the character's skills, especially if spoken language is used as the lead interaction modalitiy. To avoid frustrating the user, it is therefore often advisable to rely on cartoon-style characters or use a fantasy-style character design as these forms of embodiments may raise lower expectations.

3   Types of Conversational Settings

The choice of domain, tasks, and conversational setting imposes constraints on any prototype development. For instance, in the area of intelligent information presentation with animated characters we observe an ongoing evolution of systems as illustrated in Fig. 2. The first setting refers to applications in which a single character is deployed to present information. From the point of view of the user a generated presentation appears quite similar to watching a TV-news speaker or to the display of a video clip because no interaction is foreseen at display time. In contrast, the second setting is typical for applications with characters that are able to converse with a user in some sort of a dialogue (e.g., via spoken or typed natural language, or based on dynamically configured menus). Moving on to the third setting actually means a shift from a face-to-face character-user setting to a user-as-observer setting. That is, two or more characters talk to each other on the screen to convey information to the observing audience. However, no user intervention is foreseen during a performance. This is in contrast to the fourth scenario where we have an open multi-party dialogue setting which allows for both reactive and proactive user participation. Technically speaking the fourth scenario is quite challenging as one has to resolve on an operational level the conflict between predestination and freedom of interaction. To complicate things even further, one can think of multi-party settings with multiple characters and multiple users. However, up to now such settings remain a great challenge since in this case the characters must also be able to overhear and understand conversations among the human partners.

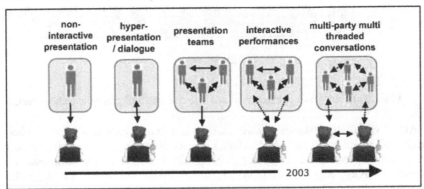

Fig. 2. Different kind of conversational settings for systems with animated characters

4   Behavior Control

Most of the current systems with animated characters distinguish between a character's embodiment and a behavior control component. Some relate this distinction to the biological body/brain dichotomy. Others take a more technically oriented view and associate embodiment with an animation engine (often called *character player*) while behavior control is related to some sort of automated behavior generation, often based on AI techniques, such as task-oriented hierarchical planning, or the simulation of certain aspects of human-like cognition. Following the latter distinction, observable behavior of a character can be regarded as the execution of a script in the character player. Thereby, a script is a temporally ordered sequence of actions including body gestures, facial expressions, verbal utterances, locomotion, and (quasi-) physical interactions with other entities of the character's immediate environment. So it comes as no surprise that behavior scripting, in one way or another, has been widely used in projects that deal with interface characters. For instance, a straightforward approach is to equip the character with a library of manually authored scripts that determine what the character might do in a certain situation. At runtime, the remaining task is to choose from the library a suitable script that meets the constraints of the current situation and at the same time, helps to accomplish a given task. What is specified in a character script is also a matter of the level of abstraction and the expressiveness of the scripting language. In some cases, the scripting language is build on top of an existing general-purpose script-based programming language. For instance, the Microsoft Agent characters can be easily scripted either in Visual Basic or in Java Script allowing the script writer to use the standard control structures of these languages like conditional statements or loop constructs. As an alternative to character specific adjuncts to programming languages, XML-compliant character scripting languages have been be defined, such as VHML (www.vhml.org) or MPML (www.miv.t.u-tokyo.ac.jp/MPML/). In any case, the script may be seen as a kind of an application programming interface (API) for the character player that allows to specify the agents behavior at a certain level of abstraction.

5   Approaches to Automated Character Scripting

A particular problem with manually authored scripts and script libraries is that the author has to anticipate scripts for all possible situations and tasks, and that the scripts must allow for sufficient variations in order to avoid characters that behave in a monotonic and too predictable way. Furthermore, the manual scripting of characters can become quite complex and error-prone since synchronization issues have to be considered. In order to avoid extensive scriptwriting but nevertheless to enable a rich and flexible character behavior, one can use a generative mechanism that composes scripts according to a set of composition rules. Our own contribution to this area of research was the development of a plan-based approach to automate the process of writing scripts that are forwarded to the characters for execution [2]. This approach has been successfully applied to build a number of applications in which information is conveyed either by a single presenter or likewise by a team of presentation agents.

While exploring further application fields and new presentation styles we identified, however, some principle limitations of scripting presentations with characters. One decisive factor is the question whether or not all information to be conveyed by a character is available before a presentation is started. Another aspect is the kind of user interactions that shall be supported during the display of a presentation.

When developing a system with more than one character one has the choice between a centralized script generator (which might rely on an AI planner or another generative approach, such as Lester's sequencing engine [4]) on the one hand, and a distributed approach on the other hand. Taking a centralised approach, the generator determines the behavior of all involved characters. Such a scripting approach facilitates the generation of well-structured and coherent presentations, however, it requires a clear separation of scripting and display time. This is only possible if all the information to be presented is a priori known. However, there are also situations in which the underlying information dynamically changes at presentation display time. Examples include the presentation of live data as well as presentations which allow for an active participation of the user. For these applications, we propose a character-centered approach in which the scripting is done by the involved characters at presentation display time. The general idea here is not specify the agents' behavior to the last detail, but give them instructions instead that they may refine and work out presentation runtime. Table 1 provides an overview of the different systems from script-based approaches to interactive performances.

Table 1. Overview of different scripting approaches

	Metaphor	Scripting Time	Script Producer	Structuring Principle	Degree of determinism	Technical Realization
tv-style presentations	scripted talk	prior to presentation, offline	separate system component	script-centered	fixed script, no interaction	centralized planning component
hyper-presentations & query /answer dialogs	scripted talk, interactive narration	switching between scripting / displaying	separate system component	script-centered	pre-defined choice points, expandable script	centralized planning component
Non-interactive pres. teams	script-based theatre	prior to presentation - offline	separate system component	plot-centered	fixed script, no interaction	centralized planning component
Reactive Presentation teams	improvisa-tional theatre	during presentation- online	involved characters	character-centered	open-ended	distributed reactive planners
Interactive performances	improvisa-tional theatre	during presentation- online	involved characters and user	character-centered	open-ended	distributed reactive planners

6   Architectures for Systems with Characters

Most systems that deploy life-like characters make a concrete commitment to one of the conversational settings illustrated in Fig. 2 and reflect this decision in a particular system architecture. However, if later on the desire emerges to support other conversational settings as well, an almost full re-implementation of the application often becomes unavoidable.

In a recent project, called MIAU [7], we wondered whether it is possible to develop a single platform which (a) can be used to construct a broad range of character applications, (b) even allows to switch on-the-fly between director- vs. character-centred scripting approaches, and (c) supports a clear separation between the specification of scripting knowledge (being a knowledge-engineering task), and the required computational machinery for behaviour generation (being an implementation task).

The architecture of the resulting MIAU platform is shown in the upper part of Fig. 3. We adopt the metaphorical distinction between a character's brain and a character's body which is typically reflected in an architecture by a separation of components for behavior planning on the one hand, and a character player component on the other hand. We further assume that the player will receive commands for direct execution from the superordinate behavior determining part. The MIAU platform itself abstracts from the player technology used for character animation, speech synthesis, and receiving user input. Rather, the platform consists of the following components:

For each character C_1... C_n MIAU foresees so-called *character components* containing a separate behavior planner as well as a separate interaction manager. The behavior planner has the task to decompose complex discourse goals into basic acts that can be executed by the character player. The interaction manager, in a certain sense, corresponds to a dialogue manager as found in NL dialogue systems since it is responsible for keeping book on interaction states and the interaction history. However, in the MIAU platform the interaction manager realizes a character's internal interface for communication with other system components by means of formalized communication acts.

To allow a user to alter settings for the performance, to take an active part in a performance, or even to intervene in the role of a director or co-director, the platform also incorporates an U box, the so-called *user component*.

However, since this time the user decides on what to do, we don't foresee a planner, but an input analyzer for mapping user input onto formalized communication acts. The internal communication with other system components is handled by the interaction manager similar to the structure of a character component. In case the user is represented in the scenario by an embodied (and possibly animated) avatar, the avatar may be employed to audio-visually indicate his or her input activity. For instance, if a text widget is used for acquiring user input, the user's avatar may speak the input sentence. Currently, we restrict ourselves to a single participating user only. Nevertheless it seems possible to extend the architecture for multi-user, multi-character scenarios by adding more user components.

In addition to character components and the user component, MIAU incorporates also a D-box, the so-called *director component*. In contrast to the characters, the director does not participate in performances and therefore has no embodiment. Rather, this component is foreseen to enable some degree of centralized control on the overall interactive performance. While the director also comprises a planner, this time the planner is used in order to influence the course of the performance depending on the degree of centralized control wanted for a certain application. Internal communication with other components is again handled via the interaction manager.

Finally, the MIAU platform comprises a message board which is shared among the different components for the exchange of internal communication acts.

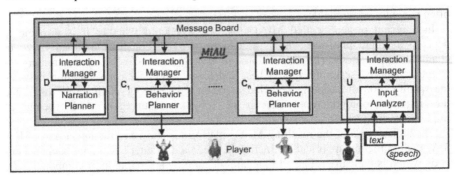

Fig. 3. Architecture of the MIAU platform for the set-up of interactive applications with a flexible number of conversational characters.

The MIAU platform is currently tested in a number of different projects (cf. Fig. 4) dealing with life-like characters including   two variants of the eShowroom [1,2] the interactive CrossTalk installation [3], and Avatar Arena [8].

Fig. 4. From left to right: the eShowroom, its interactive version, CrossTalk, and Avatar Arena

The eShowroom (first screenshot from left in Fig. 4) is an electronic car showroom in which either a single character or a team of characters are deployed to inform a user about the features of a certain car. In the interactive version of the eShowroom, a user can also take part in a "car-talk" with one or more characters (second screenshot from left in Fig. 4). The interactive CrossTalk installation (third screenshot from left in Fig. 4). has been designed for public spaces and was shown during the CeBit 2002 and the IST 2002 exhibitions. The basic idea is that a virtual stand hostess invites the user to watch a car-sales performances given by the virtual actors Tina and Ritchie who live on the opposite screen. Finally, Avatar Arena is a test-bed for the simulation of changing inter-personal relationships during negotiation dialogues. The simulation is based on socio-psychological theories of cognitive consistency [6] and captures some aspects of group dynamics.

7 Conclusions

In this paper we addressed a number of design issues that arise when building an application with one or more embodied characters. While powerful character players have become available there is no an increasing interest in research on modelling behavior and conversational skills. We argued that the choice of the conversational setting places constraints on both, the scripting approach and the architecture of a character system. We then sketched the MIAU platform that is flexible enough to switch back and forth between different conversational settings. Such a flexibility may pave the way for new engaging presentation formats. However, building an interesting character application that will be appreciated by their users is foremost a challenging design task. For instance, the number of characters, their roles as well as the foreseen role for the user need to be carefully chosen from one application to another.

References

[1]   André E, Rist T, van Mulken S, Klesen M, and Baldes S (2000) The Automated Design of Believable Dialogues for Animated Presentation Teams. In: Cassell, J., Sullivan, J., Prevost, S. and Churchill, E. (eds.): *Embodied Conversational Agents*, 220–255, Cambridge, MA: MIT Press.
[2]   André E, and Rist T (2001) Controlling the Behavior of Animated Presentation Agents in the Interface: Scripting vs. Instructing. AI Magazine 22(4):53–66.
[3]   Gebhard P, Kipp M, Klesen H, and Rist T (2003) What Are They Going to Talk About? Towards Life-Like Characters that Reflect on Interactions with Users, In Proc. of Technologies for Interactive Digital Storytelling and Environment, TIDSE 2003, Fraunhofer IRB Verlag, pp. 380–387.
[4]   Lester, J, Voerman, JL, Towns, SG and Callaway, C (1999). Deictic Believability: Coordinated Gesture, Locomotion, and Speech in Lifelike Pedagogical Agents. in: Applied Artificial Intelligence 13:383–414, 1999
[5]   McBreen H, Shade P, Jack MA, and Wyard PJ (2000) Experimental assessment of the effectiveness of synthetic personae for multi-modal e-retail applications. In Proc. of Agents 2000, pp. 39–45
[6]   Osgood C and Tannenbaum P (1955) The principle of congruity in the prediction of attitude change. Psychology Review, pp. 62, 42–55.
[7]   Rist T, André E, Baldes S (2003) In: Proc of IUI'03, A Flexible Platform for Building Applications with Life-Like Caracters ACM Press, pp 158–165.
[8]   Rist T. Schmitt M, Pelachaud C, and Bilvi M (2002) Towards a Simulation of Conversations with Expressive Embodied Speakers and Listeners. In Proc. of Computer Animation and Social Agents, CASA 2003.
[9]   van Mulken S, André E and Müller J (1998) The Persona Effect: How Substantial Is It? In Proc. of Human Computer Interaction Conference, Berlin, Springer, pp. 53–66.

Let's Run for It!: Conspecific Emotional Flocking Triggered via Virtual Pheromones

Carlos Delgado-Mata[1], Jesus Ibanez[2], and Ruth Aylett[1]

[1] Centre for Virtual Environments, The University of Salford,
C.Delgado@pgr.salford.ac.uk, R.S.Aylett@salford.ac.uk
[2] Business House, University Road, Salford, M5 4WT, Manchester, UK
jesus.ibanez@tecn.upf.es

Abstract. This paper extends Reynolds' flocking algorithm to incorporate the effects of emotions, in this case fear. Sheep are used as a typical example of flocking mammals and an autonomous agent architecture with an action selection mechanism incorporating the effects of emotion is linked to the standard flocking rules. Smell is used to transmit emotion between animals, through pheromones modelled as particles in a free expansion gas. Preliminary results show that more realistic flocking behaviour is produced.

1 Introduction

In order to obtain more believable virtual environments, some research groups are trying to model and simulate virtual animals. This objective is usually tackled from a multidisciplinary point of view. Theories and techniques from ethology, virtual reality, graphic simulation, artificial intelligence, artificial life, robotics, and software agents (among others) are used and sometimes combined.

Although modelling the behaviour of autonomous animals is really a useful task, the fact is that in nature usually animals behave as part of social groups. Therefore, if we want to populate virtual environments with believable virtual animals, we need to emulate the behaviour of animal groups.

Furthermore, our assumption of life and smartness in real animals derives from our perception of their reaction to the environment, and in particular, to their reaction to perceived actions. For example, if one runs through a flock of sheep, we expect them to move in order to avoid us. This reaction seems driven by emotional stimulus (most likely fear), and is communicated amongst conspecifics at an emotional level. Thus, believable virtual animals should display this kind of emotional response and communication.

In this paper, we propose an architecture to model and simulate animals that not only "feel" emotions, that affect their decision making, but are also able to communicate them through virtual pheromones. The virtual animals also show a group behaviour, in particular a flocking behaviour based on the boids algorithm [19] modified so that it takes into account the animals' emotions. In this sense, the emotional communication "drives" the flocking emergence. An architecture, described below, has been designed and implemented to check its feasibility.

A. Butz et al. (Eds.): Smart Graphics 2003, LNCS 2733, pp. 131–140, 2003.

The structure of the paper is as follows. First we review related work, in both group simulation and emotion areas. Next we detail the proposed architecture. Then we describe the current implementation. Finally we show the conclusions and point out future work.

2   Related Work

This section describes related work on both emotion and animation of group behaviour.

2.1   Emotions

Until recently the field of Artificial Intelligence (AI) had largely ignored the use of emotion and intuition to guide reasoning and decision-making. Minsky [13] was one of the first to emphasise the importance of emotion for Artificial Intelligence. Other models of emotion have been proposed; Picard focuses on recognising emotions [16]; Velásquez [23] synthesised emotions and some of their influences on behaviour and learning, using a similar approach to the one proposed in this work, that is a model based on Izard's Four Types of Emotion Elicitors [8].

Based on the description given above we decided to define emotions as reflective autonomic responses, that is primary emotions [3], triggered by particular stimuli. In [5] an extended review is provided.

2.2   Group Animation

As pointed out in [15], when animating groups of objects, three general classes of techniques are usually considered, depending on the number of elements being controlled and the sophistication of the control strategy. These general types of techniques are particle systems, flocking, and (autonomous) behavioural animation.

A particle system is a large collection of objects (particles) which, taken together, represent a fuzzy object [17]. Particle systems are based on physics, and particles themselves are supposed not to have intelligence, therefore this kind of technique is usually employed to animate groups of objects that represent non-living objects.

Flocking systems typically have a medium number of objects, each one of them controlled by a relatively simple set of rules that operate locally. The objects exhibit some limited intelligence and are governed by some relatively simple physics. This type of technique is usually employed to animate objects that represent living objects with simple behaviour.

Particle systems and flocking systems produce the so-called emergent behaviour, that is, a global effect generated by local rules. For example, one can speak of a flock of birds having a certain motion, even though there is not any control specific to the flock as an entity.

Autonomous behaviour is usually employed to animate one or a few objects which are supposed to be "intelligent". Therefore this kind of technique is usually employed to animate groups of objects that represent living objects. Generally each object is controlled by a sophisticated set of rules.

As we are trying to simulate the behaviour of medium-size animal flocks, we have decided to base the group animation algorithm on flocking techniques. However, we also want every animal to show a sophisticated behaviour based, among other things, on his emotional state. Therefore, our system is hybrid, in that it shows a global flocking behaviour but at the same time each object is controlled by a complicated autonomous behaviour.

Boids. The collective behaviour of flocks, herds and schools has been studied in artificial life [10] and complex systems [6] areas. This kind of behaviour seems complex, however as Reynolds suggested [19] it can be modelled by applying few simple rules to every individual. In his model of so-called boids, every individual (boid) tries to fulfil three conditions: cohesion or flock centring (attempt to stay close to nearby flockmates), alignment or velocity matching (attempt to match velocity with nearby flockmates), and separation or collision avoidance (avoid collisions with nearby flockmates). Boids has been successfully used to animate the behaviour of flocks in several famous films.

3   Our Architecture

3.1   Overall Architecture

The basic task of an animal brain has often been split into three sub-tasks as shown in figure 1a. Our model (see figure 1b) adds a fourth sub-task, emotions. The four sub-tasks in our system are therefore: perception (sensing of the environment and interpretation of the sensory signals to provide a high-level description of the environment), emotions (which affect the behaviour of the animals, exemplified by the conspecifics flight-flocking), action selection (using the perceptual and emotional inputs to decide which of the animal's repertoire of actions is most suitable at that moment) and motor control (transforming the chosen action into a pattern of "physical" actions to produce the animation of the animal).

Figure 2 shows a more detailed diagram of the designed architecture, and the next sections describe its components.

3.2   Communicating Emotions

Because agents exist in a VE and not in the real world, in principle the transmission of emotion between agents could just be carried out by 'cheating', that is by allowing agents to read each other's internal state directly. We choose not to do this however, since we see advantages in re-usability and in matching real-world behaviour (that is in real sheep for example) by trying to model emotional

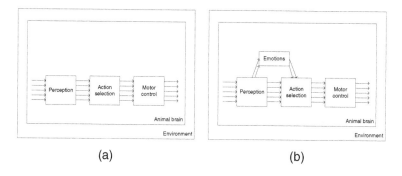

Fig. 1. Two decompositions of the functions of an animal's brain

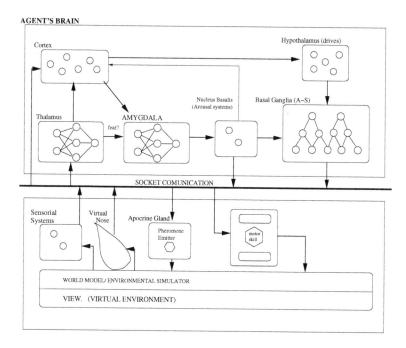

Fig. 2. Detailed architecture

interaction in a slightly more principled way. In the real-world however, emotional transmission may well be multi-modal, with certain modes such as the perception of motion being particularly difficult to model. Thus we have limited ourselves for now to a single mode, and the one we have chosen is pheromones, to be perceived by a virtual olfaction sensor.

The nose has been linked with emotional responses and intelligence. Recent experiments [7] have shown that mammals, including humans, emit pheromones through apocrine glands as an emotional response, and as means to communicate that state to conspecifics, who can adapt their behaviour accordingly; research has found that odours produce a range of emotion responses in animals, including humans [8], which is adaptively advantageous because olfaction is part of the old smell-brain which can generate fast emotional-responses, that is without the need of cognitive processes. In this respect [9] points out: "The use of pheromones to alert conspecifics or members of a social group to the presence of an intruder or a potential attacker is common in many animal species. For example, in the presence of an intruder, several species of social hymenoptera secrete pheromones which cause defensive behaviour among conspecifics. This alarm pheromone is thought to have two effects: (1) it alerts conspecifics to the threat of danger, and (2) it acts as a chemical repellent to the intruder.

Animals have a particular keen sense of smell; [12] writes: "One of the odours released by perspiration -either human or animals- is butyric acid, one gram of which contains seven thousand million billion molecules, an ungraspable number!. Imagine that this acid is spread at precise moment throughout all the rooms in a ten-story building. A man would only small it if he were to take a breath of air at the window, and then only at that precise moment. But if the same gram of odour were spread over a city like Hamburg, a dog could perceive it from anywhere up to an altitude of 300 feet!".

Every living entity, be it nutritious, poisonous, sexual partner, predator or prey, has a distinctive molecular signature that can be carried in the wind. Neary [14]points out that sheep, particularly range sheep, will usually move more readily into the wind than with the wind, allowing them to utilise their sense of smell.

In real animals chemoreceptors (exteroceptors and interoceptors) are used to identify chemical substances and detect their concentration. Smell exists even among very primitive forms of life. In our architecture we intend to model the exteroceptors which detect the presence of chemicals in the external environment.

In this work, to illustrate the use of emotion and drives to influence behaviours, sheep had been selected as the exemplar creature; to feel secure [18] claims that " A sheep need to be be with other sheep in order to be in a state of well-being and normative physiology. Sheep will always try to maintain uninterrupted visual contact with at least one other sheep, and they will flock together at any sign of danger" suggesting a specific sensor for other nearby sheep can be used to elicit a distress emotion in case of the absence of other conspecifics.

To support the communication of emotions, an environmental simulator has been developed, its tasks include changing the temperature and other environmental variables depending on the time of day and on the season, which depends on statistical historical data. An alarmed animal sends virtual pheromones to the environmental simulator and they are simulated using the free expansion gas formula in which the volume depends on the temperature and altitude (both simulated environmental variables). To compute the distribution of the pheromones a set of particles has been simulated using Boltzmann distribution formula 1, which is shown and described next.

$$n\left(y\right) = n_o e^{\frac{mgy}{k_b}T} \tag{1}$$

Where m is the pheromone's mass; g is the gravity; y is the altitude; k_b is the Boltzmann number; T is the temperature; n_o is N/V; N is number of molecules exhuded by the apocrine gland, which is related to the intensity of the emotional signal; and V is the Volume.

The virtual animal includes a virtual nose used to detect pheromones, if any, that are near the creature. To smell a pheromone the threshold set in the current experiment is $200x10^{-16}$ because [11] has shown that animals have 1000 to 10000 more sensitivity than humans and Wyatt [25] claims that the threshold in humans to detect certain "emotional response odours", like those exuded from the armpits, is 200 per trillion parts, that is $200x10^{-12}$.

3.3   Action Selection

The problem of action selection is that of choosing at each moment in time the most appropriate action out of a repertoire of possible actions. The process of making this decision takes into account many stimuli, including (in our case) the animal's emotional state.

Action selection algorithms have been proposed by both ethologists and computer scientists. The models suggested by the ethologists are usually at a conceptual level, while the ones proposed by computer scientists (with some exceptions as [22] and [2]) generally do not take into account classical ethologic theories.

According to Dawkins [4], a hierarchical structure represents an essential organising principle of complex behaviours. This view is shared by many ethologists [1] [21], and some action selection models follow this approach.

Our action selection mechanism is based on Tyrrell's model [22]. This model is a development of Rosenblatt & Payton's original idea [20] (basically a connectionist, hierarchical, feed-forward network), to which temporal and uncertainty penalties were added, and for which a more specific rule for combination of preferences was produced. Note that among other stimuli, our action selection mechanism takes the emotional states (outputs of the emotional devices) of the virtual animal.

3.4   The Flocking Behaviour

The flocking behaviour in our system is based on boids [19], although we have extended it with an additional rule (escape), and, most importantly, the flocking behaviour itself is parameterised by the emotional devices output, that is, by the values of the emotions the boids feel. The escape rule is used to influence the behaviour of each boid in such a way that it escapes from potential danger (essentially predators) in its vicinity. Therefore, in our model each virtual animal moves itself along a vector, which is the resultant of four component vectors, one for each of the behavioural rules, which are:

Cohesion - attempt to stay close to nearby flockmates.
Alignment - attempt to match velocity with nearby flockmates.
Separation - avoid collisions with nearby flockmates.

Escape - escape from potential danger (predators for example).

The calculation of the resultant vector, $Velocity$, for a virtual animal A is as follows:

$$V_A = \underbrace{(Cf \cdot Cef \cdot Cv)}_{Cohesion} + \underbrace{(Af \cdot Aef \cdot Av)}_{Alignment} + \underbrace{(Sf \cdot Sef \cdot Sv)}_{Separation} + \underbrace{(Ef \cdot Eef \cdot Ev)}_{Escape}$$

$$(2)$$

$$Velocity_A = limit(V_A, (MVef \cdot MaxVelocity)) \qquad (3)$$

where Cv, Av, Sv and Ev are the component vectors corresponding to the cohesion, alignment, separation and escape rules respectively. Cf, Af, Sf and Ef are factors representing the importance of the component vectors Cv, Av, Sv and Ev respectively. These factors allow to weight each component vector independently. In our current implementation they can be varied, in real time, from a user interface. Cef, Aef, Sef and Eef are factors representing the importance of the component vectors Cv, Av, Sv and Ev respectively, given the current emotional state of the virtual animal. That is, each of this factors is a function that take the current values of the animal' s emotions and generate a weight for its related component vector. $MaxVelocity$ is the maximum velocity allowed to the animal. In the current implementation it can be varied from a user interface. $MVef$ is a factor whose value is calculated as a function of the current values of the animal's emotions. It allows to increase and decrease the animal's $MaxVelocity$ depending on its emotional state. $limit$ is a function whose value is equal to its first parameter if this is not greater than its second one, otherwise the function value is equal to its second parameter.

The emotional factors (Cef, Aef, Sef, Eef, and $MVef$) reflects ethologic heuristic rules. Figure 3 shows an example of how emotions parameterise the flocking behaviour. In particular it shows how fear affects the component vectors of the animals' behaviour. The greater the fear an animal feels, the greater the weight of both its cohesion vector (the animal try to stay closer to nearby flockmates) and its escape vector (the boid try to stay farther from the potential danger). The resultant vector obtained by adding the four basic vectors is then scaled to not exceed the maximum speed. This maximum velocity is parameterised by the fear as well. The greater the fear an animal feels, the greater the speed it is able to reach.

4   Implementation and Preliminary Results

The implementation of the architecture is three layered. Namely the agent's brain, the world model and the virtual environment. As seen in figure 2 the agents' brains are processes that runs independently on a Linux workstation and each agent's brain receives the sensorial data via network sockets and sends (through the network) the selected action to the world's model which contains the agents' bodies and the environmental simulation. The changes to this model is reflected on each frame in the virtual environment which is developed using

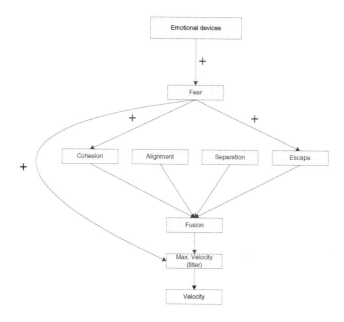

Fig. 3. How *fear* parameterises the flocking algorithm

Wildtangent's Webdriver [24] , and on a more limited scale there is an implementation using OpenGL Performer. This mechanism allows modularity and extensibility to add/modify the behaviour of the virtual animals.

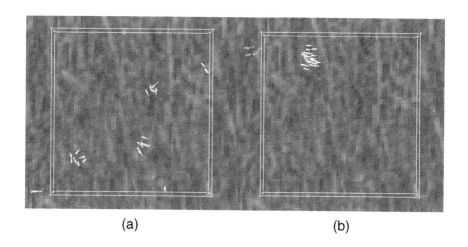

Fig. 4. Snapshot of the implemented system

The tests carried out so far, although preliminary results, show that the proposed architecture is able to cope with the problem of simulating flocks of virtual animals driven by its emotional state. For example, the emergent behaviour observed when the virtual sheep are attacked by predators (see figure 4b) seems more real than the one obtained by using classical flocking algorithms. While in models without emotional communication animals only react to a predator when it is in their field of view, in our system animals without a predator in its field of view start to react after its neighbours do so. This behaviour, which is due to the pheromones communication/perception [25], and thus emulates nature more believably.

5   Conclusions and Future Work

This work has shown that it is feasible to bring together the simple rule-based architectures of flocking with the more complex architectures of autonomous agents. Initial results suggest that this produces more believable and more specific flocking behaviour in the presence of predators. Further work will be carried out to more accurately characterise the changes in flocking behaviour obtained by this extended architecture. Transitions between grazing and reacting to predators will be carefully analysed. We further plan to validate this work by modelling a different flocking animal, for example the musk ox, which responds to predators by forming a horns-out circle of adult animals with the young inside. We argue that our extended architecture can support a much wider and more realistic spread of flocking behaviour and therefore represents a contribution to believable virtual animals.

References

1. Gerald P Baerends, *The functional organization of behaviour*, Animal Behaviour (1976), no. 24, 726–738.
2. Bruce Blumberg, *Action-selection in hamsterdam: Lessons from ethology*, Proceedings of the Third International Conference on Simulation of Adaptive Behavior (Brighton, England), 1994.
3. Antonio Damasio, *Descartes' error:emotion, reason and the human brain*, Papermac, Oxford, United Kingdom, 1996.
4. Richard Dawkins, *Hierarchical organisation: A candidate principle for ethology*, Growing Points in Ethology (Bateson & Hinde, ed.), Cambridge University Press, 1976.
5. Carlos Delgado-Mata, Rocio Ruiz-Rodarte, Ruth S Aylett, M A Perez-Cisneros, and P A Cook, *Illusion of life in palenque: Communicating emotions inside a virtual environment for maya cultural heritage*, PRICAI: Seventh Pacific Rim International Conference on Artificial Intelligence (Tokyo, Japan) (Helmut Prendinger, ed.), PRICAI, 2002.
6. G. W. Flake, *The computational beauty of nature : Computer explorations of fractals, chaos, complex systems, and adaptation*, MIT Press, 1999.
7. Karl Grammer, *5-alpha-androst-16en-3alpha-one: a male pheromone ?*, Ethology and Sociobiology **14** (1993), no. 3, 201–207.

8. Carol E Izard, *Four systems for emotion activation: Cognitive and noncognitive processes*, Psychological Review **100** (1993), no. 1, 68–90.
9. Anne Kitchell, Sharon Lynn, and Shiva Vafai, *10 smell myths: Uncovering the stinkin' truth*, Tech. report, Department of Biological Sciences, University of South Carolina, 1995.
10. C. Langton, *Artificial life: An overview*, MIT Press, Cambridge, MA, 1995.
11. D A Marshall, L Blumer, and D G Moulton, *Odor detection curves for n-pentanoic acid in dogs and humans*, Chemical Senses **6** (1981), 445–453.
12. Fernand Mery, *The life, history and magic of the dog*, Grosset & Dunlap, New York, USA, 1970.
13. Marvin Minsky, *The society of mind*, Simon & Schuster, New York, USA, 1985.
14. Mike Neary, *Sheep sense*, The Working Border Collie (2001).
15. R. Parent, *Computer animation: Algorithms and techniques*, 1998, Available at http://www.cis.ohio-state.edu/ parent/book/outline.html.
16. Rosalind Picard, *Affective computing*, MIT Press, Cambridge, MA, USA, 1997.
17. W. Reeves, *Particle systems - a technique for modeling a class of fuzzy objects*, ACM Transactions on Graphics **2** (1983), no. 2, 91–108.
18. Viktor Reinhardt and Annie Reinhardt, *Comfortable quarters for laboratory animals*, Comfortable Quarters for Laboratory Animals (Viktor Reinhardt and Annie Reinhardt, eds.), Animal Welfare Institute, Washington, DC, 2002.
19. Craig W Reynolds, *Flocks, herds, and schools: A distributed behavioral model*, Computer Graphics **21** (1987), no. 4, 25–34.
20. J.K. Rosenblatt and D.W. Payton, *A fine-grained alternative to the subsumption architecture for mobile robot control*, Proceedings of the IEEE/INNS International Joint Conference on Neural Networks (Washington DC), vol. 2, June 1989, pp. 317–324.
21. Nikolaas Tinbergen, *The study of instinct*, Oxford University Press, United Kingdom, 1969.
22. Toby Tyrell, *Computational mechanisms for action selection*, Ph.D. thesis, University of Edinburgh, Edinburgh, Scotland, 1993.
23. Juan Velásquez, *Modeling emotions and other motivations in synthetic agents*, Proceedings of the Fourteenth National Conference on Artificial Intelligence (AAAI-97) (Providence, RI), MIT/AAAI Press, 1997.
24. Wildtangent, *Wildtangent web driver*, http://www.wildtangent.com/, 2003.
25. Tristam D Wyatt, *Pheromones and animal behaviour*, Cambridge University Press, Cambrigde, U.K., 2003.

A Perception and Selective Attention System for Synthetic Creatures

Daniel Torres[1] and Pierre Boulanger[2]

[1] Department of Computing Science, University of Alberta
T6G 2E8 Edmonton, Alberta. Canada
`dtorres@cs.ualberta.ca`, `http://www.cs.ualberta.ca/~dtorres`
[2] Advanced Man-Machine Interface Laboratory, Department of
Computing Science, University of Alberta
T6G 2E8 Edmonton, Alberta. Canada
`pierreb@cs.ualberta.ca`

Abstract. This paper describes the selective attention and perception system designed for the synthetic creatures of the ANIMUS[1] project. This system allows agents to evaluate objects, other characters, properties, and events happening in their virtual environment. Perceived data is prioritized to direct the attention of the character toward salient stimuli, providing means for action-reaction and conditioned learning, automatic triggering of reflexive responses to certain stimuli, and further optimization of the cognitive processes by creating a more natural and realistic interface. The system can be customized to fit the artistic and conceptual constraints of each character, facilitating the creation of synthetic creatures with complex behavior and personality.

1 Introduction

Creating "believable" characters for interactive environments is a demanding task both in terms of art and technology. A "believable" character appears to be alive, giving the illusion of having its own thoughts, emotions, intention and personality. Thomas and Johnston[2] say:

> Consider this: a strong situation has been established. The character comes into it with a definite and interesting attitude. Confronted with the problem, he develops his own personality, grows a little, shows who he is, makes his decisions for action...(p. 375)

To support a virtual creature with such life-like behavior, we must maintain a robust and consistent system of emotions, goals and beliefs; make decisions in a changing environment; and take the character to express itself effectively to the user while remaining within the bounds of its role and personality. An acceptable perception system supports the character with all the necessary information about the world and itself in order to facilitate these tasks. Interactivity is greatly hindered without some form of perception. The quality and flexibility of such interactivity, and the performance of the character's inner systems depends on the

A. Butz et al. (Eds.): Smart Graphics 2003, LNCS 2733, pp. 141–150, 2003.
© Springer-Verlag Berlin Heidelberg 2003

ability of the perception system to convey information in a way that facilitates higher level processes. Evaluating perceived information is an expensive process. It is often needed to measure the impact and significance of the world over the agent's plans and objectives, before a response is generated. Our proposed perception system simplifies this task by means of an *early* discrimination method that prioritizes and highlights interesting stimuli, performs conditioned learning and creates primitive reactive behavior without having to analyze the meaning of sensory data. Broad agents and synthetic characters have become widely used in virtual reality simulations, video games, human training programs[3,4], therapeutic tools, support and help systems[5], virtual drama[6,7,10], and artistic projects. A flexible, customizable and robust perception system provides a solid start for the creation of characters that provoke the illusion of being alive. The rest of this paper is organized as follows: In section 2 we review some previous work. In section 3, we briefly describe the architecture of an ANIMUS system to provide a context for the perception layer. In section 4 we detail our virtual domain and its characteristics. We also define some basic concepts. The detailed description of the perception architecture, its components, and functionality is given in section 5. Section 5.6 illustrates the perception system with an example.

2   Previous Work

Several research groups are working with broad agents. We are interested in those that incorporate some model of personality, goals and emotions (such systems require more sophisticated perception methods than those which only show reactive behavior). An interesting example is C4, developed by Isla[8,9] and the MIT Media Lab: The perception system sees the world through a set of *percepts* (atomical classification and data extraction units) kept in a *percept tree*. When a stimulus is sensed, percepts are used to determine what and how much is known about it. New percepts can be created, and the existing ones refined as needed by the character, each one having its own specialized algorithm to deal with the perceived information. Bates[10] presents the Oz Project, in which agents sense the world through data objects that represent property-value pairs. Sensed data can be incomplete, incorrect, or absent. In Kline[11], perception is done by physical sensors (heat, proximity, pressure), synthetic vision (detecting objects and their features), and direct sensing (by querying the world). Sensors filter the information coming from the world or other sensors, each one reacting to a spectrum of the sensed data, while other systems get the output and construct specific numerical information that can be interpreted by higher rational systems. An example of perception systems for real robots is found in Velázquez[12].

3   The ANIMUS Project

Our perception model is part of a bigger project called ANIMUS. Here we briefly mention its basic architecture to illustrate the context in which perception is done and how it interacts with other parts of our synthetic characters. An AN-IMUS creature is a synthetic character composed of three main layers, namely **Perception** layer (described in this paper), **Cognition** layer, and **Expression** layer. The Cognition layer is a set of high-level systems that allow the character to have goals, emotions, personality, and social and rational behavior. This layer processes all information coming from the perception layer and orchestrates the actions of the expression layer. The Expression layer is a **Pose-based** animation engine similar to the ones in Isla[8] and Downie[13]. It renders a 3D graphic representation of the character and creates animations in real time to express the inner states of the creature. The Perception layer has direct connections to both the Cognition and Expression layers. An ANIMUS character can be human, animal, or otherwise.

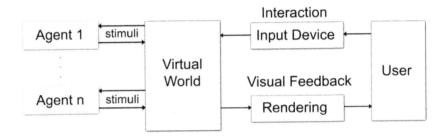

Fig. 1. The basic layout of the Virtual Environment

4   The Virtual Environment

Basic Definitions. The basic layout of the Virtual Environment can be seen in Fig. 1. It contains a number of *Virtual Characters*, the *Virtual World Agent* and an optional avatar representation of the *human user(s)*. Virtual characters are ANIMUS creatures as described in Section 3. The basic information primitive is called *feature*, a concept-value pair similar to what we find in Bates[10], representing something that can be sensed by a character. Features range from physical properties like color, weight, temperature and volume intensity, to more complex concepts like pain, hunger, and fatigue. When a feature is produced by a character it is called a *stimulus*. A *stimuli* is the set of stimulus expressed by a character at a given time.

Information Exchange. The *Virtual World* is an agent that keeps track of all existing characters and administrates a *blackboard* with the set of all stimuli at time *t*. It also synchronizes the activity of the characters by calling them to update their perception system a certain number of times per second. The Virtual Environment has any number of characters interacting in real time between themselves and the human users. When a character needs to perceive its environment, stimuli is obtained from the blackboard or by directly querying other characters. The perceived information usually contains noise or transformations induced by the Virtual World in order to make it *relative* to the character[1]. One stimuli is updated by each character and posted in the blackboard for other characters to see. This perception-reaction-expression information cycle repeats for the duration of the simulation.

5   A Selective Attention and Perception Layer

The objectives of the Perception Layer are:

1. To serve as an entry-point for the world, thus letting the character perceive its environment.
2. To segment, discriminate, and prioritize information to bias the attention of the creature toward salient stimuli.
3. To implement reflexes as an automatic response to certain stimuli
4. To perform low-level conditioned learning

The possibility of creating a selective attention model without having to analyze the meaning of perceived information was inspired from the concepts of *early* and *late* selection of human perceptual processing[18]. Early selection suggests that attention can be directed before the perceived information is semantically processed, by blocking some stimuli and preserving others. Late selection states that attention comes after the correct evaluation of information by high-level cognition systems. It was later proposed that early selection would not completely block certain stimuli, but only degrade or attenuate it before it would reach higher levels of cognition. Our perception layer is an early selection system. This creates faster response times and resource optimization since higher AI evaluation algorithms only process important information, while the rest of the stimuli remains available for late selection.

5.1   System Architecture

The modules of the Perception System are illustrated in Fig. 2. At each perception frame, the input to the Perception layer is a set of stimuli from other agents and the world. The output is a set of *prioritized* stimuli to the high level cognition system of the character. The *Reflex Agents* module can also trigger automatic reflex responses as a reaction to the perceived information.

---

[1] This principle is called *sensory honesty*. If two characters are on the same side of a wall they are able to see each other, but if one is placed at the other side, they will not be able to know their position, even though it is contained on the blackboard.

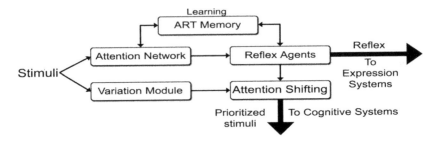

Fig. 2. The architecture of the Perception Layer

5.2 The Attention Network

The functionality of the Attention Network is inspired by Koch[16]. Each neuron contains an input weight w_i where $0 \leq w \leq 1$, and a threshold θ_i initially set to 0, and responds to a particular stimulus that may or may not be contained in the stimuli set. When a stimuli enters the network, the net input for a matching neuron is $v_{i_t} = x_{i_t} w_i$, where x_{i_t} is the magnitude of stimulus i at time t, and the output is an excitation level determined by $I_i = (v_{i_t}, \theta_i)$ (Usually a sigmoid function) if $v_{i_t} < \theta_i$ and $I_i = 1$ otherwise. There are features that can only be produced as a combination of other features (like pain, for example), thus the excitation output of some neurons is linked to other neurons, creating the network. Both the input weight and the threshold of each individual neuron changes as a function of entrant stimuli and time, giving the neuron short-term memory characteristics. A learning rate $\eta_i, 0 \leq \eta \leq 1$ controls how fast the threshold adapts to the magnitude of the stimulus, and the function $\gamma(w_{i_t}, \sigma_i)$, usually a parabolic or sigmoid decay, makes the input weight converge to 0 in σ_i frames if the input remains constant or less than the current threshold. The output of the Attention Network is an **attention stimuli** composed of the excitation magnitude of each triggered neuron. The careful selection of attention neurons and network design determines the perception capabilities of the creature. One basically controls *what* can be sensed and *how* sensible this information is. Like in real biological systems, some creatures will be able to note features ignored by others, creating a more realistic behavior and a more flexible tool for building original characters.

5.3 The Variation Module

The Variation Module is a set of variation units based on the *Inhibition of Return*[18] effect observed in human perception, which suggests that recently attended stimuli is inhibited over time. The perception of a given stimulus is inhibited when its variation is greater than a certain frequency factor[2]. We say that a stimulus produced change from one perception frame to the next one

---

[2] Such factor must be greater than 1 and smaller than the current perception rate.

if the absolute difference of their magnitudes is less than a threshold value. The output of a variation unit is 1 if variation is detected for its corresponding stimuli and the current variation rate is less than the frequency factor, and 0 otherwise. This inhibits interest in strongly repetitive phenomena like an object oscillating with constant frequency, while biasing attention to more unique events like a lightbulb that suddenly goes off. The output of the Variation Module is a **variation stimuli** composed of the magnitudes of all variation units triggered by the perceived stimuli.

5.4   Reflex Triggering

The Reflex Module is a set of *Reflex agents*. Each reflex agent is an independent unit containing two elements: a reflex stimuli and a reflex function. The reflex stimuli is a purposely chosen combination of features with attention magnitudes, and the reflex function is a unique procedure in terms of the features in the reflex stimuli. When a reflex agent finds a close correspondence between its reflex stimuli and some attention stimuli coming from the Attention Network, the original magnitudes of the perceived stimuli become the parameters of its reflex function, generating a carefuly designed reflex. Each agent handles the creation and behavior of such reflex in its own particular way, allowing flexibility and originallity between characters. In Fig. 3, an ANIMUS character perceives bullets fired by the user. When a bullet is close to its body, an evasive reflex agent appraises speed and proximity to move the body away from the bullet. This animation demonstrates that by simply using reflex agents we can create characters with interesting reactive behavior.

Fig. 3. An ANIMUS character with a simple reflex agent that moves the body away from bullets

5.5   Learning

The Conditioned Memory module is a set of ART units. For each reflex agent that has triggered a response, there exists a unique ART model that synthesizes a sample of the stimuli at the time the reflex was produced. This module is based on work by Mumford[14] and follows the suggestion that events in the environment are not arbitrarily produced but are due to hidden variables. Synthesizing coded signals for the creation of comparison points in a feed-forward, feed-backward structure helps to create knowledge about such hidden variables and hopefully teach the character to react in response to certain stimuli.

To explain the functionality of this module consider the case of *Pavlov's dog*. Pavlov discovered that dogs could be trained to salivate in response to the sound of a bell. The training consisted on simultaneously presenting the stimuli of a bell and a piece of meat to the dog. After some time, the dog relates the sound of the bell to the appearance of the meat and salivates in preparation for the feast. Similarly, our virtual dog perceives the meat and its features, triggering the salivation reflex. The conditioned memory keeps a synthetic version of the stimuli (containing both the signals from the food and the bell). After some reinforcement (done by repeating the scenario to the dog) the weight of the synthesized stimuli is enough to elicit the salivation reflex with only the presence of the bell. This happens because the bell's stimuli matches, to some extent, the template contained in the ART model of the salivation agent. In other words, the virtual dog "suspects" they are related and therefore triggers the agent. When the food appears to confirm this relation, the ART model gets updated and the bell's stimuli creates a closer match next time it is perceived.

The Attention and Variation stimuli are analyzed in the **Attention Shifting** module in order to prioritize the perceived stimuli before it is presented to the high lever cognition systems.

5.6   Alebrije: A Working Example

To demostrate the simplicity and functionality of the Perception Layer we have created a simulation called **Alebrije**. It consists of a main character (a lizard-like creature named *Alebrije*[3]) and a number of *Noise Insects*, whose only function is to emit noise as they are moved by the user or the computer. Alebrije has a perception network that responds to noise, and a reflex agent that makes him turn and face whatever stimulates his attention. The only behavior policy is that Alebrije stays awake as long as something interesting is happening and otherwise goes to sleep. Once the scenario is set the user can create any number of noise insects and move them in the virtual world. Alebrije is free to react to those who best stimulate his attention. For this experiment we use 2 noise insects: one oscillates in a cyclic fashion by the computer, while the other is controlled by the user. The perception rate is set to 20 samples per second, variation threshold is 4 samples/sec, and the decay for the noise-sensible neuron is set to 30 samples. Fig. 4 shows the noise magnitude along 350 frames as it is created by both insects. The dotted line belongs to the automated noise insect and the continuous line is the user-controlled insect. We will refer to the computer insect as $C1$, and the

---

[3] Alebrije is a term used by some Mexican artisans to describe a particular kind of imaginary creature.

human controlled insect as $C2$. At this time, the ART memory module is not completely implemented so this experiment will not reflect its features.

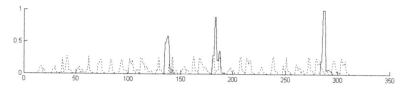

Fig. 4. The unmodified noise stimuli created by the insects.

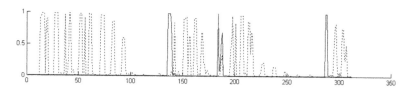

Fig. 5. Reaction to both stimuli by Alebrije's Attention Network

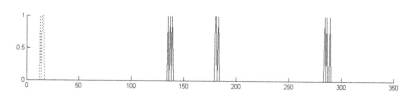

Fig. 6. Reaction to both stimli by Alebrije's Variation Module

When $C1$ begins to move, a stimuli with its noise magnitude is perceived by Alebrije's Attention Network. The noise neuron is excited with an output of aproximately 1 since its initial threshold is 0. The Variation Module detects the change and also produces 1. The reflex stimuli of the "stare" reflex agent is set to trigger when $noise_t > 0.7$, so Alebrije wakes up and stares at $C1$. At this point, w_{noise} begins to decay and θ_{noise} becomes equal to the perceived noise. As $C1$ keeps changing more than 4 times per second for the rest of the simulation, the Variation Module output quickly becomes 0 for this creature and never finds occasion to change. The cyclic peaks of noise produced by $C1$ take Alebrije's noise neuron to produce the output we observe in Fig. 5 until the weight decay causes the neuron to *adapt* to this pattern and its output converges to 0 after frame 100. At this point Alebrije looses interest and goes back to sleep. $C2$ joins the simulation at frame 135 with a noise magnitude two times greater than θ_{noise} (which had adapted to the peak noise of $C1$). The noise neuron reacts and outputs 1, adjusting its w and θ values. The Variation Module also recognizes the change and outputs 1 for $C2$, but remains in 0 for $C1$. Alebrije wakes up and turns to face $C2$, which immediately stops moving. Alebrije then turns to $C1$ since its noise magnitude is higher in comparison to $C2$ (which is now static) but around frame 170 the noise neuron adapts again and Alebrije goes to sleep. This same event repeats two more times at frame 178 and 284. Since $C2$ has a lower variation rate, the Variation Module outputs 1 every time it moves. If at frame 284 (when $C2$ moves for the last time) $C1$ and $C2$ had produced the same magnitude, the variation stimuli would have broken the tie favoring $C2$, taking Alebrije to consider it *more interesting*.

Fig. 7. The Alebrije character while sleeping (left), looking at computer's insect (center) and turning to face the user's insect(right)

6   Conclusions and Future Work

We have briefly described the ANIMUS architecture in order to provide a context for the Selective Attention and Perception System. We defined the basic units of information involved in the Virtual Environment, as well as the dynamics of the data flow and the different modules used to allow communication between characters and the user. The general architecture of the Perception System was explained and each one of its components analyzed in depth. A sample scenario was described along with its configuration and dynamics to show the system in a working case. We are pleased with the obtained results from our Perception System and believe it successfuly accomplishes its original requirements. As the Conditioned Learning Module is still not completely implemented, future work will include finishing this module and preparing test scenarios to stress the features of the system. There are many configuration variables that have to be manually adjusted at this time to get the optimal results in different characters, a group of templates will greatly save time and provide a starting point for the design of new synthetic creatures.

References

1. The ANIMUS Project: A Framework for the Creation of Emotional and Rational Social Agents. http://www.cs.ualberta.ca/~dtorres/projects/animus Computing Science Department, University of Alberta.
2. Thomas, F. and Johnston, O. Disney Animation: The Illusion of Life. Abbeville Press, New York. 1981.

3. Marsella, S. and Gratch, J. Modeling the Interplay of Emotions and Plans in Multi-agent Simulations. In Proceedings of the 23rd Annual Conference of the Cognitive Science Society, 2001.

4. Gratch, J. Modeling the Interplay Between Emotion and Decision-Making. In the 9th Conference on Computer Generated Forces and Behavioral Representation, 2000.

5. Andre, E. et al. Integrating Models of Personality and Emotions into Lifelike Characters. Proceedings of the workshop on Affect in Interactions - Towards a new Generation of Interfaces in conjunction with the 3rd i3 Annual Conference, pages 136–149, Siena, Italy, October 1999.

6. Mateas, M. An Oz-centric Review of Interactive Drama and Believable Agents. AI Today: Recent Trends and Developments. Lecture Notes in AI 1600. Berlin, NY: Springer. 1999.

7. Neal Reilly, W. Believable Social and Emotional Agents. Ph.D. Thesis. School of Computer Science, Carnegie Mellon University. USA. June 1996.

8. Isla, D. et al. A Layered Brain Architecture for Synthetic Creatures. IJCAI, Seattle, WA, August 2001

9. Isla, D. and Blumberg, B. New Challenges for Character-Based AI for Games. AAAI Spring Symposium on AI and Interactive Entertainment, Palo Alto, CA, March 2002

10. Bates, J. et al. Integrating Reactivity, Goals and Emotions in a Broad Agent. In 14th Annual Conference of the Cognitive Science Society, 1992.

11. Kline, C. and Blumberg B. The Art and Science of Synthetic Character Design. Proceedings of the AISB1999 Symposium on AI and Creativity in Entertainment and Visual Art, Edinburgh, Scotland, 1999.

12. Velázquez, J. When Robots Weep: Emotional Memories and Decision-Making. In AAAI Proceedings, 1998.

13. Downie, M. Behavior, Animation, Music: The Music and Movement of Synthetic Characters. M.Sc. Thesis, Media Arts and Sciences, Massachusetts Institute of Technology, USA. February 2001.

14. Mumford, D. Neuronal Architectures for Pattern-theoretic Problems. In Large-Scale Theories of the Brain, p. 125–152 MIT Press, Cambridge Massachusetts. USA. 1995.

15. Damasio, A. and Damasio H. Cortical Systems for Retrieval of Concrete Knowledge: The Convergence Zone Framework. In Large-Scale Theories of the Brain, p. 61–74 MIT Press, Cambridge Massachusetts. USA. 1995.

16. Koch, C. and Crick F. Some Further Ideas Regarding the Neuronal Basis of Awareness. In In Large-Scale Theories of the Brain, p. 93–109 MIT Press, Cambridge Massachusetts. USA. 1995.

17. Carpenter, G. and Grossberg, S. Adaptive Resonance Theory (ART). In The Handbook of Brain Theory and Neural Networks, p. 79–85. MIT Press, Cambridge, Massachusetts. USA. 1995.

18. Gazzaniga, M. et al. Cognitive Neuroscience, The Biology of The Mind. Norton, New York. 1998.

Intelligent Virtual Actors That Plan ... to Fail

Marc Cavazza, Fred Charles, and Steven J. Mead

School of Computing and Mathematics, University of Teesside,
UK-TS1 3BA, Middlesbrough, United Kingdom
{m.o.cavazza, f.charles, steven.j.mead}@tees.ac.uk

Abstract. In this paper, we propose a new approach to virtual actors for 3D animation, in which the actors' behaviour can generate situations of narrative interest, as a consequence of the "limited rationality" of these actors. The actors behaviour is determined by plans generated in real-time in response to a single goal acting as a narrative drive. We use Heuristic Search Planning (HSP) as a non-optimal planning technique, which generate believable plans, yet susceptible of failure. We discuss the changes required in the representation of preconditions, the role of the heuristic function, and the narrative aspects of "optimal" plans and backtracking. Throughout this paper, we illustrate the discussion with actual examples from a first prototype system.

Keywords. Virtual Actors, Heuristic Search Planning, Virtual Storytelling.

1 Introduction and Objectives

Virtual Actors are an important application for embodied 3D characters: their autonomous behaviour and their ability to interact with their environment is traditionally described as a planning problem [2][21]. Planning techniques can support the selection of actions to interact with the agents' immediate environment, as well as long-term goals that can be used to implement complex tasks in simulation applications, or a "narrative drive" in computer animation and storytelling. Several research groups have developed plan-based approaches to the implementation of autonomous characters in various applicative contexts, such as simulation [11][21], behavioural animation [9] and interactive storytelling [5][20][22], using a large range of planning formalisms and techniques. However, while a high level of intelligence is expected from tutoring agents, in entertainment applications such as storytelling and animation, there appears to be a trade-off between the agent's rationality and its believability. One objective is thus to investigate how virtual actors can be given intelligent behaviour, but with limited rationality, not aiming at optimal solutions, as it is precisely the inadequacies of the plans they generate that has potential to create interesting situations from a narrative perspective.

Early work in planning for virtual character behaviour was carried out by Badler et al. [1][21] as part of several projects using the Jack™ character for simulation applications, including the interpretation of natural language instructions in terms of high-level tasks. This work introduced a cognitive approach in which the plan's goals are

A. Butz et al. (Eds.): Smart Graphics 2003, LNCS 2733, pp. 151–161, 2003.

mapped to the agent's intentions and expectations. As part of this research, Geib has revisited some traditional planning concepts [10], in particular the notion of preconditions, in the light of specific problems facing an agent in dynamic environments, such as the relation between its expectations and the actual action outcomes. These ideas have been implemented in the ItPlans planner [11]. We shall refer to his approach in more detail in section 6 when implementing this notion of executability conditions. Funge [9] has proposed another cognitive approach to behavioural animation, based on situation calculus, in which the agents' problem solving abilities generate action sequences for computer animation. Additional work in planning for embodied agents has been described by Rizzo et al. [17], where planning was used to describe the behaviour of social agents. Monzani et al. [16] have also reported the use of planning for 3D characters, though through the use of compiled plans.

In our previous work in Interactive Storytelling [6], we have used Hierarchical Task Network (HTN) planning to describe the virtual characters' behaviours. Even though our approach was character-centred rather than plot-based, we used HTN to reflect the ordering of scenes, considering that the authoring of a basic storyline was an important aspect of interactive storytelling. The justification of the use of HTN as a formalism is by their appropriateness for knowledge-intensive domains, supporting the global authoring of a storyline through the characters' roles. One central mechanism for the creation of dramatic situations, widely used throughout many different media, is the failure of a character's plan. However, due to the nature of HTN planning, failure can only result from external causes, such as the intervention of other actors, or, in the interactive perspective, of the user. The plans themselves have a limited potential for "internal" failure and tend to behave as "ideal" plans that can only be contrasted through external factors. By contrast, in the current research we are interested in the narrative that can be generated by the virtual actor's "spontaneous" plans that it will generate from a single goal acting as a narrative drive. In particular, the bounded rationality of the agent should produce plans that fail for internal reasons and this can be the basis for the production of comic situations (in a comedy context).

2   A Test Case: Cartoon Generation

The description of stories as plans has been proposed in computational linguistics for story understanding [18] and has become a major component of interactive storytelling [6] [14] [22]. However in many cases, plans are still used as formalisms for the underlying plot. The actual emphasis on an actor's plan as part of the story varies according to different genres.

Even though cartoons rely extensively on plan failure, the extent to which this is codified within the genre is unclear. Besides, other genres, such as adventure movies often feature explicit plans as part of the narrative (e.g. bank robberies, "great escapes", etc.). In particular, the analysis of several cartoons would reveal that many of them resort to dramatisation of problem solving, or the pursuit of a single goal (e.g., catching the "Roadrunner") as a main narrative mechanism.

This is why, to support these experiments, we have opted for such a cartoon application, in the form of a short episode of the popular "Pink Panther" character. It appears that a typical Pink Panther cartoon involves problem-solving and goal-oriented activities, which tend to be contrasted by external factors (e.g. preventing a cake from being stolen, a room to be painted new, returning a cat to its owner, etc.). Many actual Pink Panther episodes can be analysed in terms of such planning aspects. For instance in the episode "In the Pink of the Night" [7], she is struggling to stay asleep despite the various wake-up mechanisms she has herself set up. In "The Pink Blueprint" [8] she is counter-planning the actions of a contractor in order to modify the design of the house to be built to fit her taste, etc.

What is it that constitutes the narrative value in a plan-based plot? It can be the apparent sophistication of the plan, that the situations that results from its execution or, more frequently, failure of the plan - or more precisely of a specific sub-part of it. A plan would essentially fail because of an interaction between sub-goals, not mastered by the agent, which emphasises the complexity of the situation in a comic manner, or because of world dynamics again ignored by the agent (including the intervention of other characters).

We have designed a simple scenario as a context, in which a single goal would provide a narrative drive but the intervening situations and their ordering are left open. This contrasts significantly from our previous work in interactive storytelling, in which the story would progress through pre-defined stages, story variability taking place within each stage. The scenario consists for the Pink Panther to get a quiet night's sleep (the "sweet dreams" scenario). Many things can get in the way, and getting rid of these constitutes various planning sub-problems: in addition, there is much room for long-range dependencies between sub-tasks that are likely to generate action failure and comic situations. For instance, in our example, if we assume that the Pink Panther's sleep goal can be contrasted by noise. The Pink Panther will have to identify various strategies for getting rid of noise, such as preventing the transmission of noise or suppressing the noise source. These strategies can be represented by (high-level) operators, while the actions constituting each strategy (closing a window, wearing ear plugs, fixing a leaking tap, calling the noisy neighbours, etc.) will be embedded in ground operators executed in the agent's environment.

Compared with the generation of stories as text, the AI-based generation of 3D computer animations emphasises the staging of characters and the creation of visual situations whose comic elements are more difficult to translate in written terms. In addition, real-time animation supports the interaction of the character's plan with background processes in the environment, which can be visualised through the same process. Finally, the real-time generation enables users to interfere with the ongoing action, in the traditional approach of interactive storytelling.

3   Planning Character Behaviour with HSP

Among the many available planning formalisms, we required one that could support several kinds of experiments, both on the representations and on the search strategies.

Heuristic Search Planning (HSP) techniques, as introduced by [3], comprise three main aspects, which can be described as: i) a domain model and its formalisation, ii) a search algorithm and iii) a heuristic function, together with an efficient calculation method. This makes possible to explore various combinations of representations, search strategies and heuristics, or to adapt the global implementation to the application requirements (for instance in terms of real-time search).

In this section, we give a brief presentation of the essential concepts of HSP, relating them to animation concepts where appropriate.

The domain formulation is generally based on a set of STRIPS operators corresponding to the various actions an agent can take. Each operator has a set of preconditions, an add-list and a delete-list. For instance, Figure 1 shows some typical operators in our system.

```
(def-operator :fall-asleep          (def-operator :cut-water           (def-operator :goto-basement
  (make-operator                      (make-operator                     (make-operator
    :pre-conditions                     :preconditions                     :pre-conditions
      '(:pp-in-bed :quiet)                '(:water-on :pp-in-basement)         '(:pp-upstairs)
    :add-list                           :add-list                          :add-list
      '(:pp-asleep)                       '(:water-off)                        '(:pp-in-basement :pp-dirty)
    :delete-list                        :delete-list                       :delete-list
      nil))                               '(:water-on)))                       '(:pp-upstairs :pp-clean)))
```

Fig. 1. Typical STRIPS-like Operators

In HSP systems, these operators are defined using atomic propositions only. States, on the other hand, are represented as conjunctions of atomic propositions. In the case of embodied virtual characters, ground operators correspond to actions that the agent can carry out in its virtual environment, which have a direct translation in the graphic world of the agent, possibly bringing the agent closer to its long-term goal. In the remainder of the paper we will still use traditional STRIPS descriptions rather than more recent PDDL ones [16].

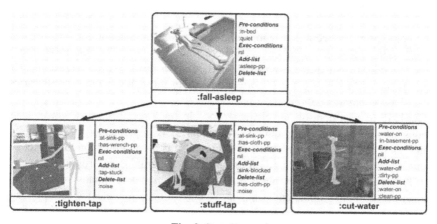

Fig. 2. State Expansion

The search algorithm explores the state space using heuristic search. Each node is expanded by considering the operators whose pre-conditions are satisfied by the current state (Figure 2). The resulting states are evaluated using a heuristic function (described below) which measures how promising this state is towards reaching the goal state. Several search algorithms have been described for early HSP systems, including weighted A* and IDA*. However, planning for character animation requires interleaving planning and execution as the environment is a dynamic one and some actions taken by the agent might fail. Also, dynamic environments provide additional variability to generate interesting stories (for instance, see the role of dynamic environments in Funge et al. [9], Cavazza et al. [6]). Rather than having to systematically replan or explore a pre-computed plan in a forward direction, we have opted to interleave planning and execution using a real-time search algorithm as the search algorithm of HSP. We have for the current experiments implemented the Real-Time A* (RTA*) algorithm [13], which can be described as a real-time version of A* using heuristic updating of previously visited states to avoid cycles in the search process.

As a heuristic function, we are using the additive heuristic as described in the HSP2 system [4]. The heuristic function evaluates each node by solving a relaxed version of the planning problem. More precisely, it approximates the cost of achieving each of the goal's propositions individually from the state considered and then combines the estimates to obtain the heuristic value of the given state [13], hence the name "additive heuristic". For instance if the goal state is the conjunction of atomic propositions expressing that the Pink Panther is in bed and her environment is quiet (`:PP-in-bed :quiet`), the heuristic function for a given state combines the estimated cost to reach each of these atomic propositions.

We are using the standard value iteration (VI) method to compute the heuristic [13], which in our context offers a good compromise between speed of calculation and complexity of implementation.

4   System Implementation and Architecture

The prototype uses a computer game engine (Unreal Tournament 2003™) to support visualisation, character animation and camera placement [19]. The Unreal Tournament engine provides high quality rendering and offers a development environment that supports the inclusion of external software modules through dynamic link libraries or socket-based communications.

Our HSP planner controls the character by selecting operators whose corresponding actions are "played" in the graphic environment. It is implemented in Allegro Common Lisp 6.2. The software architecture (Figure 3) is based on datagram socket communications (UDP) between the HSP planner and the graphic environment developed in UT. Communication takes place through bi-directional command messages. The planner sends to the graphic environment the current operator selected for application, whenever this operator corresponds to a ground operator / terminal action (for instance, `:going-to-bed`). Each ground operator is associated with a description

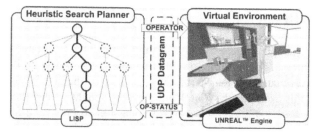

Fig. 3. System Architecture

(using the engine UnrealScript™ language), which encapsulates the low-level motion planning, such as path planning as well as the animations through which the corresponding action is displayed (in the above example, reaching the bed from its current location and getting into it). The low-level action description consists in a set of primitive operations transforming the graphic world (moving to a location, interacting with objects such as windows, water valves, etc.). These are associated specific 3D animations that have been modelled and imported from Character Studio package (part of 3ds max™). Additional animations are used in conjunction to specific events, such as action failure and evolving processes in the virtual world (e.g., flooding or a collapsing building), in order to dramatise the situations generated. These animations correspond to various stages of planning and/or the outcome of the Pink Panther's actions: having an idea, being distressed at action failure, panicking in front of external events, etc. Some typical expressions are shown on Figure 4.

Fig. 4. Dramatic Expressions

In return, the graphic environment sends back to the planner two types of messages. The outcome messages inform the planner of the outcome of the current operator application. The other type of message informs the planner of any changes taking place in the world that are not the consequences of the agent's operators postconditions and hence are not "known" to the agent. The next section describes an excerpt from an example animation produced by the system.

5 Example Result

The following example (Figure 5) illustrates the production of a comic situation as the result of an "internal" plan failure, in other words a plan which, while being overall rational, underestimates the long-term consequences of the side effects of some actions taken. In this example, the Pink Panther wants a night's sleep (her goal state can be expressed as {:in-bed, :asleep}). She has initially prepared for bed, however when trying to sleep she hears noise from a leaking tap (the :fall-asleep operator (Figure 5b) failed because the :quiet proposition is part of the preconditions of that operator, see section 6). She will devise a strategy to get rid of the noise, which is associated to the leaking tap. Several operators can be applied to solve that problem. In the first instance, she walks to the tap, trying to tighten it, but this fails (:tighten-tap is an operator (Figure 5d) with random outcome). As an alternative, she would then go down to the basement in order to cut off the main water supply. She needs first to reach the basement and once there to turn the main supply valve. However, getting down to the basement results in her being dusty on return, hence undoing the :clean-PP condition required to go to bed (:prepare-for-bed operator (Figure 5a), whose outcome, :in-bed is a pre-condition to the :fall-asleep operator that would lead to the goal state). Planning restarts by trying to restore the :clean-PP condition (in other words, washing herself). The straightforward way of doing so is to take a shower. However, this action, though carried out (the Pink Panther gets into the shower) will fail, as the main water supply has been cut off, etc. Failure here is precisely the consequence of the Pink Panther taking for granted the executability condition that water should be available to take a shower. In that specific instance, not remembering all the possible side effects of an action is modelling a form of "limited rationality", which is a key aspect is creating fallible characters prone to generate comic situations.

To conclude, while from the planning perspective, we might not have an optimal plan, this kind of failure generates good dramatic effects and is precisely the kind of results we would expect from plan-based story generation.

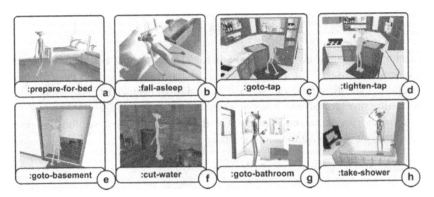

Fig. 5. Comic Strip Example

6 Discussion: Failing Plans as a Dramatic Mechanism

In this section, we discuss some important HSP concepts from the perspective of story generation: executability conditions and the need to dramatise action failure, the representational aspect of the heuristic and the narrative aspects of "optimal" plans and backtracking

There is more to the production of dramatic situations than just watching the character achieving its main goal unhindered. Actually, the unfolding of the plan itself is somehow more important than reaching the goal, as long as the struggle towards the goal is clearly visible to the spectator, as well as the external factors that contrast it. One major mechanism to create situations of narrative interest is actually the failure of the character's current plan, as long as it is properly dramatised and there is a possibility of re-planning. In planning terms, this failure often arises from conflicts in action resources, interactions between sub-plans or the side effects of operators (essentially through their delete-lists). This constitutes a difference with the use of planning by Funge et al. [9], which essentially generated dramatic actions through successful plans, for instance when the "merman" character escaped from the shark by hiding behind rocks. While both methods can succeed in generating narrative situations, in the cartoon genre we are considering, it would appear that plan failure has the greatest potential for story generation.

As a consequence, the need to produce action failure imposes a variation to the formalisation of pre-conditions. A traditional planner would simply not select a given operator whenever its complete pre-conditions are not met. However, in many cases we need to actually dramatise the failure of such a ground operator application, which consists in selecting the ground operator for application, visualising the character attempting the action and properly dramatising the action failure.

This led us, following the original proposal by Geib [10], to distinguish between pre-conditions and executability conditions in the operators' description. Executability conditions must hold for an action to be successful (i.e. to carry out the consequences intended by the agent) but, unlike pre-conditions, are not mandatory for selecting that operator. In other words, executability conditions would represent information not known to the agent, whose content varies with the environment, with the dependencies between actions, etc. For instance, the room being too warm can be part of executability conditions for falling asleep once in bed. This distinction is actually quite relevant in the planning for animation context. Without such distinction, the Pink Panther would not go to bed if the room is warm (basing herself on pre-conditions only), but this reason would not be visible to a user watching the generated animation, nor would it create a valid narrative situation. From a narrative perspective, we can now say that executability conditions correspond to conditions for success which the agent might not have an explicit knowledge of, or which it would take as granted under the circumstances (in the above example, the Pink Panther would only realise that the room is too warm once under the sheets). Examples of executability conditions include that an object or a given resource is indeed available, something that can only be known once the action is being attempted.

While HSP would still attempt at producing the shortest solution plan, this does not necessarily correspond to the most interesting course of action from a narrative perspective. For instance, faced with the possibility of either closing the window or investigating the source of the noise, the heuristic will tend to select the `:close the window` operator, as this would correspond to a smaller number of steps to reach the atomic propositions constituting the goal. Achieving the shortest plan corresponds to the agent's overall rationality, though it is not guaranteed to produce the animation sequences of greatest narrative interest. This baseline rationality makes the agent believable, in the sense that its actions are seen as meaningful, but does not always support the narrative objectives. This can be in part compensated for by associating costs to the various states, representing the desirability (or narrative interest) of a given state. These can be derived from a priori semantic categories of actions. For instance, an action that opens more possibilities of interaction and interference might have a greater narrative interest, hence a lower cost (for instance, those actions that force the Pink Panther to leave the house to investigate the cause of noise, versus just closing the window).

The use of the additive heuristic ignores the consequences of the actions in terms of delete-lists. It could be feared that the heuristic search mechanisms, by ignoring delete-lists, would not properly represent narrative intentions, such as the fact that reaching a quiet state is achieved by deleting the noise proposition. However, this can be treated as a representational problem under a closed world assumption, by explicitly maintaining the negation of atomic propositions and in the latter example using a `:quiet` atomic proposition in the add-list of corresponding operators, which will then be taken into account by the heuristic function calculation. As a result, ignoring the effects of the delete lists will not affect the quality of the heuristic as an indicator of the most rational action to take. And, because executability conditions are not taken into account at this stage, this still leaves space for unforeseen situations, avoiding again the pitfall of an "omniscient" agent whose rational behaviour towards its goal would not create situations of narrative interest. In our specific context, this ends up in being a good compromise between the overall rationality of the agent and the need for failure and replanning that supports comic situations of narrative interest.

7 Conclusions

Many interactive storytelling systems have adopted planning as their main technique for plot representation, but insist on narrative control [22] or role authoring [6]. This work, which developed from research in interactive storytelling, is an attempt at investigating the role of explicit plans in narratives and considers planning for plot formalisation rather than representation. The ability to generate plans for the actors within the constraint of a set of possible actions, which is where the "scriptwriting" aspect takes place, could constitute an interesting research tool to explore the role of explicit plans in narrative genres.

We have discussed the generation of plans for embodied agents from a single goal acting as a "narrative drive" and its ability to produce various comic (hence relevant) situations. A specific advantage of HSP techniques is that they can generate computer animations of narrative value by relying on a single goal as a global narrative drive, which creates a great potential for diversity of courses of actions, hence for story generation. It also supports believability of the character's behaviour, in the sense that it shows an overall rational behaviour, tending towards the most reasonable actions in a given situation, yet leaving space for failure and re-planning when using specific executability conditions. Such dramatised failures actually constitute the main source of situations of narrative interest.

We also have shown that the main components of HSP planning, whether in terms of knowledge representation or the actual search mechanisms, could be adapted to the requirements of story generation. Further, due to the generic nature of representations used and the performance demonstrated by HSP techniques, this approach should have a greater potential for scalability than more traditional approaches in AI-based animation.

Acknowledgments. We thank Eric Jacopin for many enlightening discussions and Hector Geffner for his advice on the use of HSP techniques.

References

[1] Badler, N. Interactive humans: from behaviors to agents, Dynamic Behaviors for Real-Time Synthetic Humans, Course 11 Notes of SIGGRAPH'95, 1995.
[2] Badler, N., Webber, B., Becket, W., Geib, C., Moore, M., Pelachaud, C., Reich, B., and Stone, M. Planning for animation. In N. Magnenat-Thalmann and D. Thalmann (eds), Interactive Computer Animation, Prentice-Hall, pp. 235–262, 1996.
[3] Bonet, B. and Geffner, H. Planning as Heuristic Search: New Results. Proceedings of ECP'99, pp. 360–372, 1999.
[4] Bonet, B. and Geffner. H. Planning as Heuristic Search. Artificial Intelligence Special Issue on Heuristic Search, 129(1), pp. 5–33, 2001.
[5] Cavazza, M., Charles, F. and Mead, S.J. Interacting with Virtual Characters in Interactive Storytelling. ACM Joint Conference on Autonomous Agents and Multi-Agent Systems, Bologna, Italy, pp. 318–325, 2002.
[6] Cavazza, M., Charles, F. and Mead, S.J. Character-based Interactive Storytelling. IEEE Intelligent Systems, special issue on AI in Interactive Entertainment, pp. 17–24, 2002.
[7] Chiniquy, G. "In the Pink of the Night" in Jet Pink, The Pink Panther Cartoon Collection (DVD), MGM Home Entertainment Inc., 1999.
[8] Chiniquy, G. "The Pink Blueprint" in Jet Pink, The Pink Panther Cartoon Collection (DVD), MGM Home Entertainment Inc., 1999.
[9] Funge, J., Tu, X., and Terzopoulos D. Cognitive Modeling: Knowledge, Reasoning and Planning for Intelligent Characters, SIGGRAPH 99, Los Angeles, CA, August 11–13, 1999.
[10] Geib, C. Intentions in means-end planning, Technical Report MC-CIS-92-73, University of Pennsylvania, 1992.
[11] Geib, C. The Intentional Planning System: ItPlanS, Artificial Intelligence Planning Systems, pp. 55–60, 1994.

[12] Korf, R.E. Real-time heuristic search. Artificial Intelligence, 42:2-3, pp. 189–211, 1990.

[13] Liu, Y., Koenig, S. and Furcy, D. Speeding Up the Calculation of Heuristics for Heuristic Search-Based Planning. In Proceedings of the National Conference on Artificial Intelligence, pp. 484–491, 2002.

[14] Mateas, M. and Stern A. A Behavior Language for Story-Based Believable Agents. IEEE Intelligent Systems, special issue on AI in Interactive Entertainment, pp. 39–47, 2002.

[15] McDermott, D. PDDL the planning domain definition language. Technical report, Yale University, http://www.cs.yale.edu/users/mcdermott.html, 1998.

[16] Monzani, J-S., Caicedo, A. and Thalmann, D. Integrating Behavioural Animation Techniques, Eurographics 2001, Computer Graphics Forum, Volume 20, Issue 3, 2001.

[17] Rizzo, P., Veloso, M.V., Miceli, M. and Cesta, A. Goal-based personalities and social behaviors in believable agents, Applied Artificial Intelligence, 13, pp. 239–27, 1999.

[18] Schank, R.C. and Abelson, R.P. Scripts, Plans, Goals and Understanding: an Inquiry into Human Knowledge Structures. Hillsdale (NJ): Lawrence Erlbaum, 1977.

[19] Special issue on Game engines in scientific research, Communications of the ACM, 45:1, January 2002.

[20] Swartout, W., Hill, R., Gratch, J., Johnson, W.L., Kyriakakis, C., LaBore, C., Lindheim, R., Marsella, S., Miraglia, D., Moore, B., Morie, J., Rickel, J., Thiebaux, M., Tuch, L., Whitney, R. and Douglas, J. Toward the Holodeck: Integrating Graphics, Sound, Character and Story. in Proceedings of the Autonomous Agents 2001 Conference, 2001.

[21] Webber, B., Badler, N., Di Eugenio, B., Geib, C., Levison, L., and Moore, M. Instructions, intentions and expectations. Artificial Intelligence J. 73, pp. 253–269, 1995.

[22] Young, R.M. Creating Interactive Narrative Structures: The Potential for AI Approaches. AAAI Spring Symposium in Artificial Intelligence and Interactive Entertainment, AAAI Press, 2000.

Extracting Emotion from Speech: Towards Emotional Speech-Driven Facial Animations

Olusola Olumide Aina, Knut Hartmann, and Thomas Strothotte

Department of Simulation and Graphics
Otto-von-Guericke University of Magdeburg
Universitätsplatz 2, D-39106 Magdeburg, Germany
{aina, hartmann, tstr}@isg.cs.uni-magdeburg.de

Abstract. Facial expressions and characteristics of speech are exploited intuitively by humans to infer the emotional status of their partners in communication. This paper investigates ways to extract emotion from spontaneous speech,
aiming at transferring emotions to appropriate facial expressions of the speaker's
virtual representatives. Hence, this paper presents one step towards an emotional
speech-driven facial animation system, promises to be the first true non-human animation assistant. Different classifier-algorithms (support vector machines, neural
networks, and decision trees) were compared in extracting emotion from speech
features. Results show that these machine-learning algorithms outperform human
subjects extracting emotion from speech alone if there is no access to additional
cues onto the emotional state.

1 Introduction

Emotion is a fundamental and cross-cultural primitive and a vital communication mechanism that complement speech. Often a spoken message will be misunderstood if accom-
panied by the wrong emotional signal. The emotional status cannot be *directly observed*
but can to be inferred. For this reason, emotions require some medium of expression,
such as facial expressions, words, music, tone of voice, or body language — often in
parallel. In addition, other less accessible physiological indicators (e.g., the heart-rate,
sweating, goose-pimples, and muscular-tightness) provide cues to the emotional status
of a speaker.

Ironically, there is no clear and comprehensive definition of what emotions are.
However, psychologists agree on *fundamental* or *basic* set of emotions — a combination
of which suffices to define all other *complex* or *secondary emotions*. Again, the content
of this ideal subset of fundamental emotions has been the subject of much debate. This
paper adopts the popular classification of the psychologist EKMAN, who considers these
emotions as basic ones for which a distinctive facial expression exists (i.e., fear, anger,
sadness, happiness, and disgust) [7,6].

Because emotion has for long been considered irrational or contrary to reason, it
have been thought-of as undesirable in scientific endeavors. Recent thinking, however,
suggest that emotions do play a significant role in learning. In fact, emotions have been
argued to be the ultimate source of intelligence and may provide machines which the
autonomy they need to function like humans in some respect. The framework for such

A. Butz et al. (Eds.): Smart Graphics 2003, LNCS 2733, pp. 162–171, 2003.
© Springer-Verlag Berlin Heidelberg 2003

a system has been drawn out by PICARD [20], who coined the term *affective computing* to represent the design and implementation of systems that understand, respond to, and perhaps synthesize emotions. This paper exploits speech as a vehicle for delivering emotions to a synthetic character.

Although the initial motivation for research in facial animation was for entertainment purposes (i.e., character animation in film), a growing number of applications are emerging in computer games, education, broadcasting, teleconferencing, and e-commerce. These intelligent agents or avatars need to talk, laugh, wink, cry, sing, or even scream. In order to give these character a desired personality, a broad range of facial expressions have to be represented and transformed into each other. Unfortunately, as humans are accustomed to faces, they recognize the slightest nuances and deviations from normal facial patterns and expressions. Therefore, realistic facial animation often requires a small army of animators laboring for great lengths of time in a production environment. Thus, any scheme that helps to cut-down the man-hour requirement or to increase the quality of animation is much welcome.

There are at least 5 fundamental approaches to facial animation. While offering significant advantages, each has its own limitations. In practice, two or more of these methods are used in combination for greater efficiency. These methods include:

Keyframing: Human animators define keyframes representing individual extreme (facial) postures, gestures, or expressions to be performed by the character. Subsequently, all in-between values for adjacent extremes are computed automatically. This technique represents the standard approach for relatively simple tasks. For complicated geometries, especially those undergoing a large variety of complex deformations, keyframing is impractical.

Parametric Methods subdivide the face into several (possibly overlapping) regions — each representing some major animatable facial feature (e.g., the eyes, brows, or lips). Subsequently, the minimum and maximum deformation is often specified. Hence, the number of animatable parameters is reduced; making complex surface deformations more intuitive. However, the construction of this parameter hierarchy is a very difficult task.

Muscle-Based Techniques: Parametric methods cannot (re)produce the infinite variety of subtle contortions (e.g., creases, dimples, and wrinkles) which the face is capable of. Therefore, muscle or physics-based techniques are used to construct mechanical models to simulate the dynamic deformation of skin, muscles, and other tissues of the face. Thereby, an accurate skin and muscle-based model implicitly encodes a wide range of facial actions. However, these models are notoriously complicated to construct, as doing so requires a thorough understanding of human (facial) anatomy *and* mathematics.

Performance-Based Systems capture facial expressions of an actor and transfer them to animate a synthetic character. Usually, the positions of artificial or natural facial markers are tracked; leaving the animators to establish links between the markers on the actor and the corresponding points or regions on the synthetic character. Unfortunately, these systems generate a torrent of data and are very expensive.

Speech-Driven Systems attempt to reconstruct facial expression by analyzing the speaker's voice. Here, the synthetic character mimics the speaker's lip movements.

Recent research approaches aim at inferring the emotional status of speakers automatically and thus produce facial expressions appropriate to the tone of their voice. Unfortunately, this approach is non-trivial and effective speech-driven facial animation system are rare.

This work focuses on the recognition of emotion from speech. We apply machine-learning algorithms on speech features extracted from individual phonemes, words, and the duration of voiced utterances. The system adds appropriate facial expression to a speech-driven facial animation system, which computes the position of speech articulators considering co-articulation phenomena between phonemes. This is essential for a tight synchronization between audible and visual speech. Due to its complexity, a new theory on co-articulation has to be discussed elsewhere [1]. A set of videos demonstrate the capabilities of our system.[1]

This work is organized as following: After reviewing the related work in Section 2, we present the concepts of a pattern recognition approach to extract emotion from speech in Section 3. Section 4 highlights implementation aspects of the architecture proposed in this papers. The results achieved in this work are presented in Section 5. Finally, we discuss possibilities for further improvements in Section 6.

2   Related Work

Historically, research in speech processing has been geared towards answering the questions: *"What was said?"* (speech recognition) and *"Who said it?"* (speaker identification). More recently increasing attention has been given to a third question: *"How was it said?"*, i.e., emotion recognition.

Emotion recognition systems where successfully applied to extract emotion from infant-directed speech [23], to interact with and to train autonomous robots [3,18,4,8], to detect critical situations in automatic call centers [11,15], and for the facial animation of virtual characters [17,16].

Regrettably, the recognition of emotion from speech alone is anything but trivial. Research in the recognition of emotion from speech is markedly dogged by a dearth of suitable corpora and ad-hoc decisions as to which emotions are to be recognized. In fact, almost every study done on the subject considers a different subset of emotions and employs a different corpus. The accuracies reported in literature depend on a number of factors such as: the number of emotions to be distinguished, the choice of classifier-algorithm, and the type of experiment (i.e., speaker dependent vs. speaker independent). Hence, a general comparison of all these experiments is neither fair nor possible.

Some of the machine-learning algorithms applied in previous studies include support vector machines, neural networks, nearest neighbor classifiers, Mahalanobis-distance classifiers [2], Gaussian mixture models [3], Fisher linear discriminant method [22], and supra-segmental hidden Markov models [21].

In general, computers outperform humans subjects (untrained listeners) in the recognition of emotion from speech when there is no access to facial or linguistic information. Research in multi-modal emotion recognition systems (e.g., [10] or [14]) showed that

---

[1] http://wwwisg.cs.uni-magdeburg.de/~aina/emotions.html

by considering facial information in addition to speech much higher accuracies can be obtained.

3   Recognizing Emotion from Speech

The design of an emotion recognition system typically involves the choice of or the construction of an emotional speech database, the selection of a suitable set of speech features to be analyzed and the choice of an effective classifier algorithm.

3.1   Speech Database of Emotions

The suitability of the test corpus ultimately determines the success of the experiment. With respect to emotion, three types of speech corpora exist:

Spontaneous Speech is often argued to contain the most direct and authentic emotions, as it involves a speaker who is oblivious to the recording. Besides being un-ethical, obtaining a usable amount of such data is exceedingly difficult and expensive. Those corpora are not generally circulated due to copyright issues. Moreover, spontaneous speech is often likely to contain background noise.

Acted Speech: In the absence of the spontaneous speech, it is very common to resort to recorded speech. However, because acted speech is an attempt to "fake" emotions, questions have been raised as to its naturalness and therefore its suitability. Professional actors may however be used to produce seemingly authentic emotions.

Elicited Speech: These kind of databases strive to obtain genuine emotional speech that could be considered spontaneous — but with the ease with which acted speech can be recorded. Certain emotions such as happiness and fear can be induced. Unfortunately, elicited speech is often too mild and inconsistent. Besides, it is very hard to collect a suitable amount of speech that would be truly representative.

3.2   Speech Features to Be Analyzed

The recognition of emotion from speech can be considered as a pattern recognition problem. This requires the computation of relevant speech features to train the classifier. The following features have been consistently identified as effective indicators of emotion [13]:

Time-Related Measures include the rate and duration of speech as well as silence measures (i.e., the length of pauses between words and phrases) and can serve to distinguish excitement and therefore emotions.

Intensity-Related Measures: The intensity of speech signals reflect the amount of effort required to produce the speech. Therefore, this measure provide indications to the emotional status of the speaker.

Frequency-Related Measures are used in speech recognition to identify phonemes by its pattern of resonant frequencies. Variations in voice's quality due to changes in the emotional state will most certainly influence the number and size of the resonant peaks (i.e., the amplitude and bandwidth of *formants*).

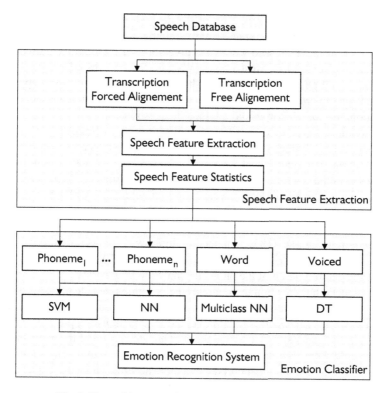

Fig. 1. The architecture of the emotion recognition system.

Pitch-Related Measures are the most frequently used vocal cues of emotion. Here, the frequency of the vibrating vocal cords in the glottis indicate vocally-expressed excitement and it is measured in terms of *pitch* or *fundamental frequency* (F_0).

Because the measured features (e.g., the degree of stress, rhythm, or intonation) may extend the duration of phonemes or syllables, speech features must often embrace higher units of the utterance. Linguistics refer to these long-time speech features as *supra-segmental* or *prosodic* in contrast to *phonetic*, i.e., phoneme-related speech features. Prosodic features better correlate voiced emotions [9].

4   An Emotion Recognition Architecture

Figure 1 illustrates the components of the emotion recognition system presented in this paper. The following sections focus on its basic modules: the speech database, the extraction of speech features, and the emotion classifier algorithms.

4.1   The Construction of an Emotional Speech Database

An speech corpus was derived from 336 short sentences, expressing the fundamental emotions *joy* (115), *anger* (121), and *sorrow* (100). Each sentence was constructed in such a way that the vocal expression of the desired emotion peaked over a word or group of words (*stressed words*) in the early or latter part of the utterance[2]. On average, two-thirds of all these stressed words had no emotional bias and were used to express all fundamental emotions. Most importantly, the list of stressed words is phoneme-balanced, i.e., all phonemes in the English language are represented in approximately equal numbers. In order to avoid the characteristic rise in intonation that can be mistaken for emotion, the speech corpus did not include questions.

All utterances were read by a female native speaker of English with an American accent and recorded under studio conditions at 44 kHz 16 bit stereo. All sentences were repeated till the expected tone of voice was achieved (i.e., the actor reached the desired emotional extreme) — some as often as 11 times. In addition, each utterance was reread twice in a neutral tone in order to create a group of utterances without any emotion.

After recording, the emotional stressed words were excised from the utterances. In this process, 1628 audio files were generated. 1443 contained single-word utterances, while the remaining files (185) contained multiple-word phrases of varying length. All audio files were annotated using the HIDDEN MARKOV TOOLKIT [25] (the annotation involves the determination of the phoneme and word boundaries).

The phonetic transcription incorporates the machine-readable phonetic alphabet defined by the Carnegie Mellon University (CMU). The transcription employs the *free* as well as the *forced alignment* paradigm. Forced alignment uses a preliminary transcription as an initial guess and tries to find the start and end points of the given phonemes in the speech file. Free alignment on the other hand does not require any additional information. Hence, forced alignment produces a more accurate phonetic segmentation if the speaker's pronunciation matches the supplied phoneme transcription and words are enunciated clearly. Unfortunately, forced alignment will often recognize eluded phonemes in fast, sloppy, or careless speech. Moreover, it often adds intra-word pauses where they are none. As free alignment purely relies on training data, it is slightly less accurate than forced alignment, but it transcribes only those sounds that are actually pronounced.

4.2   Speech Feature Extraction

The pitch or fundamental frequency (F_0), the smoothened pitch contour, the vocal energy as well as the amplitudes and bandwidths of the first five formants ($F_1 \ldots F_5$) were computed for (annotated and segmented) audio files using the SPEECH FILING SYSTEM (SFS) [12].

Subsequently, the minimum and maximum values, their difference, the mean and median value as well as the standard deviation over the duration of each phoneme, voiced segment, and word interval where calculated for these features using the SPEECH MEASUREMENT LANGUAGE (SML) of the above mentioned utility. The SFS was chosen primarily as it appears to compute pitch more accurately than other (free-ware) speech processing utilities. Specifically, it did not award pitch values to non-voiced segments.

The decision to measure features over a the duration of a word was guided by the assumption that:

---

[2] In effect, the entire sentence was used as a "spring board" to help enunciate the desired emotion adequately.

> *While the emotion of a speaker may vary within a sentence or phrase, it is*
> *likely to remain constant over the duration of a single word.*

This is in contrast to the approach taken in other studies - where speech features are computed over entire utterances (too coarse a measure) or indiscriminate time-spans.

On the other hand, the decision to measure features over the the duration of a phoneme was taken in order to achieve a introduce a measure of context-dependence into the experiment. In lay terms:

> *It seems rather awkward to compare features computed over one word with*
> *features computed over another (non similar) word.*

The problem with this approach is that, there are far too many words in the lexicon! A reasonable compromise is therefore to select another speech sub-unit with a far smaller lexicon. Incidentally, the phoneme is the only speech (sub)unit that meets this criteria. Syllables do not. (While the English language has about 48 phonemes, it has several thousand syllables!)

4.3   Emotion Classifier Algorithm

The classifier stage actually consists of 3 sub-stages: the *training*, *test*, and *operation* phases. The 1443 single-word utterances were reserved for training and test phases, while the classifier operated on the remaining 185 multiple-word utterances. Training and testing was done with the following classifiers in order to determine the most suitable classifier for the operation phase: support vector machines (SVM), neural networks (NN), an ensemble of neural networks (multiclass-NN), and decision trees (DT).

The training, testing, and operation was done in the WEKA machine-learning and knowledge discovery environment [24]. WEKA is a collection of machine-learning algorithms and tools for data pre-processing, classification, regression, clustering, attribute-selection, and visualization written in Java. Several distributed versions of WEKA exist. The current experiment made use of WEKA-PARALLEL [5]. WEKA-PARALLEL enables the cross-validation portion of a WEKA-classifier to be performed simultaneously using any number of machines on the Internet. This helped to significantly reduce the amount of time required to run a classifier on a large dataset, especially when the classifier was to run with a very large number of folds.

5   Results

The classification accuracies for the 10-fold cross-validation recognition experiments performed on phoneme-based, voiced segment, and word-based datasets are listed in Figure 2-a. Results obtained for the per-phone experiments clearly indicate that features measured over *vowels and diphthongs better indicate emotion* (see also [19]). Moreover, features computed on a word-by-word basis are more useful for the recognition of emotion in comparison to those features computer over voiced utterances.

Both support vector machines and neural networks outperform decision trees (up to 9%) for word segments. In most cases, both neural networks achieved better results than

Data Set	SVM	NN	Multiclass-NN	DT
Consonants	63.78	**69.50**	68.11	63.60
Vowels	77.25	**79.38**	78.97	71.57
Voiced Segments	73.37	76.96	**78.70**	71.52
Words	**86.69**	84.41	**86.69**	77.69

(a) Classification accuracy

	SVM	NN	Multiclass-NN
Perfect	**63**	50	55
Fair	**32**	39	36
Poor	**5**	10	9

(b) Contiguous classification accuracy on the multiple-word dataset

Fig. 2. Classification results of several machine-learning algorithms.

support vector machines. This is probably due to the fact that both networks use a very large number of nodes in the hidden-layer. Unfortunately, this led to considerably long training times for both networks, specially the multiclass-NN (up to several hours). In contrast, it took only a few minutes to train support vector machines.

This second category of experiments distinguishes between contiguous and non-contiguous classification accuracy. By the former, we mean that the correct classification is *consistently* made on each word or phoneme of the utterance. That is to say, the correct classification must be made on each word in a n-word utterance. When this is the case the classification is termed *perfect*. However, if an incorrect classification is made on at least one (but not all) word, the classification is deemed *fair*; and by extension if the wrong classification is made on all words, the performance is deemed *poor*. This rigorous criteria reflects the need of the target application i.e., facial animation, for which the *correct* and *unchanging* facial expressions must be generated. The results are presented in Figure 2-b. Clearly, word-based classifier are nearly 70% better than phoneme-based — reflecting that *emotions are a prosodic feature* and therefore better over supra-segmental features. In this experiment, support vector machines reached the best results (63% perfect), followed by the ensemble of neural networks (55% perfect) and lastly the neural network (50% perfect) on the word-based feature dataset.

A final test was designed to compare the accuracy of machine-learning classifiers and the performance of humans. Therefore, the same multiple-word dataset was presented to 4 human subjects; Two of which spoke no English at all. The other two subjects were non-native speakers of English. As expected, human recognition was quite high — averaging 71% if the listener had access to the linguistic content of the utterance, but fell to 56% for subjects without any knowledge of English. Not surprisingly, these figures almost match the 63% contiguous accuracy obtained by the SVM.

6   Future Work

In spite of the encouraging results that are obtained in this paper, significant enhancements can be made by applying attribute and instance selection algorithms (as a pre-processing step to train the classifier), considering the fact, that the training and test databases were quite noisy. Moreover, our speech-based classification could be augmented with linguistic and visual information. Furthermore, we plan to explore supra-segmental hidden Markov models [21] to the recognition of emotions from speech. This approach is particularly appealing in that it is theoretically sound and able to look at speech signal at the acoustic and prosodic level at the same time.

Finally, training data could be considered as being fuzzy with respect to emotion [2]. Although in truth, emotions are at best a subjective phenomena and cannot thereby be measured on a numerical scale. However, they can be thought of as being fuzzy on account of the difficulty with they can be measured accurately. Fuzzy emotions would include non-precise terms that reflect the degree of emotion in the voice (e.g., *very angry, quite sad*, or *a little bit happy*). The concept of fuzzy emotions also make it possible to classify mixed emotions. However, this might pose additional restrictions on classification results as certain emotions as joy and anger are mutually exclusive and cannot co-exist.

7 Conclusion

Speech-driven facial animation systems require a contiguous accuracy on the recognition of emotion. This paper first takes this requirement into consideration.

Although some researchers argue that acted speech do not contain genuine emotions, we maintain that this is not an issue in facial animation, where speech is acted and actors are required. In conclusion, we stress that speaker-dependent emotion recognition is suited for the work-flow in the production process; whereby *one* actor's voice used to animate a *single* character. In such an environment, such a system can be trained to recognize emotion in the voice of one specific actor. To be truly workable however, such a system must embody functionality for *online training* that enables it to *further* learn from the human animator. In the process of time (or in the course of a project), it is conceivable that such a system will make few fewer and fewer mistakes, thereby reducing the work-load of the animator and cutting down production cycles. When that day arrives we will have birthed a *true animation assistant*.

References

1. O. O. Aina. Speech-Driven Facial Animation. Master's thesis, Department of Simulation and Graphics, Otto-von-Guericke-University Magdeburg, Germany, 2003.
2. N. Amir and S. Ron. Towards an Automatic Classification of Emotions in Speech. In *International Conference on Spoken Language Processing (ICSLP'98)*, pages 555–558, 1998.
3. C. Breazeal and L. Aryananda. Recognition of Affective Communicative Intent in Robot-Directed Speech. *Autonomous Robots*, 12(1):83–104, 2002.
4. T. Brønsted, T. D. Nielsen, and S. Ortega. Affective Multimodal Interaction with a 3D Agent. In *Language, Vision & Music*, pages 67–78. John Benjamins, 2002.
5. S. Celis and D. R. Musicant. Weka-Parallel: Machine Learning in Parallel. Technical report, Department of Mathematics and Computer Science, Carleton College, Northfield, MN, USA, 2002.
6. P. Ekman. Basic Emotions. In T. Dalgleish and M. J. Power, editors, *Handbook of Cognition and Emotion*, chapter 3. John Wiley & Sons, New York, 1999.
7. P. Ekman. Facial Expressions. In T. Dalgleish and M. J. Power, editors, *Handbook of Cognition and Emotion*, chapter 16. John Wiley & Sons, New York, 1999.

8. S. C. Gadanho and J. Hallam. Emotion-Triggered Learning in Autonomous Robot Control. *Cybernetics and Systems*, 32(5):531–559, 2001.
9. A. Gardener and I. A. Essa. Prosody Analysis for Speaker Affect Determination. In *Proceedings of Perceptual User Interfaces Workshop*, 1997.
10. T. S. Huang, L. S. Chen, and H. Tao. Bimodal Emotion Recognition by Man and Machine. In *ATR Workshop on Virtual Communication Environments*, 1998.
11. R. Huber, A. Batliner, J. Buckow, E. Nöth, V. Warnke, and H. Niemann. Recognition of Emotion in a Realistic Dialog Scenario. In *International Conference on Spoken Language Processing (ICSLP'00)*, pages 665–668, 2000.
12. M. A. Huckvale, D. Brookes, L. Dworkin, M. Johnson, D. Pearce, and L. Whitaker. The SPAR Speech Filing System. In *European Conference on Speech Technology*, 1987.
13. T. Johnstone and K. R. Scherer. Vocal Communication of Emotion. In M. Lewis and J. M. Haviland-Jones, editors, *Handbook of Emotions*. Guilford Press, 2000.
14. T. Kitazoe, S.-I. Kim, Y. Yoshitomi, and T. Ikeda. Recognition of Emotional States using Voice, Face Image and Thermal Image of Face. In *6th International Conference on Spoken Language Processing (ICSLP 2000)*, pages 653–656, 2000.
15. C. M. Lee, S. Narayanan, R. Pieraccini, and R. Pieraccini. Combining Acoustic and Language Information for Emotion Recognition. In *International Conference on Spoken Language Processing (ICSLP 2002)*, 2002.
16. Y. Li, F. Yu, Y.-Q. Xu, E. Chang, and H.-Y. Shum. Speech-Driven Cartoon Animation with Emotions. In *Proceedings of the 9th ACM International Conference on Multimedia*, pages 365–371. ACM Press, New York, 2001.
17. R. Nakatsu, A. Solomides, and N. Tosa. Emotion Recognition and Its Application to Computer Agents with Spontaneous Interactive Capabilities. In *IEEE International Conference on Multimedia Computing and Systems*, pages 804–80. IEEE Press, 1999.
18. P.-Y. Oudeyer. The Production and Recognition of Emotions in Speech: Features and Algorithms. *International Journal of Human Computer Interaction*, 2003.
19. C. Pereira and C. Watson. Some Acoustic Characteristics of Emotion. In *International Conference on Spoken Language Processing (ICSLP'98)*, pages 927–930, 1998.
20. R. W. Picard. *Affective Computing*. MIT Press, Cambridge, 1997.
21. T. Polzin and A. Waibel. Detecting Emotions in Speech. In *Proceedings of the Second International Conference on Cooperative Multimodal Communication (CMC/98*, 1998.
22. D. Roy and A. Pentland. Automatic Spoken Affect Analysis and Classification. In *Proceedings of the Second International Conference on Automatic Face and Gesture Recognition*, pages 363–367, 1996.
23. M. Slaney and G. McRoberts. Baby Ears: A Recognition System for Affective Vocalizations. In *International Conference on Acoustics, Speech and Signal Processing (ICASSP'98)*, 1998.
24. I. H. Witten and E. Frank. *Data Mining: Practical Machine Learning Tools and Techniques with Java Implementations*. Morgan Kaufmann Publishers, San Franscisco, 1999.
25. S. Young. *The HTK Book*. Entropic Ltd, Cambridge, 1995.

A Constraint-Based Approach to Camera Path Planning

Marc Christie and Eric Languénou

IRIN, Université de Nantes
B.P. 92208, 44322 Nantes Cedex 3, France
`christie,languenou@irin.univ-nantes.fr`

Abstract. In this paper, we introduce a constraint-based approach to camera control. The aim is to determine the path of a camera that verifies declarative properties on the desired image, such as location or orientation of objects on the screen at a given time. The path is composed of elementary movements called hypertubes, based on established cinematographic techniques. Hypertubes are connected by relations that guarantee smooth transitions. In order to determine the path of the camera, we rely on an incremental solving process, based on recent constraint solving techniques. The hypertube approach provides a nice global control over the camera path, as well as fine tuning in the image via cinematographic properties.

1 Introduction

Much research in computer animation has led to realistic movements for objects or characters. For instance, some delicate tasks such as animating hair or tissue are now automated in modelers. However, few effort has focussed on camera control, which is an important task in story telling. The aim is to assist the control of the camera parameters in order to ease the creation of camera paths. The rightmost scene in Fig. 1 presents a possible camera path derived from three pictures: the camera must follow the cowboy during a linear movement and then turn around the indian such that both characters appear in the image when the camera is behind the indian.

Early works in computer graphics use low-level spline interpolation and smooth transitions. However, computed paths are generally non-realistic and far from the user's mind. Moreover, the user has to determine a set of points that compose the trajectory of the camera, thus spending precious time in a tedious generate-and-test process (place the camera and check the result).

Since then, various techniques have been proposed to assist the control of the parameters of a camera (see Section 2.2).

Our research follows Jardillier and Languénou's work [7]. Their approach is based on the following ideas: (1) the user provides a high-level cinematograhic-based description; (2) each property given in this description is written as a constraint; (3) a constraint solver, which implements pure interval methods, computes solution sets in which the animator navigates.

A. Butz et al. (Eds.): Smart Graphics 2003, LNCS 2733, pp. 172–181, 2003.

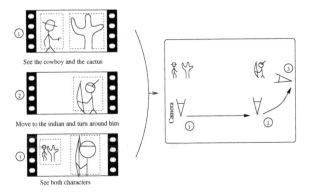

Fig. 1. A Simple Shot.

In this paper, we propose to describe trajectories of cameras as sequences of parameterized elementary movements, called *hypertubes*: linear movement (traveling), rotation of a camera around its horizontal or vertical axes (panoramic), zoom-in, zoom-out and arcing that allows one to turn around objects. The user has to fix the sequence of elementary camera movements as well as the desired properties on objects.

In order to compute the parameters of the hypertubes, we propose an incremental solving process based on recent interval solving techniques. Our solver implements the following algorithms: (1) interval-based filterings [8] on the first hypertube to remove areas without solutions; (2) choice of a solution among the set of remaining areas with respect to an optimization criterion in order to determine starting conditions for the next hypertube; (3) backtracking for inconsistent hypertubes.

The outline of this paper is as follows. The next section shortly introduces CSP and camera control background. Section 3 describes our main contribution, namely the hypertube model, and Section 4 presents the experimental results.

2   Preliminaries

In this section, we briefly introduce the necessary background on Numeric Constraint Satisfaction Problems (CSPs) [8] and camera control.

2.1   Numeric CSPs

In the following, we consider the set of closed intervals whose bounds are floating-point numbers. A n-ary box **B** is a Cartesian product of intervals $B_1 \times \cdots \times B_n$.

A numerical CSP is a triple $\langle \mathcal{C}, \mathcal{V}, \mathcal{B} \rangle$ where $\mathcal{C}$ is a set of constraints over the real numbers, $\mathcal{V}$ is the set of variables occurring in $\mathcal{C}$ and $\mathcal{B}$ is a union of boxes representing the variable domains. Given a numerical CSP P with n variables, the set of solutions of P is the set of reals $r \in \mathbb{R}$ that satisfy all the constraints, *i.e.*

$$Sol(P) = \{r \in \mathbb{R}^n \mid r \in \mathcal{B} \ \wedge \ \forall c \in \mathcal{C} \ (r \text{ verifies } c)\}.$$

A box $\mathbf{B}$ is an *outer box* for P if $Sol(P) \subseteq \mathbf{B}$, and $\mathbf{B}$ is an *inner box* for P if $Sol(P) \supseteq \mathbf{B}$. In the following, we use the algorithm IntervalConstraintSolving(P) that computes a set of inner boxes of P.

2.2 Camera Control

The aim of camera control is to assist the user in the computation of the camera parameters. Some works are based on constrained optimization [4] for computing optimal camera positions. For this category of algorithms, it may be difficult to determine objective criteria and such methods are very sensitive to starting points. An interesting declarative approach [3] offers high-level control over the camera. The proposed framework automatically generates predefined camera positions considering character events in the 3D scene (start, stop, turn, pick-up) and user-defined properties. Yet, camera positions are computed via vector algebra and cannot manage complex properties on the screen.

Further approaches rely on differential equations [9,5]. The camera parameters are expressed through the relationship linking the motion of objects in the 3D scene and the motion of their projected images on the 2D screen. However, these approaches are well suited for real-time environments but they do not provide a global control on the camera path.

Recently, several constraint-based approaches [7,1,6] have been investigated. In this framework, the aim is to give the user declarative tools for animation modeling. The main problem here is the size and the under-constrained nature of constraint systems. We may recall that a camera has seven degrees of freedom (translation, rotation and focus) and each property of the desired image, *e.g.*, the location of an object on the screen, leads to a set of non-linear constraints over all these degrees. Moreover, to animate the camera, the constraint system should be solved for every frame, *i.e.*, 24 times per second or more likely for every key-point composing the camera's path, *i.e.*, 28 variables for a basic spline involving four key-points.

The main feature of Jardillier and Languénou's work [7] is the specification of camera movements by a high-level intelligent process. However, a number of drawbacks can be identified. The path of the camera is restricted to very basic movements, namely a hyperbola for each parameter. The whole problem is modeled by one "global" and under-constrained constraint system, which requires expensive computations. In fact, increasing the number of variables and constraints exponentially increases computation time. Finally, navigation in the set of solutions is not very satisfactory: too many similar solutions are computed in an undefined order and no classification assists the animator.

The hypertube approach introduced in Section 3 overcomes these main shortcomings, namely expensive computations, restricted movements and poor interactivity.

3   The Hypertube Model

The hypertube model is a new constraint-based approach to camera control. In this framework, the user acts as a film director. He provides (1) a sequence of elementary and generic camera movements to model the shot, and (2) properties such as locations or orientations of objects on the screen. The goal is to instantiate the given camera movements that verify the desired properties. The geometrical description of the scene (dynamic of characters and objects) is generally given by a modeler and is an input to our system.

3.1   From Cinema to Constraints

Movements. We introduce a set of elementary camera movements, the cinematographic primitives called *hypertubes*, that allow the modeling of arbitrary movements by composition. Table 1 recalls the main camera primitives.

Table 1. Various camera primitives.

Camera primitive	Nb. Variables	Property
Traveling	10	Trav(name, time)
Local traveling	10	LTrav(name, object, time)
Panoramic	7	Pan(name, time)
Local panoramic	10	LPan(name, object, time)
Arcing	9	Arc(name, time)
Local arcing	9	LArc(name, object, time)
Zoom-in	7	ZoomIn(name, time)
Zoom-out	7	ZoomOut(name, time)

Each movement depends on a set of parameters, for example:[1]

- Traveling is a linear movement of the camera for both descriptive or object tracking purposes. Dolly and track are specific travelings where the point of view of the camera is respectively parallel or orthogonal to the movement. In our tool, traveling is parameterized by two points: the initial camera location (variables T_{X1}, T_{Y1}, T_{Z1}) and the final location (variables T_{X2}, T_{Y2}, T_{Z2}). Orientation is controled by variables $T_{\theta1}$ and $T_{\theta2}$ (vertical axis) and T_ϕ (horizontal axis). The zoom factor is represented by one variable (T_γ).
- Panoramic realizes a rotation of the camera around its horizontal axis (tilt) or vertical axis (pan). Similar to traveling, a pan is used for descriptive or tracking purposes. Panoramic is parameterized by a fixed camera location (variables P_X, P_Y, P_Z), the initial camera angles ($P_{\theta1}$ and $P_{\phi1}$) and final camera angles (variables $P_{\theta2}$ and $P_{\phi2}$). The zoom factor is given by P_γ.
- Arcing allows the camera to swivel around an object or group of objects. This movement is parameterized by the center of arcing (variables A_X, A_Y, A_Z),

---

[1] Note that in this paper we do not consider the rolling axis of the camera.

the initial and final locations of the camera in polar coordinates (the radius A_r and the angles $A_{\psi 1}, A_{\psi 2}$), the initial and final horizontal orientation ($A_{\theta 1}$, $A_{\theta 2}$, the vertical orientation A_ϕ, and a zoom factor A_γ.

Any other movement may be defined as a merge of elementary movements, e.g., doing a zoom while the camera is executing a traveling. Furthermore, we introduce *local* movements, that is, movements defined in the local basis of an object. In other terms, the camera moves along with an object, typically when a camera is attached to a car.

Properties. In our modeling framework, classical cinematographic properties are made available (see Table 2).

Table 2. Available cinematographic properties.

Property	Function	Description
Location	Frame(object, frame, time)	Constrains an object in a frame.
Orientation	Orient(object, side, time)	Constrains the camera to view an object's side (front, rear, top, ...).
Collision	Collision(time)	Avoids collision between the camera and any obstacle.
Occlusion	Occlusion(object, time)	Avoids occlusion between objects (when an object hides another).
Camera Distance	CDist(object, distance, time)	Constrains the camera-to-object distance.
Object Distance	ODist(obj1, obj2, distance, time)	Constrains an object-to-object distance on the screen.

Each property is rewritten as constraints in terms of the hypertube variables. In the following, we describe how to rewrite the location property Frame(object, frame, time) considering a traveling hypertube. Location areas are defined by rectangles on the screen called frames (see Fig. 2). Frames restrain the projection area of objects. In Figure 2, the object's location is defined by (I_X, I_Y, I_Z) and the frame is given with two intervals $[F_{X1}, F_{X2}]$ and $[F_{Y1}, F_{Y2}]$. Such a property leads to the following set of inequalities on the variables of the traveling primitive:

$$\begin{cases} z' & \geqslant 0 \\ x'/(z'/T_\gamma) \geqslant F_{X1} \\ x'/(z'/T_\gamma) \leqslant F_{X2} \\ y'/(z'/T_\gamma) \geqslant F_{Y1} \\ y'/(z'/T_\gamma) \leqslant F_{Y2} \end{cases}$$

The intermediate variables (x', y', z') define the object's coordinates in the local basis of the camera and are defined as follows:

$$\begin{cases} x' = -(I_X - T_{X2})\sin T_\theta + (I_Y - T_{Y2})\cos T_\theta \\ y' = -(I_X - T_{X2})\cos T_\theta \sin T_\phi + (I_Y - T_{Y2})\sin T_\theta \sin T_\phi + (I_Z - T_{Z2})\cos T_\phi \\ z' = -(I_X - T_{X2})\cos T_\theta \cos T_\phi + (I_Y - T_{Y2})\sin T_\theta \cos T_\phi + (I_Z - T_{Z2})\sin T_\phi \end{cases}$$

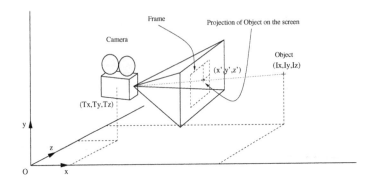

Fig. 2. Projection of a $3D$ Point in a Frame Through a Pinhole Camera.

These constraints express the nonlinear relationship between the location of an object in the $3D$ scene and its projection through a camera; therefore constraining the projection area of an object on the screen constrains the parameters of the camera. This location property allows correct camera placements for photographic composition.

The Occlusion and Collision properties are written via simple distance constraints. In the first case, we consider the distance between two objects on the screen space. This should be greater than the sum of the objects' projected radiuses. Whereas in the second case, we consider the distance between the camera and the objects in the 3D space.

3.2   A Camera Path as a Sequence of Hypertubes

The path of the camera is defined by a sequence of hypertubes interlaced with *intertubes*, namely relations between two successive hypertubes that guarantee continuity. Fig. 3 illustrates the connection between two horizontal travelings where continuity is guaranteed by a simple Bézier interpolation.

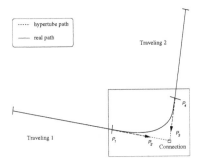

Fig. 3. Linking two traveling hypertubes.

More formally, an *intertube* between two hypertubes $\mathcal{H}$ and $\mathcal{H}'$ is a set of equations between variables of $\mathcal{H}$ and $\mathcal{H}'$. A camera shot is therefore defined by the sequence

$$\mathcal{H}_1, \mathcal{I}_{1,2}, \mathcal{H}_2, \mathcal{I}_{2,3}, \ldots, \mathcal{I}_{p-1,p}, \mathcal{H}_p,$$

where each $\mathcal{H}_i$ is a hypertube and each $\mathcal{I}_{i,i+1}$ is an intertube between $\mathcal{H}_i$ and $\mathcal{H}_{i+1}$. A hypertube is here considered as a constraint satisfaction problem (CSP) associated with an elementary camera movement, a set of properties and a duration.

In this work, we are interested in determining approximate solutions of $\mathcal{H}$.

3.3 Constraint Solving

We define a search algorithm that combines constraint propagation and enumeration to compute a solution of the global CSP $\mathcal{H}$. This algorithm is detailed in Table 3. First, a set $\mathcal{B}_i$ of *inner boxes* is computed for the hypertube $\mathcal{H}_i$ using constraint solving. Second, a choice function (ChooseBest) selects and extracts some best box $\mathbf{B}$ in the set $\mathcal{B}_i$. At last, the box $\mathbf{B}$ is propagated through the next intertube $\mathcal{I}_{i,i+1}$.

Table 3. General Search Algorithm.

```
1  Solve (ℋᵢ, 𝓘ᵢ,ᵢ₊₁, ..., ℋₚ)  returns  inner box
2  begin
3       B_r := empty box
4       found := false
5       ℬⁱ := IntervalConstraintSolving(ℋᵢ)
6       while (ℬⁱ ≠ ∅ and not (found))  do
7            B := ChooseBest(ℬⁱ)
8            if (i = p) then        %  no more hypertubes to process
9                 found := true
10                B_r := B
11           else
12                ℋ'ᵢ₊₁ := PropagateViaIntertube(ℋᵢ₊₁, 𝓘ᵢ,ᵢ₊₁, B)
13                B_r := Solve(ℋ'ᵢ₊₁, 𝓘ᵢ₊₁,ᵢ₊₂, ℋᵢ₊₂, ..., ℋₚ)
14                found := (B_r ≠ empty box)
15           end
16      end
17      return (B_r)
18 end
```

Let us shortly detail the three steps:

− Constraint solving. The constraint solver we rely on computes a set of inner boxes of a constraint system. The underlying technique is based on propagation algorithms from artificial intelligence coupled to recent local consistency methods [2]. It boils down to pruning whole areas from the search space that are inconsistent.

- Enumeration. The ChooseBest function selects a box, within a set, that maximizes a set of quality functions. This set is defined by the properties. Let us consider an orientation property Orient($obj1$, $front$, 0): the best solution occurs when the $front$ vector of the object $obj1$ faces perfectly the camera. The corresponding quality function is defined by a simple dot product over the $front$ vector and the camera's orientation.
- Propagation. The PropagateViaIntertube function connects hypertubes by merging the final point of $\mathcal{H}_i$ with the initial point of $\mathcal{H}_{i+1}$ (see Fig. 3). As a result, some variables of $\mathcal{H}_{i+1}$ are directly instantiated, therefore reducing the next step search space.

4   Experimental Results

A C++ prototype allows to specify the camera primitives and cinematographic properties. In Table 4 the results of two benchmarks are reported, which show the computation time w.r.t. the size of models. The first example relies on a 3D scene composed of two mobile characters (A and B) and a static object C (see Fig. 4). The user's description is the following (leftFrame, rightFrame and middleFrame are user-defined frames):

```
Trav('trav', 2);                        % create a traveling for 2 s.
LArc('arc', 'A', 1);                    % create an arcing around object A for 1 s.
Pan('pan', 2);                          % create a pan for 2 s.
Connect('trav', 'arc');                 % connect movements together
Connect('arc', 'pan');                  % connect movements together
Frame('A', rightFrame , [0..5]);        % frame A for the whole sequence (5 s.)
Orient('A', RIGHT-SIDE, 0)              % see A's right side at the beginning
Frame('B', leftFrame , 5);              % frame B at the end of the sequence
Frame('C', middleFrame , 5);            % frame C at the end of the sequence
```

Example #2 (see Fig. 4) relies on the same 3D scene. Yet, obstacles have been added with occlusion and collision properties:

```
Collision([0..5]);         % avoid collisions for the whole sequence.
Occlusion('A', [0..5]);    % avoid occlusion of A for the whole sequence.
```

The computed camera paths are presented in Figure 4 as solid lines. Figure 5 presents the rendering of the second benchmark.

Table 4. Execution times for 2 benchmarks (PC Pentium III/800MHz under Linux)

Problem	Hypertubes	Variables	Constraints	First solution (ms)
Example #1	3	26	17	3170
Example #2	3	26	25	6090

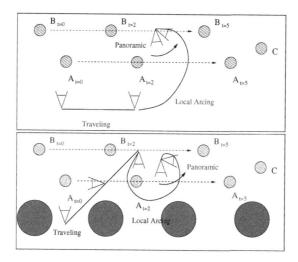

Fig. 4. Results of Example #1 (at the top) and #2 (at the bottom) based on a Traveling, a Local Arcing and a Panoramic (red circles represent the obstacles). Due to the obstacles, the second path is entirely different but the properties are preserved.

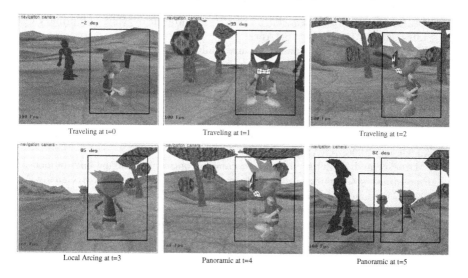

Fig. 5. Evaluation: Obstacle and Occlusion Avoidance. On the last stamp, character A is on the right, character B on the left and C in the middle. The trees represent the obstacles.

Time spent to generate camera paths are around 3 to 6 seconds, which must be compared to the duration of the whole sequence (5 seconds). A precise comparison with the former approach [7] is difficult: the paths computed by the hypertube approach are more complex; the solutions are *natural* since established camera movements are used; and good quality solutions are propagated.

Nevertheless we can state that our results are very encouraging: the previous approach needs important execution times (more than 10 minutes for the first solution) for problems defined over more than 7 variables.

5   Conclusion

This paper has proposed a CSP approach to camera control based on established cinematographic techniques. The hypertube model offers a global control over the camera path as well as fine control in the image via cinematographic properties. Experimental tests have shown very encouraging results thereby enforcing the choice of our hypertube model. This opens exciting perspectives for our application, especially regarding real-time applications. The aim is to generate the hypertubes on the fly considering events in the 3D scene such as an actor entering a room or two actors meeting.

References

1. W. Bares, S. McDermott, C. Bourdreaux, and S. Thainimit. Virtual $3D$ camera composition from frame constraints. In *Proceedings of the eighth ACM international conference on Multimedia*, pages 177–186, Marina del Ray, California, United States, 2000. ACM Press New York.
2. F. Benhamou and F. Goualard. Universally quantified interval constraints. In *Proceedings of the 6th Int. Conf. on Principles and Practice of Constraint Programming (CP'2000)*. LNCS, Springer, 2000. Singapour.
3. D. Christianson, S. Anderson, L. He, D. Salesin, D. Weld, and M. Cohen. Declarative camera control for automatic cinematography (video). In *Proceedings of the Thirteenth National Conference on Artificial Intelligence and the Eighth Innovative Applications of Artificial Intelligence Conference*, pages 148–155, Menlo Park, August4–8 1996. AAAI Press / MIT Press.
4. S. Drucker and D. Zelter. Intelligent camera control in a virtual environment. In *Proceedings of Graphics Interface '94*, pages 190–199, Banff, Alberta, Canada, May 1994. Canadian Information Processing Society.
5. M. Gleicher and A. Witkin. Through-the-lens camera control. In Edwin E. Catmull, editor, *Computer Graphics (SIGGRAPH '92 Proceedings)*, volume 26-2, pages 331–340, July 1992.
6. N. Halper, R. Helbing, and T. Strothotte. A camera engine for computer games: Managing the trade-off between constraint satisfaction and frame coherence. In *Proceedings of the Eurographics'2001 Conference*, volume 20, 2001.
7. F. Jardillier and E. Languénou. Screen-space constraints for camera movements: the virtual cameraman. In N. Ferreira and M. Göbel, editors, *Eurographics'98 proceedings*, volume 17, pages 175–186. Blackwell Publishers, 108 Cowley Road, Oxford OX4 IJF, UK, 1998.
8. O. Lhomme. Consistency techniques for numeric CSPs. In Ruzena Bajcsy, editor, *Proceedings of International Joint Conference on Artificial Intelligence (IJCAI-93)*, pages 232–238, Chambery, France, August 1993. Morgan Kaufmann.
9. E. Marchand and N. Courty. Image-based virtual camera motion strategies. In *Graphics Interface Conference, GI 2000*, May 2000.

Declarative Camera Planning
Roles and Requirements

Jonathan H. Pickering[1] and Patrick Olivier[2]

[1] University of York, Heslington, York, YO10 5DD, UK, jhp@cs.york.ac.uk
[2] Lexicle, York Science Park, York, YO10 5DG, UK, plo@lexicle.com

Abstract. Static camera planning is a fundamental problem for both interactive and non-interactive computer graphics. We examine the nature or the problem, contrasting procedural and declarative specifications of camera position. In establishing the desirability of the declarative approach, we identify the a number of components: an image description language; an object ontology; and a framework for performing constrained optimization.

1 Pictorial Communication

Pictures have formed part of human communications since ancient times. Scholars have used maps and diagrams in their literature, while illustrations form part of most types of literature other than novels. Television, cinema, video and computer games are hugely important styles of entertainment and occasional education. Computer graphics systems now allow users to generate sophisticated model worlds and render still or moving images of these worlds using a representation of a virtual camera that can be set up within a model world. Currently these cameras are positioned manually or are under the procedural control of a simple software component that adapts the camera set-up to a changing environment such as the automatic tracking of characters seen in computer games.

Such is the utility of using pictures that inevitably future computer system will have a greater demand for three dimensional graphics, and the limits of small dedicated pieces of software to control them will soon be reached. For example, automated help tools are being developed to support the maintenance and repair of very complex machinery, such as spacecraft. These systems communicate with the user using a specialist explanation generator which can convert a logical description of a repair task into natural language and pictures. Defining what information the picture is intended to convey is a relatively straightforward task of maintaining correct coreference between a list of properties of a picture and the natural language being generated. Camera planning can be defined as solving the problem of how to locate a virtual camera so that a set of properties in the resulting image are achieved, or maintained.

Camera planning is one component of the automated presentation pipeline. Such a pipeline is likely to make use of artificial intelligence techniques to generate views driven by formally specified input goals. This can be contrasted with

A. Butz et al. (Eds.): Smart Graphics 2003, LNCS 2733, pp. 182–191, 2003.

the imperative approach where a user provides a procedural description of how to achieve a desired view. Such a declarative approach to camera planning is often suggested, yet never have the requirements of such a system been articulated in details. The goal of this paper is to formalise the requirements of such a system, and in particular the input requirements, in such a way that a generic multi-domain camera planning package could be developed.

2   State of the Art

An early attempt to build a camera planner was by Blinn [1]. His work involved setting up virtual cameras to view the flight of a space craft by a planet so that the planet and craft appeared at specified screen locations. Furthermore, the camera needed to be a fixed distance from the space craft, with a fixed field of view, and the spin axis of the planet needed to be parallel to the screen vertical. Blinn was able to to find an iterative solution that solved the problem by producing successively better approximations. Although a closed form solution was also found, the iterative solution was preferred as it was able to produce approximations even when the problem as specified was insoluble. From this early effort three themes can be observed that will prove to recur in camera planning research.

Declarative specification: the input to the camera planner is in the form of a description of properties that should hold in the final image on the screen. In effect the camera planner acts like a declarative programming package, which takes as its input a description of what the problem is and returns a solution, if one exists.

Optimization techniques: for Blinn, the preferred method of solving the problem was to use a method of successive approximations. This is essentially a form of optimization in which an answer that is *good enough*, if not exactly correct, is chosen. This is a feature of most camera planning systems, if only because in the real numbered domain in which virtual cameras are defined small errors are acceptable and may not even be noticeable. It is therefore natural to use an optimization process that tries to minimize some measure of how bad the image is relative to the initial declaration of what it should look like.

Infeasible specifications: with any system of declarative programming it is possible that a declaration may be made of a problem that is insoluble. In the case of camera planning the problem is complicated by the acceptability of minor errors in the camera set-up. For example, if for a given fly-by the declaration of image properties requires that the space craft and planet are half a screen width apart, and the best solution has the positions of the space craft and planet in error by a few pixels, such an image will in most circumstances be acceptable. If, however, the error is so great that the space craft and planet are indistinguishable, being covered by a single pixel (e.g. the craft to camera distance being far too high) the result in not acceptable.

IBIS was more general presentation planning system developed by Seligmann [2]. In the specification of IBIS, Seligmann identified the need for the inputs to the picture generating package to describe the intended effect on the user. In this sense her approach was higher level than Blinn's declarative effort (which referenced screen properties alone), for example, commands such as locate(X), which indicates that the picture will be used to find an object X, were preferred to commands such as show(X). The former indicates that X and its surrounding objects should be visible and recognizable, while the command show(X) means any picture that contains X. The additional information about how the picture should be use has the effect of reducing the size of the search space.

In a similar spirit to IBIS, Butz's CATHI [3] system incorporated a camera planner that took a high level goal as input and decomposed it into atomic actions using a context sensitive recursive descent parse. Although this involved far more than just camera planning, including lighting and arrangement of model objects, it is important to note that use of a hierarchical language with stylistic information contained in the parse. As with Seligmann's work the system required the declarative presentation of high level goals, which implied constraints on the how the picture could be achieved.

The first explicitly declarative approach was that of Christianson [6] who developed a the Declarative Camera Control Language (DCCL). This was a hierarchical language that decomposed a description of an intended screen into a cinematic idiom. Idioms are standard lay outs of cameras that allow continuity to be maintained during editing. For example, if a character A is to the left of character B in the first shot of a screen, that the sense of left and right must be maintained during all subsequent cuts to other shots.

The CONSTRAINTCAM system [4] used a purer constraint system to allow a character in a model world to be followed. The virtual camera was assumed to be positioned on a hemisphere centred on the character; pointing at the character; and have a head-up vector parallel to the natural up of the scene. Objects in the world that potentially occluded a view of the character could be projected onto the hemisphere, represented as a bitmap with occluded regions set to zero. The globally feasible region, in which a camera could be positioned, was found by intersecting the feasible regions for each constraint. This had the advantage of allowing the detection of incompatible pairs of constraints.

Approaches that treat camera planning as a constrained optimization problem are typified by Drucker and Zeltzer [5]. In their approach the input specified that the objects be positioned at certain screen positions with a target size and be unoccluded. The problem was transformed into a set of equations that had to be optimized representing properties such as screen position, screen size, and a set of inequalities corresponding to constraints such as occlusion. The problem was solved using a sequential quadratic program, which is a numerical implementation of the method of Legrange undetermined multipliers. This method of solving camera planning problems can be seen as a generalization of that of Blinn [1].

Finally, two techniques for finding paths for moving camera are worthy of explicit discussion, although dynamic camera planning is not the topic of this paper, both use methods of constraints and optimization. Languénou [7], developed the *Virtual Cameraman* which found paths for dynamic cameras satisfying certain constraints such as maintaining view of given objects. The problems were solved using a method based on interval arithmetic, in which the space of control parameters for the camera was successively subdivided. At each level of the subdivision interval arithmetic was used to determine which, if any, of the subspaces contained solutions, and so drive the next level of subdivision. Marchand and Courty [8], have also developed a system for finding paths for cameras satisfying certain constraints, but in this case the path was found using a differential control techniques to find an optimal path.

Drawing together these examples, two main features that must be addressed in the area of camera planning emerge.

- A formal means of specifying input to the camera planner is needed. The language should be declarative in the sense that it specifies properties of the final images rather than how to achieve those properties.
- A method of solving the problems specified in the input language is required, this method should be some form of optimization in the space of camera parameters. Wherever possible constraints should be derived from the problem and used to accelerate the optimization by reducing the search space.

Most of the remainder of this paper will be dedicated to an analysis of the first of these two problems. The second problem of finding solutions will briefly be addressed in the section 5.

3   Domain and Requirements

As was stated in the previous section, camera planning can be reduced to the two problems of specifying the input the planner and finding a means of constrained optimization to solve the resultant problems. The first step towards analyzing the possible inputs to a system is to carry out a requirements analysis of the problem domain, which requires an understanding of how the system will be used and what role it will play in the larger system in which it will be deployed. This section describes a simple requirements analysis of the camera planning domain; we concentrate on two *use cases* (examples of possible uses): providing pictures to illustrate explanations, and providing spectator views of computer games and simulations. From these cases features defining the general form of a camera planner's input are extracted.

In computer graphics a virtual world is viewed using a virtual camera, which is defined by three[1] components: position, orientation and field of view. Camera planning is defined as an automated method of finding the three components of a

---

[1] Aspect ratio is a fourth component but will be ignored here as it is usually defined by the user or the demands of an output device.

camera, in effect positioning the camera and specifying where it is to look. Cameras are dynamic objects whose properties can change with time giving rise to flying or zoom shots, however in this analysis only static cameras viewing static models will be considered. In effect we attempt to automate still photography.

The objective is to intelligently define a virtual camera based on a description of properties that must hold in the resultant picture. This can illustrated with an example from photo-journalism: on the eve of an important state visit an editor may ask a photographer to "get a picture of the President shaking hands with the Queen". The editor would not advise the photographer to "position yourself between seven and ten meters from the Queen at right angles to the line of approach of the president with a 250mm zoom lens, and get a picture of the President shaking hands with the Queen". The detail of how to photograph the handshake can be left to the photographer who will adjust them to suite prevailing conditions. So, for example, if security requires the photographer to be at least 20m away, a more powerful lens has to be used to accommodate the greater range.

The example illustrates the operation of a camera planner, the user of the planner should only have to reason about the properties that are required of pictures that the virtual camera will take. This principle can be transformed into two related rules that govern the design of camera planners.

- The input to the camera planner should consist of a declaration of the properties of the picture that are of interest to the user that requests the picture.
- The user that requests a picture should not have to reason about the model world beyond specifying what properties it requires to hold in a picture of that world.

We can illustrate the impact of these two rules by considering a number of examples of the operation of camera planners.

3.1   Providing Images for Explanation Systems

Automated reasoning systems are becoming available that can be used for problems such as fault diagnosis in machinery. These systems necessarily contain representations of the problem domain upon which they operate, usually in the form of a set of logical forms naming the parts and defining their relationships. This is differs from a graphical model which names parts but associates each name with a set of polygons and textures.

Likewise, the output of such a reasoning system consists of formal description of the cause of a fault and possibly the actions that must be taken to remedy it. To communicate this to a conventional user, an explanation of the repair needs to be made in natural language augmented with pictures. Such a specialist natural language generation package would provide the natural language and specifications for the associated pictures. The natural language generation package can not be expected to reason about the graphical model of the problem domain, in order to define virtual cameras or set up lights.

Such a system, can only be expected to define the information that is to be communicated to the user. For example, if the reasoning system had specified that a cable release must be loosened, the natural language interface may request a picture showing the location of the cable release. It is the job of the camera planning component to find a camera set-up that gives a picture showing the cable release in sufficient detail to be recognizable and with sufficient surrounding objects visible to be located. A typical output would be show_location(cable_release), which names the cable release and indicates that its location is to be shown. It is the job of a camera planner to reason that showing the location of an object means showing the object itself large enough to be recognizable together with surrounding objects that can be used to locate the target object. In this example the camera planner might have a simple input language that would allow statements requiring ! objects to be shown in various way such a show_location or show_close_up.

3.2   Spectator Views of Computer Games and Simulations

Ever larger simulations are being constructed, some of these have a inherent visual component such a flight simulators, others such as simulations in computational fluid dynamics require a scientific visualization package to produce graphical models. A particular form of simulation is the role playing game, which can now run across a network allowing many users to participated in what is referred to as a multiuser dungeon. Both participants and spectators of these systems have a need to see specific events or objects.

There are currently two methods of providing such views, the simplest is to have the users drive cameras about the world, the alternative is to provide fixed cameras at various locations and allow users to switch between them. Both of these approaches have obvious drawbacks. Driving a camera round a large model world is difficult and if the simulation or game is happening in real time, the user is bound to miss action. Multiple fixed cameras can be a good solution provided the number of cameras is small. If the number of cameras grows the user is presented with a growing problem of how to select the correct camera. The problem is that the user will usually want to observe some object or action, but the cameras are fixed to location, hence the user must find the location of the object to be viewed and then find the nearest cameras to that location. Alternatively, if camera selection is automatic, the risk of disorienting a user increases with the number of *cuts* between ! different cameras.

The problem that emerges is similar to that described in section 3.1. If users want to see something in a model world, they will be concerned with that which they are trying to see and not the coordinates of the world. The users will want to request views of certain actions or objects and a camera planner should find a virtual camera set-up that satisfies the request. It is of course possible that the users may modify the initial camera set-up to suite there personal needs but the initial set-up should be provided for the user as a result of a request to show something. As in the previous section the input to the camera planner would consist of logical forms defined on objects or actions in the model world but specifying how the objects or actions are to appear in an image.

3.3   An Image Description Language

From the two examples it is clear that what is needed is a formal language that can be used for the description of images. We refer to this as an *image description language* (IDL) which must declare properties of images as predicates taking as arguments the objects or named actions in a model world. Consequently, an IDL will consist of statements such as show(Person_1), which is defined on the object Person_1, which specifies that the camera planner needs to reason over the model world to try and find a solution.

High-level propositions, which are aesthetic judgements (and often take no arguments), such as elegant, are not used. Such descriptions are the result of intrinsically subjective judgements and difficult to formalize or even agree on. Even if a definition for elegant were to be agreed on, for example "must have two objects symmetrically positioned in the foreground", this could only be used to drive a random search for an image with a pair of objects in the foreground. If an elegant picture were requested the camera planner would have to search the Cartesian product of all the objects in the model world to find a set-up that satisfied the conditions for elegance. This is perfectly possible, but somewhat useless as our analysis of possible applications indicated that what users need is to view specific objects or actions.

It might be argued that propositions such as elegant should not be used alone but only in conjunction with predicates defining the content of the image. Indeed, we do not preclude the possibility of such high-level descriptions, but believe that they can only be formalized in terms of, or in conjunction with, the an objective IDL. In such an approach statements of the form show(Person_1, Person_2) ∧ elegant would be allowed. Yet there two problems remain in such approach. Firstly the term elegant has to be defined in such a way that it is comparable will all possible definitions of content. A more serious problem is that it that elegance is something that we always want in our pictures and should somehow be built into the definition of showing two persons. This may be achieved by allowing higher level predicates to be defined in terms of low-level predicates with the requirements such as elegance built into the decomposition. In the examp! le given such a system would be as follows.

$$\text{show(P\_1, P\_2)} \mapsto \begin{array}{l} \text{show(P\_1)} \quad \wedge \quad \text{show(P\_2)} \quad \wedge \\ \text{symmetric\_about\_centre(P\_1, P\_2)} \end{array}$$

Finally, we note that all the objects or actions in the world will be identified, or if they are not it is not the responsibility of the camera planner to name them. As a result descriptions along the lines of "show the thing on the left" will not be required. In formal terms this means that quantifiers and variables will not be needed in the language as the arguments of all the predicates will be instantiated.

4   Design of an IDL

In this section the design of an IDL is investigated. The basis of an IDL will be low-level *atomic* predicates that map directly to constrained optimization problems. Higher level predicates must be defined in terms of conjunctions and disjunctions of low-level predicates. The decomposition should occur in such a was as to enforce the rules of picture composition.

4.1   The Need for Typing and Polymorphism

In order to establish the need for a type system in the IDL we can consider an additional *use case*, as in section 3. Consider the problem of establishing the relationship of two objects, this would imply a shot in which both objects were visible and positioned symmetrically about the center of the screen. Following the pattern of section 3.3 this could be represented by a statement of the form.

$$\texttt{establish(P1, P2)} \mapsto \begin{array}{l} \texttt{show(P1)} \quad \land \quad \texttt{show(P2)} \quad \land \\ \texttt{symmetric\_about\_centre(P1, P2)} \end{array}$$

Suppose however that the two objects are people, in this case it is essential that the heads are shown and at least one face should be visible. This may be achieved by the following definition.

$$\texttt{establish(P1, P2)} \mapsto \begin{array}{l} \texttt{show(P1.head)} \quad \land \quad \texttt{show(P2.head)} \quad \land \\ \texttt{symmetric\_about\_centre(P1, P2)} \quad \land \\ \texttt{(show(P1.face)} \quad \lor \quad \texttt{show(P2.face))} \end{array}$$

This example demonstrates that the objects in the model world must have a type system associated with them and that the predicates of the IDL must be polymorphic (defined differently on different types). Also the objects of a given type such as *person* must have identifiable subcomponents, as in the preceding example, which makes reference to a face and a head.

These are unusual properties for data structures in computer graphics, the concern of which is more typically hierarchical containers for geometrical data, each node of which can contain an arbitrary number of child nodes. In artificial intelligence however, such a notion is very familiar, for example, Minsky [9] introduced the notion of a frame to allow just such formal reasoning as is required in the IDL. Frames are compound data structures that contain named items, which can themselves be frames, called slots. So, for example, a frame representing the object room, would have slots for walls, windows, floor and so on.

It is not difficult to modify the existing data structures used in computer graphics to operate in this way, however great care must be used in identifying the types and type hierarchy that is built up. The type hierarchy represents an ontology of objects that will have a consequence how they are to be treated by the camera planner. Building such a ontology will require analysis of the composition rules used in the arts of photography, cinema, painting and drawing, as it will have to represent the cognitive classes used in those rules.

4.2   Properties of Low-Level Predicates

As described in section 3, a camera consists of three components, position, orientation and field of view. To further complicate matters orientation can be represented in several way with differing numbers of components, for example, a rotation matrix with nine components, or a quaternion with four components for example. Whichever choice is made the space of camera parameters is real numbered, high (> 6) dimensional and non-homogeneous.

Atomic level predicates must define properties that can be realized as functions of the camera parameters: position, orientation, and field of view. For example, the property of occlusion is dependent only on position because if object A is hidden behind object B, altering the the field of view or direction of view of your camera will not make object A visible. The only way to make object A visible is to move to another position. Other properties such as the apparent size of an object are dependant on more than one camera parameter, position and field of view in the case of apparent size.

Constraints are best implemented on position because we can use spatial modelling techniques, standard in computer graphics, to build models of the feasible regions of space. Also, in cluttered model worlds a large amount of occlusion occurs and it is desirable to exploit the resultant reduction in the search space to the full. For example, if an object to be viewed is in a room with an open door and window, the search space consists of the inside of the room and a pair of frusta extending from the door and the window. Multiple constraints can be joined by using intersection when the constraints are in conjunction and union when they are in disjunction. If, after an intersection, the volume of the feasible region falls to zero, then the constraints in the conjunction are incompatible.

The remaining predicates that cannot be transformed into spatial models can be cast as optimization problems. So the predicate center(X) becomes an objective function that returns a measure of the distance that the image of X lies from the center of a picture. A optimization procedure can operate in the space of camera parameters, restricted in position to the region modelled by the spatial constraints, and try to minimize the value of the objective function.

5   Summary

A camera planning package should consist of three related components. A interface, or IDL, which should provide predicates defined at the highest possible level of abstraction. A means of converting the specified problems into constrained optimization problems, which is available if all the high-level terms of the IDL can be transformed into low-level atomic predicates. Finally a constraint optimization system that can solve the problems that are generated from the IDL, this system should be able to leverage the considerable reduction in search space implied by the spatial constraints.

The IDL will need to be typed to allow for the fact that different ruled of composition apply to different types of object. This in turn requires that the 3D models need augmenting. Object typing is required as the rules for presenting images of objects differ depending on the object. For example, when asked to show an object in such a way as to ensure it is identifiable, objects which posses fronts such as people or televisions must be shown in a different way from objects which do not have a front, such as a ball or table. Identifiable subcomponents are required as for composite objects finding certain subcomponents may be essential to correctly photographing them. For example, when asked to photograph people the head should normally be included. This requires that objects have a type `person` and that person has a subcomponent slot `head`. This is a much more rigid data structure than is normal in computer graphics.

We conclude by observing that past treatments of camera planning are relatively thin on the ground, especially when we consider how fundamental the problem is to the automatic generation of computer graphics. Yet, nearly all interactive 3D applications have some form of implicit procedural control. By taking a smart graphics approach, and applying notions and techniques that are commonplace in artificial intelligence, we have established both the requirements and the outline design of static camera planner.

References

1. Blinn J., Where am I? What am I looking at? IEEE Computer Graphics and Applications, (July, 1988), 76–81.
2. Seligmann D. D. and Feiner S., Automated Generation of intent based 3D illustrations Computer Graphics **25**, (1991), 123–132.
3. Butz A.: Animation with CATHI, Proceedings of American Association for Artificial Intelligence/IAAI, AAAI Press, (1997), 957–962.
4. Bares W. H. and Rodriguez D. W. and Zettlemoyer L. S. and Lester J. C.: Task-Sensitive Cinematography Interfaces for Interactive 3D Learning Environments, Proceedings Fourth International conference on Intelligent User Interfaces, (1998), 81–88.
5. Drucker S. M. and Galyean T. A. and Zeltzer D.: CINEMA: A System for Procedural Camera Movements, Proceedings of the 1992 Symposium on Interactive Graphics, Computer Graphics, Special Issue (1992), 67–70.
6. Christianson D. B. and Anderson S. E. and He L. and Salesin D. H. and Weld D. S. and Cohen M. F.: Declarative Camera Control for Automatic Cinematography, Proceedings of the American Association for Artificial Intelligence, (1996), 148–155.
7. Jardillier F. and Languénou E.: Screen-Space Constraints for Camera Movements: the Virtual Cameraman, Eurographics '98, Computer Graphics, Special Issue, **17**, **3**, (1998), 174–186.
8. Marchand É. and Courty N.: Image-Based Virtual Camera Motion Strategies, Graphics Interface, (May 2002), 69–76.
9. Minsky M. L.: A Framework for Representing Knowledge, The Psychology of Computer Vision, Wilson P. H. (ed.) McGrawHill, New York, (1977), 211–277.

Automatic Video Composition

M. Zancanaro, C. Rocchi, and O. Stock

ITC-irst
Panté di Povo, Trento Italy
{zancana,rocchi,stock}@itc.it

Abstract. This paper introduces an approach to generate video clips starting from an annotated commentary. The novelty of the approach lies in the use of rhetorical structure of the accompanying audio commentary in planning the video. The basic notions of cinematography are briefly introduced together with the Rhetorical Relation Theory to model the structure of a discourse. Then, the architecture of a video engine to automatically build video clips from the audio commentary annotated with respect to rhetorical relations is described. Finally, an application for a multimedia mobile guide in a museum is described.

1 Introduction

This paper introduces an approach to generate video clips starting from an annotated commentary and a database of still images. One of the first case studies of the generation of "motion presentations" is the work of (Karp and Feiner, 1993). Their system generates scripts for animation using top down hierarchical planning techniques. (Christianson et al. 1996) presents a successful attempt to encode several of the principles of cinematography in the *Declarative camera control language*.

Similar systems are BETTY (Butz, 94) and CATHI (Butz, 98). BETTY is an animation planner, which generates scripts for animated presentations. The CATHI system generates on-line descriptions of 3D animated clips for the illustration of technical devices, in the context of a coordinated multimedia document.

Animated presentations have been successfully employed also in multimodal frameworks for the generation of explanations (Daniel et al. 1999) and in learning environments (Bares et al. 1997).

A totally different approach is proposed by (Lindley and Nack, 2000). In this work, a planning mechanism is employed to select video clips from a video database and sequencing them into a meaningful presentation for viewers.

The novelty of our approach lies in the use of rhetorical structure of the accompanying audio commentary in planning the video. In particular, knowledge of rhetorical structure is extremely useful in taking decisions related to the punctuation of the video, in order to reflect the rhythm of the audio commentary and its communicative goals. In our view, the verbal part of the documentary always drives the generation of the visual part.

The language of cinematography (Metz, 1974), including shot segmentation, camera movements and transition effects, is employed in order to plan the animation and to synchronize the visual and the verbal parts of the presentation.

A. Butz et al. (Eds.): Smart Graphics 2003, LNCS 2733, pp. 192–201, 2003.

Following, we briefly summarize the basic terminology of cinematography and we shortly introduce the Rhetorical Structure Theory to describe the structure of the audio commentary. Then, we will discuss how these conventions can be expressed both in terms of constraints on camera movements and in terms of strategies related to the discourse structure of the associated audio commentary. Finally, a case study of a mobile museum guide that employs automatically composed video clips starting from personalized commentaries will be presented.

2   The Language of Cinematography

According to (Metz, 1974), cinematic representation is not like a human language that is defined by a set of grammatical rules; it is nevertheless guided by a set of generally accepted conventions. These guidelines may be used for developing multimedia presentations that can be best perceived by the viewer.

The shot is the basic unit of a video sequence. In the field of cinematography a shot is defined as a continuous view from single camera without interruption. Since we only deal with still images, we define a shot as a *sequence of camera movements applied to the same image*.

The basic camera movements are *pan*, from "panorama", a rotation of the camera along the x-axis, *tilt*, a rotation along the y-axis, and *dolly*, a rotation along the z-axis.

Transitions among shots are considered the punctuation symbols of cinematography; they affect the rhythm of the discourse and the message conveyed by the video.

The main transitions used are *cut, fade*, and *cross fade*. A cut occurs when the first frame of the following shot immediately replaces the last frame of the current shot. A fade occurs when one shot gradually replaces another one either by disappearing (fade out) or by being replaced by the new shot (fade in). A particular case of a fade happens when instead of two shots, there is one shot and a black screen that can be, again, faded in or faded out. Finally, a cross fade (also called dissolve) occurs when two shots are gradually superimposed during the moment when one is faded out while the other is faded in.

3   Rhetorical Structure Theory

Rhetorical Structure Theory (Mann and Thompson, 1987) analyses discourse structure in terms of dependency trees, with each node of the tree being a segment of text. Each branch of the tree represents the relationship between two nodes, where one node is called the nucleus and the other is called the satellite. The information in the satellite relates to that found in the nucleus in that it expresses an idea related to what was said in the nucleus. This rhetorical relation specifies the coherence relation that exists between the two portions of text contained in the nodes. For example, a *Cause* rhetorical relation holds when the satellite describes the event that caused what is contained in the nucleus. Figure 1, shows an example of a rhetorical tree. Here the second paragraph (the satellite) provides background information with respect to the content expressed in the first paragraph (the nucleus). This additional information acts as a sort of reinforcement for what was previously said in the first paragraph and consequently facilitates the absorption of information. In the original formulation by Mann and Thompson the theory posited twenty different rhetorical relations, while other scholars have since added to this theory.

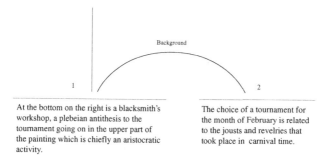

At the bottom on the right is a blacksmith's workshop, a plebeian antithesis to the tournament going on in the upper part of the painting which is chiefly an aristocratic activity.

The choice of a tournament for the month of February is related to the jousts and revelries that took place in carnival time.

Fig. 1. An example of a rhetorical tree (simplified).

RST was originally developed as part of work carried out in the computer-based text generation field. In a previous work (Not and Zancanaro, 2001), we described a set of techniques to dynamically compose adaptive presentations of artworks from a repository of multimedia data annotated with rhetorical relations. These techniques have been exploited in an audio-based, location-aware adaptive audio guide described in (Not et al., 2000).

4   Video Clips on Still Images

Video clips are built by first searching for the sequence of details mentioned in the audio commentary, deciding the segmentation in shots and then planning the camera movements in order to smoothly focus on each detail in synchrony with the verbal part. In building a video clip, a set of strategies similar to those used in documentaries are employed. Two broad classes of strategies have been identified. The first class encompasses constraints, imposed by the grammar of cinematography, while the second deals with conventions normally used in guiding camera movements in the production of documentaries. While the constraints are just sequence of forbidden camera movements, the conventions are expressed in terms of rhetorical structures found in the audio commentary. In our view, the verbal part of the documentary always drives the visual part.

4.1   Constraints on Camera Movements

In order to assure a pleasant presentation, constraints on camera movements have to be imposed. The role of the constraints is to avoid, during the planning of the shots, the creation of a sequence of "unpleasant" camera movements. For example, a pan from right toward left should not follow a pan from left to right. In general, applying any given movement (pan, tilt and zoom) and then immediately reapplying it on the reverse direction is discouraged because this action renders the video awkward to watch. Figure 2 shows an example of constraint.

```
(defconstraint zoom-in
   (var mv (get-previous-movement))
   (var mv2 (get-previous-movement mv)
   (and
        (not (equal (mv zoom-out)
        (not (equal (mv2 zoom-out))))))
```

Fig. 2. An example of constraint

This constraint controls the application of the zoom in, which can be used except when the previous or the last but one movement is a zoom out. During the planning of the shots, whenever a camera movement is proposed, all the constraint related to that movements are checked. If they are all satisfied the movement can be applied, otherwise two tricks can be used: either choosing a different way of focusing the detail required by the verbal part (for example a zoom out can often effectively replace a pan) or starting a new shot altogether. In the latter case, the two shots should be linked by a transition effect that suggests continuity, such as a short fade.

There is a lot of works investigating the issues of coherent camera movements in 3D environments (see for example, Butz, 1994, 1997, Christianson, 1996 and Bares et al, 2000), in future works we are planning to employ those techniques yet our main research interest lies in the use of rhetorical strategies as explained in the next section.

4.2   Rhetorical Strategies

Constraints on camera movements alone are sufficient to ensure a pleasant presentation, yet they do not impact the effectiveness of the video clip. In order to have a more engaging presentation, the visual part should not only focus on the right detail at the right time, but it should also support the presentation of new audio information by illustrating its relation to information that has been already given. In this manner continuity between the information is built, which in turn facilitates the viewing of the video clip while stimulating the absorption of new information.

The text in figure 3 can be visually represented with two shots of the same image (that is, the tournament) linked by a long cross fade. Technically, having two shots is not necessary, since the image is the same, but the cross fade helps the user understand that background information is going to be provided. The first image is thus presented while the first paragraph is heard over the audio, then when the audio switches to, in this case, the background information, the image is enlarged to cover the entire panel and finally refocused on the detail once the audio has stopped.

A rhetorical strategy suggests, on the basis of a rhetorical tree configuration, what shot segmentation and which transition effect should be applied. The strategies employed in the present prototype were elicited by a focus group activity with a documentary director.

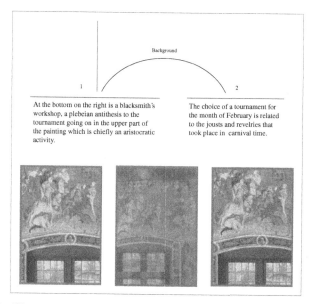

Fig. 3. The "Tournament" example: a cross fade entailed by a background relation

5   Architecture of the Video Engine

The engine is a rule-based system. When a video for a given commentary is requested, the engine analyses the discourse structure of the commentary and selects an appropriate set of images to be presented. The generation chain consists of four phases:

- **Detail Association:** a detail, retrieved from a database of images, is associated with each segment of the commentary;
- **Shot initialization and structure planning:** a candidate structure for the final presentation is elaborated, taking into consideration the rhetorical structure of the commentary;
- **Shot Completion:** camera movements between details are planned. Constraints are considered in order to avoid "inconsistencies";
- **Editing:** transitions among shots are selected according to the rhetorical structure of the commentary.

The input is an XML representation of the audio commentary. The annotation encompasses the segmentation, the rhetorical relations among segments as well as the duration in seconds and the topic (that is the main concept relative to a simple domain taxonomy) of each segment. The output is the script of the video and the audio channels encoded in a XML. Each shot is represented as an image, the camera movements that will be applied on it and the audio file to be played.

```
<segment id="01" parent="root"        <movie id="February">
relname="none"                        <shots>
topic="tournament"                    ...
audio="castle.wav"                    <play audio="blacksmith.wav"/>
duration="3" >                        <audio-pause duration="1.5"/>
At the bottom on the right is         </audio-track>
a blacksmith's                        </shot>
workshop, a plebeian                  <shot id="shot20645" image="01">
antithesis to the                     <video-track>
tournament going on in the            <pause duration="7"/>
upper part of the                     </video-track>
painting which is chiefly an          <audio-track>
aristocratic                          <play audio="young-women2.wav"/>
activity.                             </audio-track>
</shot>
<segment id="02" parent="01"          </shots>  <editing>
relname="elaboration"                 <display shot="shot20474"/>
topics="castle"                       <cut duration="1"/>
audio="windows.wav"                   <display shot="shot20480"/>
duration="2"} />                      <crossfade shot="shot20522"
   The differences between the        duration="1.5"/>
various styles                        <crossfade shot="shot20645"
   of construction have been          duration="1"/>
reproduced extremely                  </editing>
   carefully.                          </movie>
```

Fig. 4. Representation of an audio commentary and the corresponding generated script.

5.1   Phase 1: Detail Association

In this phase the system assigns one or more details to each segment of the commentary. This operation consists in searching a database of images for details with the same topic of the segment. The images in the database were segmented with respect to the details contained and annotated with respect to simple domain taxonomy. The concepts in the taxonomy are the same used in the annotation of the audio commentary. The result of this phase is the same sequence of segments taken in input such that each segment refers to an image.

5.2   Phase 2: Shot Initialization

In this phase, shots are initialized taking into consideration the rhetorical structure of the commentary. At the moment the nucleus/satellite distinction is not taken into account. The result of phase 2 is a candidate structure for the final presentation: a sequence of shots to be completed.

The processing is guided by a set of rules, which are fired when particular configurations of rhetorical relations are matched. For example a relation of type elaboration or sequence signals a smooth transition from the current topic to new information that is strictly related to it; it is thus preferable to aggregate segments in the same shot and to exploit camera movements. Background and circumstance tend to highlight the introduction of new information that provides a context in which the following or the previous messages can be interpreted. They tend to break the flow of the discourse. It is thus preferable to split the segments in two different shots so that, in the next phase, it is possible to exploit proper transition effects in order to emphasize that change of rhythm.

There are cases in which the structure planned in this phase is revised during successive stages of computation. For example, to avoid the "seasickness" effect the system can apply constraints and then modify the previously planned structure by adding new shots.

5.3   Phase 3: Shot Completion

This is the phase in which the engine incrementally completes each shot by illustrating each of its segments. In performing this task the engine traces the camera movements already planned. When a candidate move is proposed the system verifies whether it is suitable or not according to the list of past camera movements and the constraints imposed over that type of movement. Figure 5 shows a completed shot, where the list of the segments is empty whereas audio- and video-track contain a sequence of action applied to images or audio files.

```
(shot
     id : sh01
     image: "January.jpg"
     segments: empty
     audio-track: ((play :sound "january.wav")
                   (a-pause :duration 2))
     video-track: ((pause :duration 2)
                   (zoom :scale 1.20 :duration 3)))
```

Fig. 5. An example of a completed shot.

Constraints encode the cinematographer's expertise in selecting and applying camera movements in order to obtain "well-formed" shots. For instance, when a panning movement is proposed where the previous movement is also a panning, the system has to check if the resulting sequence is suitable. Simple constraints include: (i) When the previous movement is a dolly-out a dolly-in cannot be applied; (ii) When the previous movement is a dolly-in a dolly-out cannot be the subsequent movement; (iii) When a panning or a tilting is along a similar path and in the opposite direction of the previous movement that panning or tilting cannot be applied.

Constraints encode *schemes* of forbidden movements and when one of them is not satisfied the proposed move is rejected. In this case the engine initializes a new shot, declares the previous one completed and associates the remaining segments to the new shot.

5.4   Phase 4: Movie Editing

This is the phase in which the engine chooses the "punctuation" of the presentation. Movie editing is achieved by selecting appropriate transitions among shots. In order to reflect the rhythm of the discourse, the choice of transition effects is guided by the rhetorical structure of the commentary. The system retrieves the last segment of the shot displayed and the first segment of the shot to be presented and plans the transition according to the following rules:

- If two segments are linked by a relation of type elaboration a short cross fade applies;
- If two segments are linked by a relation of type background or circumstance a long cross fade applies.
- If two segments are linked by a relation of type sequence a cut applies.
- If a relation of type enumeration holds among two or more segments a rapid sequence of cut applies.

These rules have been selected according to the observations about the usual employment of transition effects in the field of cinematography (Arijon, 1976) and from focus group with a documentary director. Fade effects are fit for smooth transition, when there is a topic shift or when the center of interest changes but the new topic is related to the old one, as in the case of elaboration or background. Cut is more appropriate for abrupt and rapid changes, to emphasize the introduction of a new concept, as in the case of sequence. A special case holds when the verbal commentary enumerates a set of subjects or different aspects of the same object; in those cases a rapid sequence of cuts can be used to visually enumerate the elements described. The output of this phase is a complete script with the descriptions of shots and the sequence of transition effects, i.e. the editing, to be applied to shots.

6 Cinematography for a Mobile Multimedia Guide

As a test case of the generation of video clips, we are investigating the use of video clips in a multimedia mobile guide in a museum. Many research projects are exploring the new possibilities offered by Personal Digital Assistants (PDAs) in a museum setting. Usually, these multimedia guides use static images, while others employ pre-recorded short video clips about museum exhibits. Our hypothesis is that using video clips to present the description of a painting allows the visitor to better identify the details introduced by the audio counterpart of the presentation.

At present, we have completed a first prototype for the famous XV century fresco "The Cycle of the Months" at Torre Aquila in Trento, Italy. It illustrates the activities of aristocrats and peasants throughout the year and covers all four walls of a tower. It introduces a number of characters as well as many different activities from falconry to wine harvesting.

The guide is implemented on a PDA, which by means of infrared sensors is capable of identifying the visitor position within the frescoed Tower of the castle. Interaction with the system is both proposed by the system itself and accepted by the user, thus sharing the responsibility of information access. When the system detects that the visitor is in front of one of the four walls, a picture of that wall is displayed on the PDA and, after a few seconds, if the user has not changed her position the panel she is facing is highlighted. At this point, the visitor can click on the panel and receive the video documentary of the panel she has chosen. This modality has been chosen in order to allow the visitor to retain control of an inherently proactive guide.

Preliminary studies and pilot tests show encouraging results and interesting effects. All users became acquainted with the system very quickly. Most of them used the PDA as a "3D mouse", pointing directly to the infrared emitters to speed up the localization. In the future, we will propose a new interface where the user can be explicitly involved in the process of localization. Most of the users complained before actually using the system that a video sequence on a PDA would distract their attention from the real artwork. After a short interaction with the system, however, they appreciated the possibility of quickly localizing small details on the fresco. This demonstrates that use of cinematic techniques in a multimedia guide can be effective, particularly when explaining a complex painting.

7   Conclusions and Future Work

The paper describes an engine to compose video clips starting from an annotated audio commentary and a repository of images. An application for a multimedia mobile guide in a museum has been introduced. The novelty of the approach lies in the idea of using the Rhetorical Structure Theory to describe the semantics of the transitions among shots.

To improve the quality of the resulting presentation we are planning to introduce new rules in order to allow: (i) the use of composed camera movements, (ii) the variation of the speed of the camera and (iii) the use of "metagraphics" (arrows, bounding boxes, blurred areas) as an alternative to zoom in, in order to highlight also the very detailed parts of the images.

At the moment the application does not take into account users features like age, preferences, level of expertise, etc. We are planning to develop a new version of the software that can also allow the variation of the rhythm of the documentary according to the needs of a particular user.

Acknowledgment. This work has been supported by the PEACH and TICCA projects, both funded by the Autonomous Province of Trento and the latter co-funded by CNR.

References

1. Arijon D.. 1976. *Grammar of the film language*. Silman-James Press, Los Angeles.
2. Bares W. and Lester J. 1997. Realtime generation of customized 3D animated explanations for knowledge-based learning environments. In AAAI97 Proceedings of the Fourteenth National Conference on Artificial Intelligence, pages. 347–354.

3. Bares W., McDermott S., Bourdreaux C., and Thainimit S.. Virtual 3D camera composition from frame constraints. In Proceedings of the eighth ACM international conference on Multimedia, pages 177–186, Marina del Ray, California, United States, 2000. ACM Press New York.

4. Butz, A.. 1994. BETTY: Planning and generating animations for the visualization of movements and spatial relations. In Proceedings of *Advanced Visual Interfaces*, Bari Italy.

5. Butz, A. 1997. *Anymation with CATHY*. In Proceedings of *AAAI/IAAI*, Vol. 1, pages. 957–962.

6. Christianson, D, Anderson S., He L. W., Salesin D., Weld D., and Cohen M. 1996. Declarative camera control for automatic cinematography. In AAAI/IAAI, Vol. 1, pages 148–155.

7. Daniel B., Callaway C., Bares W. and Lester J. 1999. Student-sensitive multimodal explanation generation for 3D Learning Environments. In Proceedings of the Sixteenth National Conference on Artificial Intelligence, pages. 144–120.

8. Lindley, C. and Nack, F. 2000. Hybrid Narrative and Associative/Categorical Strategies for Interactive and Dynamic Video Presentation Generation. In: New Review of Hypermedia and Multimedia (volume 6, pages 111–145).

9. Mann W. and Thompson. S.1987. Rhetorical Structure Theory: A Theory of Text Organization, In L. Polanyi (ed.), The Structure of Discourse, Ablex Publishing Corporation.

10. Metz C. 1974. Film Language: a Semiotics of the Cinema. Oxford University Press, New York.

11. Not and Zancanaro, 2001. E. Not, M. Zancanaro. "Building Adaptive Information Presentations from Existing Information Repositories". In Bernsen N.O., Stock O. (eds.), Proceedings of the International Workshop on Information Presentation and Multimodal Dialogue, Verona, Italy.

12. Karp P. and Feiner S.. 1993. Automated presentation planning of animation using task decomposition with heuristic reasoning. In Proceedings of Graphics Interface, pages 118–127.

Beyond Encoding: It Has Got to Move

Marius Hartmann

Ph.D-student

IT University of Copenhagen
Glentevej 67, 2400 Kbh. NV, Denmark
hartmann@it-c.dk

Abstract. The challenges related to constructing autonomous bodies, which may effectively interact with their environment are well recognized within the field of Artificial Intelligence. Within this field encoding approaches are increasingly abandoned in favor of interactive or decentralized perspectives. In this poster I will argue the combination of non-encoded visual cues and motion may present rich information to us, the ability to form large coherent relational structures from minimal visual information is an onboard capability of humans and may prove a viable solution to the problems of occlusion in conventional displays. The possibility of creating taxonomy of movement could present us with a pre-attentive non-encoding approach of visualizing information.

1   Introduction

Matching the difference between the speed at which technology can deliver information with the speed at which humans are capable to receive and react to this is one of the fundamental challenges to technology.

The advent of dynamic and contextual aspects of information has shown the conventional ways of delivering information lacking. This communicational shortcoming may have the consequence of producing a widening gap between human decision-making and technological filtering due to the limited communicational properties of the tools and methods in use.

The way we choose technology to present information digitally is predominantly encoded and sets narrow limits to the agility of which we may interact with information as the encoding doesn't facilitate our embodied perceptual mechanisms, but requires translation or decoding. One may argue that by relying so heavily on encoding, we have achieved what Rodney Brooks calls the sense-think-act bottleneck [1], although this is originally referring to a robot vs. real-world scenario, I here compare it to the human vs. virtual-world scenario, in the sense that we, in the digital situation, currently are put in an alien environment. However in contrast to the robot-population, humans have been thoroughly tested and fine-tuned by evolution, we just need to take advantage of this. If we want to interact dynamically with digital technology, we need the creation of situations where we may act with the speed of intuition, hence a rein-

A. Butz et al. (Eds.): Smart Graphics 2003, LNCS 2733, pp. 202–205, 2003.

corporation of the body as an interactive and contextual generator of information is necessary.

2 Motion

Motion is a promising candidate for representing information that has not to be decoded. We perceive the world by movement- "Observation implies movement, that is, locomotion with reference to the rigid environment, because all observers are animals and all animals are mobile" [2], just as the psychologist James Gibson demanded life-like experiments where the subject where able to move their heads, we should enable motion as a support to digital communication. In the display of information motion holds a very usable feature in that it promotes interaction rather than the sense-think-act cycle, motion also has positive usability issues in terms of constancy [3].

Apart from having a potent aspect of attention motion also present a pre attentive level of grouping, which may add to the perception of complex structures [4]. The potency of introducing motion graphics as a communicational tool may hold the solution of how to present large amounts of data and especially relational aspects.

3 Causality

In order to represent a relational property of motion graphics it is necessary to understand the way we perceive causality. Causality contains latent perceptual levels we have come to take for granted, without realizing the omniscience of this phenomenon. In 1946 psychologist Albert Michotte first reported a series of experiments on the perception of causality, he devised an elaborate mechanical apparatus that allowed him to manipulate the animation of two objects on the projection screen. These animations could be as simple as moving a dot at various speeds and with various delays. However small variations in the display of movement would result in significant variations in the description of what his subjects reported seeing. Their reports could vary from the factual "A launches B". At other times the description would contain words attributing motivation, emotion, gender, age or relationships between the two objects, for example, "It is as if A's approach frightened B, and B ran away"[5].

"The impression of causality is dependent on specific and narrowly limited spatial-temporal features of the event observed. The spatio-temporal organization is such that it directly unleashes this impression in us. Alter the relevant variables by a small but measurable amount and the impression disappears" [6].

Movement may have potentials of escaping encoding or even objectification. In Michotte's discoveries concerning object-removal he wrote: "It follows that the movement of an object is liable in some circumstances to survive phenomenally the removal of the object, and there can be an apparent *continuation* of the movement of the object which has ceased to exist and is consequently not itself being displaced" [5]. Subjects would in some cases experience the causal relations between dots – even in cases where there was only one dot visible at the time of the impression.

The possibility of creating taxonomy of movement could present us with a pre-attentive non-encoding approach of visualizing information. For instance the paradoxical cases as Michotte named the situations in which an experimental event would cause an impression which real life bodies would not, is a field which is laid out to us to be explored in the context of communicational structures. In a superficial way motion shares some of the characteristics as the interactive process of 'internal book-keeping' as put by Mark Bickhard [7] in that it doesn't contain encoding, and yet is capable of signifying states.

The use of animation has also been examined in an ecological context, perhaps most notable are Gunnar Johansson's point-light experiments, in which actors wearing small lights performed action in darkened rooms. The actions or situation were unrecognizable to subjects whenever the actors where not in motion. However in motion the groupings and relations among the lights made it possible for the subjects to perceive gender, weight, action performed and moods of the actors.

Experiments within experimental psychology has demonstrated the combination of non-encoded visual cues and motion may present rich information to us, the ability to form large coherent relational structures from minimal visual information is an onboard capability of humans and may prove a viable solution to the problems of occlusion in conventional displays.

The use of animation as communicational tool was accentuated by R. Baecker, his use of animation visualized abstract relations in real time in the case of sorting algorithms. His claim was that a student having watched the 30-minute animation carefully would be capable of programming some of them, although this was never documented or tested, interviews with the students supported the usage of animation to communicate concepts. Simultaneously the nine different algorithms illustrated in the animation are compared for efficiency. On explaining why animation is such an effective method of displaying real time data Baecker adds: "The film also go beyond a step-by-step presentation of the algorithms, communicating an understanding of them as dynamic processes. We can see the programs in process, running, and we therefore see the algorithms in new and unexpected ways. We see sorting waves ripple through the data. We see data reorganize itself as if it had a life of its own. These views produce new understandings which are difficult to express in words" [8].

The problem of handling the world in a non-verbal way may seem odd or disturbing to us, as we generally perceive of the human-made environment as a rational construct using the probes of symbolism and language. However, in some cases the sheer scale of digitized information makes is disadvantageous to rely so heavily on encoded representations. For instance one may think of the low number of search results we actually perceive out of the many found in the average search engine. For instance when was the last time you went down three pages in a search engine on the web? The findings within the research of animation and causality, as presented in this paper, may produce resources invaluable to the development of communicational structures capable of handling the challenges that we are confronted with in relation to dynamical sources of information, as well as vast information sources found in e.g. database search results.

References

[1]   Brooks, Rodney. Intelligence without representation. Artificial Intelligence. 1991.

[2]   Gibson, James J. The Ecological Approach to Visual Perception, 72. 1979.

[3]   George G. Robertson, Stuart K. Card, and Jock D. Mackinlay. Information Visualization Using 3d Interactive Animation, *Communication of the ACM*, Vol.36,No.4. April 1993.

[4]   Bartram, L., and Ware, C., Calvert, T., (in press) Filtering and Brushing with Motion. Information Visualization,

[5]   Michotte, Albert. The perception of causality, 121,138. Methuen 1963.

[6]   Oldfield, R.C. vii in the foreword to [6].

[7]   Bickhard, Mark and Richie, Michael,D. On the nature of representation: A case study of James Gibson's Theory of perception. New York: Praeger Publishers 1983.

[8]   Baecker, R., Sherman, D. Sorting out sorting, 9. Morgan Kaufman 1981.

3D Graphics Adaptation System on the Basis of MPEG-21 DIA

Hae-Kwang Kim[1], Nam-Yeol Lee[1], and Jin-Woong Kim[2]

[1] Dept. of Software Engineering, Sejong University, 143-747 Seoul, Korea
{hkkim, nylee}@sejong.ac.kr
[2] Radio Broadcasting Technology Lab., ETRI,
305-350 Daejun, Korea
jwkim@etri.re.kr

Abstract. In this paper, adaptation of 3D graphics on the basis of the MPEG-21 DIA (Digital Item Adaptation) standard is presented. The MPEG-21 DIA standard covers a general usage environment description framework for adapting multimedia contents including computer graphics. The adaptation parameters for the 3D graphics consist of user characteristics and terminal capability. The user characteristics parameters represent the user's quality preferences on graphics components of geometry, material and animation as well as 3D to 2D conversion preference. The terminal capability parameters represent the graphics format and the graphics processing capacity of vertex processing rate, fill rate and memory bandwidth. MPEG-21 3D graphics DIA adaptation system adapts 3D graphics to these usage environment parameters input from the user for the best experience of the graphics contents.

1 Introduction

Content is transmitted to and consumed by a user in a typical usage environment so that the information on the target usage environment is a critical factor for the content creation and adaptation. Digital content adaptation technologies have been developed recent years. Scalable coding technologies decompose an original high quality content into a base layer and more than one enhanced layers. The base layer conveys low quality content. High quality content can be obtained, when enhanced layers are added to the base layer. These scalable technologies are targeted for adaptation to different network and terminal capabilities.

Metadata-based content adaptation techniques [1] are developed in the concept of UMA (Universal Machine Access) and reflected in MPEG-7 and UAProf (User Agent Profile) standards. MPEG-21 DIA (Digital Item Adaptation) deals with UMA technologies covering description of usage environments such as networks, terminals, user characteristics and natural environment. The 3D graphics DIA in this paper was proposed by the authors and adopted in the current adaptation model document of the MPEG-21 DIA [2].

The paper is structured as followings: section 2 describes the 3D graphics related MPEG-21 DIA. A graphics adaptation system is presented in section 3. The paper concludes in section 4 with future research directions.

A. Butz et al. (Eds.): Smart Graphics 2003, LNCS 2733, pp. 206–211, 2003.

2   MPEG-21 DIA for 3D Graphics Adaptation

Technologies for adaptation of graphics contents to different usage environments are demanded as graphics contents are expanding its usage to various applications on different platforms such as mobile phones, PCs and PDAs [3]. There are various techniques and formats for representing graphics contents and MPEG-21 DIA description is designed to cover these various representation technologies. Table 1 shows MPEG-21 DIA usage environment parameters for the graphics adaptation.

Table 1. MPEG-21 DIA usage environment elements related to 3D graphics adaptation

Parameters	Description
Geometry Emphasis	User preference on the degradation of geometry (Float number from 0 to 1)
Material Emphasis	User preference on the degradation of material (Float number from 0 to 1)
Animation Emphasis	User preference on the degradation of animation (Float number from 0 to 1)
Multiview3Dto2D	For converting to 2D graphics (Camera parameters)
Graphics File Format	For converting the graphics format (Format name)
Vertex processing rate	Maximum vertex processing rate of a codec (vertices/sec)
Memory bandwidth	Maximum memory bandwidth of a codec (bits/sec)
Fill rate	Maximum fill rate of a graphics codec (pixels/sec)

With the first 3 elements of Geometry Emphasis, Material Emphasis and Animation Emphasis, the user can express preference on the quality degradation of the geometry, material and animation components of graphics contents. For example, when the terminal can not process the original full 3D graphics, the user may express preference to the maximum quality of geometry information sacrificing texture and animation quality.

The Multiview3Dto2D element provides arbitrary number of views with different configuration of camera parameters. For instance, the user's terminal has 2D image processing capability with HMD (Head Mount Display). The user may describe a stereo camera configuration with this element. When the adaptation server receives this information, it converts 3D graphics to stereo 2D images calculated by the left and the right virtual camera parameters for the user to have immersive 3D experience without 3D graphics capability.

Graphics File Format element is used by the server to convert the file format of graphics contents to the file format that the terminal can handle. Currently there are various file formats for the graphics contents.

The last 3 elements of vertex processing rate, memory bandwidth and fill rate represent the animation processing capability of the terminal's graphics engine. These elements may be used for the adaptation server to control animation quality of graphics contents so that the adapted animation can be processed in the user's terminal.

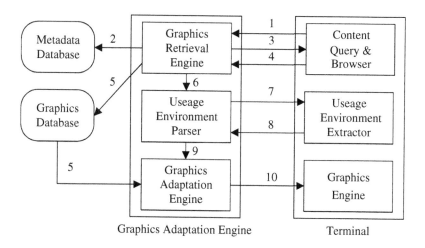

Fig. 1. Architecture of an MPEG-21 DIA based Graphics Adaptation System

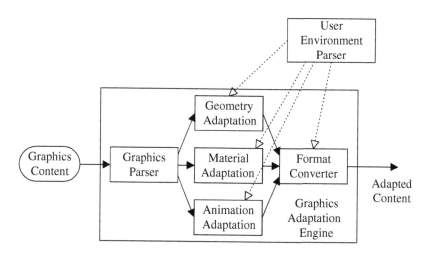

Fig. 2. Block diagram of an MPEG-21 DIA based Graphics Adaptation Engine. The dotted line represents the flow of corresponding environment description for each component adaptation tools. The dashed line represents the flow of graphics contents

The following XML code shows an instance of graphics DIA description for a user's graphics preference. This example shows that the user prefers full geometry information while he can accept degradation of animation and material quality by half.

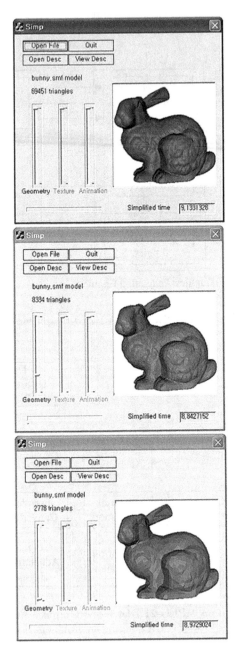

Fig. 3. A user interface for graphics contents adaptation tool. User preference of graphics quality is controlled by slide bars. The top, middle and bottom images of Bunny model correspond to Geometry Emphasis set to 1 (69451 triangles), 0.12 (8334 triangles) and 0.04 (2778 triangles), respectively

```
<?xml version="1.0" encoding="UTF-8"?>
<DIA
xmlns="urn:mpeg:mpeg21:dia:schema:2003"
xmlns:bt="urn:mpeg:mpeg21:dia:schema:BasicTypes:2003"
xmlns:mpeg7="urn:mpeg:mpeg7:schema:2001"
xmlns:xs="http://www.w3.org/2001/XMLSchema"
xmlns:xsi="http://www.w3.org/2001/XMLSchema-instance"
<Description xsi:type="GraphicsPresentationPreferenceType">
  <geometryEmphasis> 1.0 </geometryEmphasis>
  <animationEmphasis> 0.5 </animationEmphasis>
  <materialEmphasis> 0.5 </materialEmphasis>
</Description>
</DIA>
</xml>
```

3   MPEG-21 Based Graphics Adaptation System

Fig. 1 shows the architecture of an MPEG-21 based 3D graphics adaptation system. MPEG-21 DIA only standardizes the description itself. So the extraction and the parser tools for the DIA usage environment description are required to be implemented conforming to the standard.

The user at the terminal (1) sends a query for a specific graphics contents to the graphics retrieval engine of the adaptation server. The retrieval engine (2) searches its metadata database and (3) returns the search result. The user selects a graphics contents and (4) sends its *url* to the retrieval engine. The retrieval engine (5) retrieves the graphics contents from the graphics database and sends it to the graphics adaptation engine. The retrieval engine (6) requests the usage environment parser retrieve the usage environment from the terminal. The usage environment parser (7) sends the request of usage environment to the terminal. The usage environment extractor extracts the environment description and (8) sends it to the parser. The parser (9) sends the retrieved environment description to the graphics adaptation engine. The graphics adaptation engine adapts the retrieved graphics contents to the input environment description and (10) sends the adapted graphics contents to the graphics engine of the terminal that will present it to the screen.

Fig. 2 shows a block diagram of a graphics adaptation engine. The graphics parser of the adaptation engine parses the input graphics contents into geometry, material and animation parts and sends each part to the corresponding adaptation tool. Each specialized adaptation tool adapts the received component of graphics to the usage environment description input from the usage environment parser. The format converter aggregates the adapted components and converts to the graphics format of the usage environment description.

For geometry adaptation, QEM (Quadratic Error Metrics) based simplification algorithm can be used for polygonal mesh representation. For material quality, a size reduction method can be used. For animation quality, frame rate reduction can be used. Fig. 3 shows the user interface of a 3D graphics adaptation software tool developed as an application of the MPEG-21 graphics DIA. The user interface has three slide bars for geometry, material and animation preference. An ordinary user can control the quality of graphics without knowledge of inside graphics technology as he does for JPEG image compression without knowledge of image coding. The top image in Fig. 3 shows original Bunny model consisting of 69451 triangles obtained with the Geometry Emphasis set to 1. The middle image of the Bunny model consists of 8334 triangles with Geometry Emphasis set to 0.12. The bottom image of the Bunny model consists of 2778 triangles with Geometry Emphasis set to 0.04.

4   Conclusion

In this paper, a graphics adaptation system on the basis of MPEG-21 DIA is presented. We are currently working on refining the design of the adaptation system and implementing the standard reference software for the MPEG-21 graphics DIA. As future work, we are planning to research on various algorithms for geometry, material and animation adaptation not only to the presented usage environments, but also to other graphics related MPEG-21 DIA usage environment description such as user characteristics of color vision deficiency and natural environment of illumination.

References

1. Rakesh, M., John R. S., Chung-Sheng, L.: Adapting Multimedia Internet Content for Universal Access. IEEE Trans on Multimedia, Vol. 1, No. 1. (1999)
2. MPEG MDS Group: MPEG-21 Digital Item Adaptation AM (v.5.0). MPEG document No. N5613. Pattaya (2003)
3. Rist, T., Brandmeier, P.: Customizing Graphics for Tiny Displays of Mobile Devices. Personal and Ubiquitous Computing, Vol. 6, Issue 4 Springer-Verlag, London (2002) 260–268

Analogical Representation and Graph Comprehension

Aidan Feeney and Lara Webber

Department of Psychology, University of Durham Queen's Campus, Thornaby,
Stockton-on-Tees TS17 6BH, United Kingdom
{aidan.feeney, l.j.webber}@durham.ac.uk

Abstract. In this paper we argue that people sometimes construct analogical representations of the information that they extract from simple graphs and that these representations are subject to the same nomic constraints as the original graphical representations. We briefly review behavioural and neuro-psychological findings across a range of tasks related to graph comprehension, which suggest that people spontaneously construct analogical representations with a spatial quality. We describe two experiments demonstrating that the representations constructed by people reasoning about graphs may also possess this spatial quality. We contrast our results with the predictions of current models of graph comprehension and outline some further questions for research.

1 Introduction

People may extract, and represent, a variety of information from a graph or a diagram. For example, from a simple bar graph containing information about the values along a scale of two different levels of a variable, one may extract information about the value of each level of the variable or the relative value of the levels. Thus, each of the statements in Figure 1 is consistent with the information presented in the graph.

A is high on the scale
B is low on the scale
A is higher on the scale than B

Fig. 1. A simple graph and three extracted pieces of information

The third statement in Figure 1 specifies the relationship between the entities depicted in the graph. One of the advantages of graphs and diagrams is that they support the easy encoding of such relational information perhaps via a process of perceptual inference [1]. In this paper we will argue that people may represent such relational information analogically rather than propositionally. Our focus will be on the representations constructed of graphical information for high-level cognition such as inference. We will not be concerned with perceptual or attentional processes and representations [see 2].

A. Butz et al. (Eds.): Smart Graphics 2003, LNCS 2733, pp. 212–221, 2003.

Although the argument that we wish to make here would be relatively uncontroversial in many areas of psychology (see section 2 below) it does not yet appear to have been made in the literatures on graph comprehension and design. Paradoxically, most current theories of graph and diagram comprehension make the assumption that viewers build up a wholly propositional description of the graph with which they are interacting [e.g. 3; 4]. Whilst this assumption may be convenient for the purposes of modelling, it is psychologically implausible. One problem with the assumption is that there is a range of behavioural and neuropsychological evidence demonstrating that analogical representations with a spatial quality are built up in the course of a range of activities related to graph comprehension. These activities include comprehending text, reasoning about relations and thinking about number. In addition, we have gathered behavioural evidence from a number of graphical tasks demonstrating that people build analogical representations of the relational information contained in a graph. We will review both types of evidence below.

Before reviewing empirical evidence, we will describe why, a priori, we mistrust the assumption that all of the information extracted from a graph or a diagram is represented propositionally. Our mistrust is based, in part, on recent attempts to distinguish sentential from pictorial representations [5; 6]. According to Shimojima, the most satisfactory criteria for distinguishing between the two is whether a particular representation obeys nomic or stipulative constraints. Nomic constraints arise out of natural laws, such as the laws of physics, whereas stipulative constraints arise out of convention. Shimojima argues that pictorial representations tend to satisfy nomic constraints whereas sentential representations do not. Although there are problems with this distinction particularly with the claim that pictorial representations are not subject to stipulative constraints [see 6], the results of experimental research suggest that the notion of nomic constraints may be an important one. For example, Cheng [7] has demonstrated the advantages for teaching of diagrammatic representations that encode the laws of the domain being taught. Thus, the principles of electricity are better learned when the representations used for teaching encode the relationships which hold between variables in the world. In a similar vein, Gattis and Holyoak [8] have demonstrated that graphical representations in which the variables represented obey the physical constraints that apply in the world are more clearly understood, and more easily used as the basis for reasoning, than graphs which do not adhere to these constraints. Both of these studies support the notion that adherence to nomic constraints facilitates learning and reasoning about a domain and may be one of the factors that make pictures more efficient than sentential representations.

According to theories of graph comprehension that assume propositional descriptions of graphical information, there is no qualitative difference between mental representations derived from text and those that are derived from graphical displays. Of course, the graphical display may index information more efficiently and facilitate perceptual inferences [1]. It may also exploit Gestalt perceptual principles in order to communicate efficiently [3]. Nonetheless, the internal representational medium for pictures is assumed to be the same as it is for text. Our objection to this assumption is that we think it unlikely that information processors will always fail to represent those aspects of graphs and diagrams that often make them more efficient than sentences. In deriving a representation from a diagram or a graph, the reader is constructing a mental structure which may later be used as the basis for an inference. If this mental structure were to adhere to the constraints which applied in the domain to which the graph of diagram referred, then subsequent inferences based upon that representation are likely to be facilitated. Particularly in cases where people must reason about the relationships described in a graph, our claim is that they will represent that relational information analogically. We will now review the evidence that people spontaneously construct such analogical representations.

2   Representations for Tasks Related to Graph Comprehension

In this section we will review behavioural evidence that analogical representations are spontaneously constructed during a variety of tasks related to graph comprehension. As space precludes a very extensive review of any one literature we will briefly describe studies in two different areas. We will also describe some recent evidence from fMRI studies of reasoning which suggest that the brain mechanisms involved in reasoning about relations are the same as those previously shown to underlie a range of spatial tasks.

2.1   Behavioural Evidence

Text Comprehension. Relevant work in the areas of text comprehension is motivated by the idea that people construct mental models [see 9; 10] or situation models [for a review see 11] of the information contained in a textual description. The notion of a mental model is also to be found in the literatures on multi-media learning [12] and reasoning about both simple [13] and complex [14] displays. Some model theories emphasize a spatial aspect to people's models [e.g. 9]. Such theories view models as analogical to that which they represent. Other applications of model theory instantiate mental models via a set of production rules [e.g. 13] or some other propositional device. Only the former version of model theory results in a representation that is subject to nomic constaints. For example, in Johnson-Laird's mental model theory, the statement 'A is to the left of B' results in a representation containing a token for A and a token for B where A in the representation is placed to the left of B. Thus, the structure of the model is analogical to the situation in the world and the model is subject to the same nomic constraints as the situation it represents.

The literature on model construction is very large (see 11). However, one very convincing demonstration that people's representations of text may have a spatial dimension comes from work by Glenberg and colleagues [15]. Participants were asked to read a series of sentences, presented one at a time, describing a jogger. In the second critical sentence the jogger was described as *putting on* or *taking off* a sweatshirt. Participants subsequently read a number of filler sentences describing the jogger's progress. Immediately after the critical sentence or after the first or the second filler sentence participants received the word *sweatshirt* as a probe and were asked to say whether it had occurred in the text. The time taken to make this judgment varied according to whether the jogger was said to have put on or taken off his sweatshirt. Thus, when the probe appeared after the first filler sentence, participants were slower to verify the appearance of the probe when the jogger was said to have taken off his sweatshirt than when he had put it on. This finding is taken as evidence that people represent the spatial structure of the situation described as well as its propositional content.

Mathematical Cognition. Another research area that appears to offer support for the notion that analogical representations are constructed for a wide variety of tasks related to graph comprehension comes from the literature on mathematical cognition. Dehaene [16] has suggested the existence of three cardinal types of representation of number. These are an auditory verbal representational code, a visual Arabic code and a magnitude representation along an oriented analogical number line. Evidence for an analogical representation of number comes from the literature on the so-called SNARC effect (Spatial-Numerical Association of Response Codes).

In a typical SNARC experiment [see 16], participants are asked to make judgements about whether numbers are odd or even. To indicate their response, participants have to present one of two keys and the assignment of even and odd responses to right and left keys is systematically varied. The SNARC effect consists of an interaction in the speed of participants' responses between number magnitude and side of response. Thus larger numbers are responded to more quickly when the correct response involves the right rather than the left hand whilst smaller numbers produce a quicker response when they require the left-hand button to be pressed. The effect is obtained when handedness is controlled for and when participants respond with their hands crossed but is reversed when the participants are from cultures where the writing system is right-to-left.

The primary task in the SNARC paradigm (making a numerical parity judgement) is irrelevant to judgements about magnitude. Thus, participants do not have to adopt an analogical representation in order to accomplish the task. Nonetheless, they appear to spontaneously represent number along an analogical number line and this representation underlies the interaction between magnitude and side of response. Although there is debate about the origins and significance of the SNARC effect [17], it seems unquestionable that the effect indicates the use of an analogical representation for judgements of parity.

2.2 The Neural Substrates of Reasoning about Relations

There is substantial behavioural evidence that people construct analogical representations whilst reasoning about relations [see 18]. However, researchers have recently begun to investigate the neural substrates of reasoning. Goel and Dolan [19] have investigated the brain mechanisms involved in reasoning about simple spatial relationships (e.g. ahead of) and non-spatial relationships that are easily mapped onto spatial relations (e.g. heavier than). Content was also manipulated in this study so that participants received problems with concrete or abstract content. However, the activation differences due to this manipulation will not be discussed here. Goel and Dolan used an event-related fMRI methodology in which participants were presented with sets of premises consisting of two sentences followed by a third, conclusion sentence. The sentences were added, one at a time, to a computer display. Each set of premises contained three terms. One of these terms was mentioned in both premises and is known as the repeated term, whilst the other two terms (known as non-repeated terms) appeared in the conclusion (e.g. A is ahead of B; C is ahead of A ∴C is ahead of B). Participants' task in the experimental trials was to indicate whether the conclusion was logically necessary given the premises. The baseline condition in this experiment involved the presentation of a third sentence which was unrelated to the first two sentences (e.g. A is ahead of B; C is ahead of B ∴F is above X). The experimenters were interested in the reasoning component of the task (that is, the period from the first appearance of the conclusion until participants gave a response).

The main finding in this study is that, relative to the baseline condition, and across both the spatial and non-spatial items, three-term relational reasoning implicated a widespread dorsal network involving occipital, parietal and frontal lobes of the brain. Similar patterns of activation have been observed in studies of the manipulation of visuo-spatial information [20] and allocentric relations [21].

Although it is possible that information may be represented non-analogically in parietal areas of the brain, in conjunction with the behavioural evidence, Goel and Dolan interpret their findings as strong evidence for the construction of analogical representations during relational reasoning. Interestingly, another simple reasoning task, involving picture sentence verification (see below), has been shown to recruit greater parietal involvement when a visual-spatial strategy is reported than when a linguistic strategy is used [22]. In addition, Dehaene and colleagues [23] have found evidence for bilateral parietal involvement in the kind of mathematical judgments described in the previous section.

3 Analogical Representations and Graph Comprehension

We have briefly reviewed the substantial evidence in the literature for the spontaneous construction of analogical representations with a spatial quality. Evidence for these representations is to be found in the text comprehension, mathematical cognition and reasoning literatures. In addition, there is evidence for the involvement of neurological systems previously associated with spatial cognition in reasoning about relationships. In this section we will describe the results of two sets of experiments that we carried out in order to provide evidence that people represent the relationship between the entities referred to in graphs using analogical representations with a spatial quality. Our tactic in both sets of experiments has been to design graphical versions of tasks from the literature on the cognitive psychology of reasoning [see 18]. Thus we will briefly describe the results of two experiments. The first of these involved a graph sentence verification task whilst the second involved a graphical relational reasoning task.

3.1 Graph Sentence Verification
In our first set of studies we used a graph sentence verification task similar to the picture sentence verification task that was extensively studied in the 1960s and 1970s. We asked participants to verify that the relationship between two referents described in a graph was the same as the relationship described in a sentence, which was presented immediately below the graph. Although we ran the task using bar graphs and line graphs, we will describe only the bar graph data here. A fuller description of this experiment is to be found in Feeney et al [24].

In the experiment we presented 50 participants with 64 displays like those shown in Figure 2. Each display consisted of a bar graph specifying the position of two referents on a scale and a verbal description of the relationship between these referents. We manipulated the slope of the graph so that it was ascending (the rightmost bar taller than the leftmost bar) or descending (the leftmost bar taller than the rightmost bar). We manipulated the relational term in the verbal description (less than vs. greater than) and the order of the labels on the X-axis in the graph. Finally, we manipulated whether the state of affairs described in the verbal description matched the state of affairs depicted in the graph. These manipulations resulted in a total of 16 experimental trials and participants received four trials in each condition. We measured participants' error rates and reaction times in the experiment but will discuss only reaction times here.

Table 1. Sample arrays and means for the interaction between Slope, Relational Term and Match between Descriptions from Feeney et al (2000).

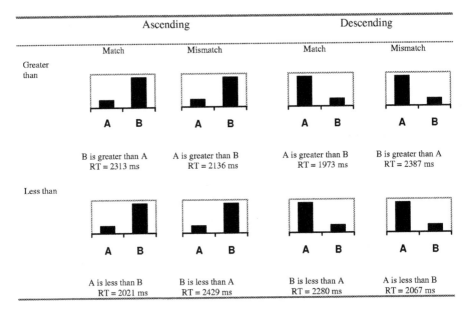

We used a 2x2x2x2 within participants ANOVA to analyse the time it took participants to make their verification decisions. This analysis showed that participants were faster to make a verification decision where the pictorial and linguistic descriptions were matching (mean = 2146 ms) than when the descriptions described different states of affairs (mean = 2254 ms). In addition, there was a highly significant interaction between the slope of the graph, the relational term used in the linguistic description and whether the descriptions were matching. The means involved in this interaction are presented alongside corresponding sample arrays in Table 1. Examination of these means and the corresponding arrays reveals that the significance of the interaction is explained by whether the order of the labels was the same in both descriptions. Thus participants were only faster to verify matching trials than mismatching trials when label order was same in both descriptions.

Feeney et al [24] interpreted these results as suggesting that participants construct representations of the relationship depicted in the graph which they inspect from left to right. This spatial aspect to their representations is difficult to reconcile with current theories of graph comprehension [3; 4]. We have replicated these findings with line graphs and similar results have been reported by Fischer [25] who also interprets the alignment effect as evidence for analogical representations of the information presented in the graph.

3.2   Graphical Relational Reasoning

In the second set of experiments that we will describe, in order to test for analogical representations of the relationships depicted in graphs, we designed a graphical reasoning task isomorphic in structure to the relational reasoning task described in an earlier section. Although we have run experiments using this paradigm where we asked people to reason with bar and line graphs, in this paper we will briefly describe the results of an experiment using line graphs. A more detailed description of this experiment is to be found in Webber and Feeney [26].

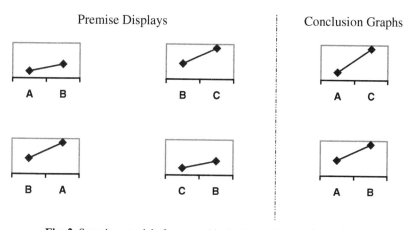

Fig. 2. Sample materials from graphical relational reasoning task.

In the experiment we presented 52 participants with a set of 112 graphical relational reasoning problems. In each problem participants initially saw a pair of line graphs each of which specified the relationship between two entities (see Figure 2). One of these entities was common to both graphs (the repeated term). We will refer to this display as the premise display. The premise display disappeared from view and on the next screen participants saw a conclusion graph only which specified the relationship between two of the entities shown on the previous screen. The conclusion graph either integrated the two non-repeated terms from the first screen (see upper portion of Figure 2) or it concerned the entities described in just one of the graphs on the first screen (see lower portion of Figure 2). We manipulated two aspects of the premise display: the data points were either ascending or descending and the non-repeated terms appeared either together or separated by the repeated term (see Figure 2). We also manipulated two aspects of the conclusion graph: either the conclusion logically followed from the premise display (see upper portion of Figure 2) or it did not (see lower portion of Figure 2) and the order of the referents in the graph was either consistent (see upper portion of Figure 2) or inconsistent (see lower portion of Figure 2) with the order of the referents in the premise display. We measured the time taken to inspect the premise displays, how long it took participants to indicate whether the conclusion was logically necessary given the premise display and the number of errors that they made.

Predictions. If people construct an analogical representation of the relationships between the entities described in the premise display and subsequently use that representation in order to assess the logical necessity of the conclusion then some very simple predictions may be made for their inspection and decision latencies as well as for their error rates. In particular, we would expect evidence for reordering in premise display inspection times such that participants will inspect premise displays where the non-repeated terms appear together for longer than they do premise displays where the non-repeated terms are separated by the repeated term. This is because in constructing a spatial representation to stand for the relationship between the referents in the graph, people are likely to integrate the information in the premises and to order the referents in terms of size [see 27].

The use of analogical representations leads to related predictions concerning conclusion verification times and error rates. The easiest way to reorder the referents in premise displays where the non-repeated referents occur together is to reverse the order of the referents. Thus, a graph with the referent order BACB is reordered as CBBA and likewise, the BCAB graph becomes ABBC. This has the effect of making conclusion graphs who referents were consistent with the order of the terms in the premise display inconsistent with the order of the referents in participants' likely mental representation of the relational information in that display. As consistent conclusions are very likely to be verified more quickly and more accurately than inconsistent conclusions, we predict opposite effects of conclusion consistency for trials in which the non-repeated terms in the premise display occur together versus trials in which the non-repeated terms are separated by the repeated term.

Table 2. Conclusion verification times and error rates (in italics) for the interaction between Consistency and End Term Position in the graphical relational reasoning task.

	Label Order Consistent		Label Order Inconsistent	
End Terms Separate	2045	*3.41*	2267	*8.81*
End Terms Together	2252	*7.39*	2184	*4.26*

Results. We used a 2x2 repeated measures ANOVA to analyse the inspection times of all 44 participants whose error rate was less than one standard deviation (S.D. = 18.76%) above the mean error rate (mean = 13.28%) for the entire experiment. The results of this ANOVA showed that premise displays in which the non-repeated terms appeared together were inspected for significantly longer than were premise displays in which the end terms were separated (4344ms vs. 3990ms). Analysis of the conclusion verification times revealed the predicted interaction between consistency and the position of the end-terms. This interaction also accounted for a significant amount of variance in the error data. Verification times and error data are presented in Table 2.

4 Implications for Smart Graphics

We have shown that people construct analogical representations when making inferences about the relationships described in bar and line graphs. Whilst we recognise that people may construct propositional or non-conceptual representations [see 2; 28] when interacting with graphs, our findings suggest that if the goal of the interaction is to extract information about a pattern in some data or the relationship between different levels of a variable, then spatial forms of representation might be preferred. Recent work on text comprehension [29] has shown that spatial and causal information extracted from text are held in separate working memory stores. It is possible that the relational and quantitative information extracted from graphs is likewise supported by different cognitive resources.

Our findings have several applied consequences. We have found increased errors and slower latencies when people have to manipulate graphical information in order to construct an ordered analogical representation. Graphing software might facilitate inference by allowing the user to manipulate the information on the screen. Thus, users might be offered the option of reordering the information on the screen or of interrogating the graph for relational information in a variety of ways. It may even be possible to design software to produce the most easily encodable graphs possible given a particular dataset.

A more general implication of our research is that when choosing diagrammatic conventions and representing data, designers should ensure that the ensuing graphics are faithful to the constraints that operate in the domain that is being represented. In many cases, this is likely to facilitate the construction of analogical representations with a spatial quality to be used by high-level cognitive processes such as inference.

References

1. Larkin, J. & Simon, H.A. Why a diagram is (sometimes) worth ten thousand words. Cognitive Science (1987) Vol. 11, 69–100
2. Rensink, R.A. Internal vs. external information in visual perception. In Proceedings of the Second International symposium on Smart Graphics. ACM Press, NY (2002) 63–70
3. Pinker, S. A Theory of Graph Comprehension. In R. Freedle (Ed.) Artificial Intelligence and the Future of Testing. Lawrence Erlbaum Associates Ltd, Hillsdale, NJ (1990) 73–126
4. Carpenter, P.A. & Shah, P. A Model of the Perceptual and Conceptual Processes in Graph Comprehension. Journal of Experimental Psychology: Applied (1998) Vol. 4, 75–100
5. Shimojima, A. The graphic linguistic distinction. Artificial Intelligence Review (1999) Vol. 13, 313–335
6. Stenning, K. Seeing reason: Image and language in learning to think. Oxford University Press, Oxford, UK (2002)
7. Cheng, P.C.H. Electrifying diagrams for learning: Principles for complex representational systems. Cognitive Science (2002) Vol. 26, 685–736
8. Gattis, M. & Holyoak, K.J. Mapping Conceptual to Spatial Relations in Visual Reasoning. Journal of Experimental Psychology: Learning, Memory and Cognition (1996) Vol. 22, 231–239
9. Johnson-Laird, P.N. Mental Models. Cambridge University Press, Cambridge, UK (1983)
10. Gentner, D. & Stevens, A.L. (Eds.) Mental models. Lawrence Erlbaum, Hillsdale, NJ (1983)

11. Zwann, R.A. & Radvansky, G.A. Situation models in language comprehension and memory. (1998) Psychological Bulletin, Vol. 123, 162–185
12. Mayer, R.E. Multimedia learning. The Psychology of Learning and Motivation (2002) Vol. 41, 85–139
13. Hegarty, M. Mental animation: Inferring motion from static diagrams of mechanical systems. Journal of Experimental Psychology: Learning, Memory & Cognition (1992) Vol. 18, 1084–1102
14. Trafton, J.G., Kirschenbaum, S.S., Tsui, T.L., Miyamoto, R.T., Ballas, J.A. & Raymond, P.D. Turning pictures into numbers: Extracting and generating information from complex visualizations. International Journal of Human Computer Studies (2002) Vol. 53, 827–850
15. Glenberg, A.M., Meyer, M. & Lindem, K. Mental models contribute to foregrounding during text comprehension. Journal of Memory and Language (1987) Vol. 26, 69–83
16. Dehaene, S., Bossini, S. & Giraux, P. The mental representation of parity and number magnitude. Journal of Experimental Psychology: General (1992) Vol. 122, 371–396
17. Giaquinto, M. What cognitive systems underlie arithmetical abilities? Mind and Language (2001) Vol. 16, 56–68.
18. Evans, J.St.B.T., Newstead, S.N. & Byrne, R.M.J. Human Reasoning: The Psychology of Deduction. Lawrence Erlbaum Associates Ltd, Hove, UK (1993)
19. Goel, V. & Dolan, R.J. Functional neuroanatomy of three-term relational reasoning. Neuropsychologia (2001) Vol. 39, 901–909
20. Corbetta, M., Miezin, F.M., Shulman, G.L. & Petersen, S.E. A PET study of visuospatial attention. The Journal of Neuroscience (1993) Vol. 13, 1201–1226
21. Mellet, E., Tzourio, N., Crivello, F., Joliot, M., Denis, M. & Mazoyer, D. Functional anatomy of spatial mental imagery generated from verbal instructions. The Journal of Neuroscience (1996) Vol. 16, 6504–6512
22. Reichle, E.D., Carpenter, P.A. & Just, M.A. The neural bases of strategy and skill in sentence-picture verification. Cognitive Psychology (2000) Vol. 40, 261–295
23. Dehaene, S, Spelke, E., Pinel, P., Stanescu, R. & Tsivkin, S. Sources of mathematical thinking: Behavioural and brain-imaging evidence. Science (1999) Vol. 284, 970–974
24. Feeney, A., Hola, A.K.W., Liversedge, S.P., Findlay, J.M. & Metcalfe, R. How people extract information from graphs: evidence from a sentence-graph verification paradigm. In M. Anderson, P. Cheng, & V. Haarslev (Eds.) Diagrams 2000, LNAI 1889, pp 149–161 (2000)
25. Fischer, M.H. Do irrelevant depth cues affect the comprehension of bar graphs? Applied Cognitive Psychology (2000) Vol. 14, 151–162
26. Webber, L.J. & Feeney, A. How people represent and reason from graphs. (Under review)
27. Johnson-Laird, P.N. & Byrne, R.M.J. Deduction. Lawrence Erlbaum Associates Ltd, Hove, UK (1991)
28. Pylyshyn, Z.W. Visual indexes, preconceptual objects, and situated vision. Cognition (2001) Vol. 80, 127–158
29. Friedman, N.P. & Miyake, A. Differential roles for visuospatial and verbal working memory in situation model construction. Journal of Experimental Psychology: General (2000) Vol. 129, 61–83

Optimization Strategies for a Scalable Avatar

Uwe Berner

Technische Universität Darmstadt, Interactive Graphics Systems Group,
3D Graphics Computing, Fraunhoferstraße 5,
64283 Darmstadt, Germany
uberner@gris.informatik.tu-darmstadt.de
http://www.gris.informatik.tu-darmstadt.de

Abstract. Computers are moving more and more from the desktop into our eve-ryday life. Today's challenge is to build a suitable visualization architecture for anthropomorphic conversational user interfaces which will run on different de-vices like laptops, PDAs and smart phones. Concrete implementations as part of conversational interfaces are User-Interface Avatars which are anthropomorphic representatives on the base of artificial 3D characters. The existing system methods, the graphical output chain and different optimization strategies are discussed.

1 Introduction

Computers are becoming more and more ubiquitous. You can see it, if you look around you: Laptops, PDAs, smartphones and other gadgets like MP3-Players. They are moving from the desktop into our everyday lives. This leads to the important question of how the user interfaces should look like for this new generation of com-puting.

An important field of activity at the Interactive Graphics Systems Group (GRIS) are Conversational User Interfaces where the primary goal is to give the computer a face to talk with. Conversational User Interfaces uses natural dialog-centric communication patterns to interact with the computer. The user is migrating from the paradigm of direct manipulation to the usage of assistance functionality [1]. The goal is the devel-opment of software architecture to shift complex tasks to human like assistants (ava-tars) which can be incorporated on different stationary and mobile devices like lap-tops, PDAs and mobile phones.

Concrete implementations at the Interactive Graphics Systems Group (GRIS) as part of conversational interfaces are User-Interface Agents/Avatars which are anthropo-morphic representatives on the base of artificial 3D characters. They represent a hu-man-computer interaction with the explicit presence of emotional aspects contained in every communication using facial expressions, gestures, and poses [2], [3]. The over-all human-machine dialogue is controlled by a preceding dialogue control, which manages all user-interface components and modalities. It also decides on given sen-

A. Butz et al. (Eds.): Smart Graphics 2003, LNCS 2733, pp. 222–230, 2003.

tences to be generated by a speech synthesis software, and delivers them to the avatar platform.

The main idea behind this paper is to make this avatar interface available on different devices and optimize the graphical output. This includes different types of avatars (3D, 2D and pseudo-3D) and optimization methods for them. We will describe possible optimizations for the 3D-avatar including the whole graphical processing chain. In figure 1 the idea of the different renderers and the adaptation is illustrated.

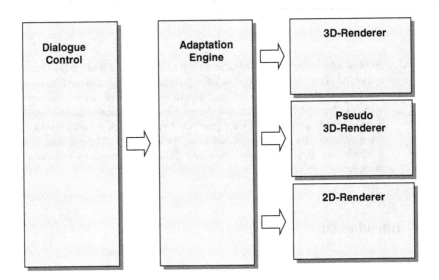

Fig. 1. Adaptation and Renderers

As far as known there are no efforts to implement an avatar with such different graphical output. The systems uses either 3D or 2D output and often stream the graphical data in a mobile context. Furthermore nobody scales the complexity of the avatar automatically while the system is running. Of course there are systems where you can load avatars with different graphical complexity at the beginning. Some examples of avatars, even in a mobile context can be found on the sites [4].

2 Overview

Our goal is to make this conversational user avatar available for different use cases, different users and different devices. This leads to the following requirements of a scalable avatar. The user interface avatar should be adaptable to different performance conditions, environments and devices. To achieve this goal the graphical representation should be scalable depending on the graphic performance, the environment, the conversation modus and the available devices. After all the graphical output should satisfy visual fidelity at all optimization levels.

At the same time the generation of the avatar animations and the interface to the dialogue controlling parts of the software system should be unchanged. One advantage of using morph targets with corresponding weights is the independence of the animation. Every animation generated from the dialogue control can be used to control any renderer. Another advantage is the independence of the graphical models used from the renderer, they could be human or comic-like and are not restricted to a physical model or special mesh structure.

There are three classes of renderers. 3D-renderer uses real 3D systems and require the highest performance of the hardware. Pseudo 3D-renderer uses images of 3D heads and produces a stream of pictures. 2D-renderer uses points to illustrate an icon-like head (note that the 2D version should be used on small devices, for example, mobile phone displays). The advantage is to scale the avatar among different devices and under varying performance conditions. Even it could be necessary to switch between different renderers to reduce the system load.

Here the objective was to improve the 3D–renderer in order to have the possibility to scale the graphical output of the system. To achieve this we examined three possible ways to do it covering the whole graphical processing chain. (illustrated in figure 2)

1. Manipulate the weights of the morph targets
2. Analyse different mesh reduction methods
3. Improve the morph node of Java3D

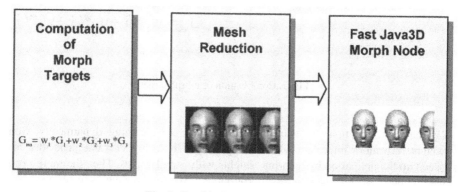

Fig. 2. Graphical processing chain

3 Optimized Weights for Morph Targets

The key idea behind the animation with morph targets is to combine different geometries corresponding to their weights (see figure 3).

The facial structure is based on morph targets and efficiently realized as a morph node (Alexa et. al. 2000) [5]. Hereby, a wide range of facial expressions can be provided, while the parameterization of the face is kept simple and can be realized with just a few key values. Key-frames defining the state of the animated character may consist only of a small number of such values and playback is possible even over low-bandwidth networks and on small portable devices. Moreover, facial animations can easily be mapped to different geometries, thus further extending the possible choices for the user interface designer. In this way, photo-realistic avatars or comic-like characters can be displayed and animated.

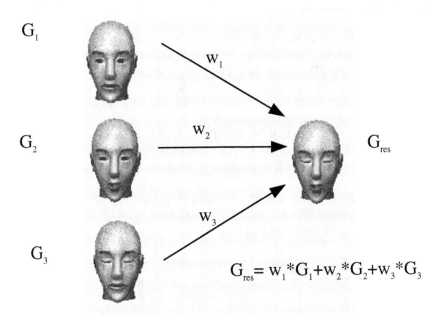

Fig. 3. Combination of morph targets

During the animation the value of the weights are changing dynamically. Some weights are more important which is represented by a higher value. The idea is to speed up the animation by ignoring weights with small values. Then the morph process computes the results with less morph-targets. We set the weights under a specified value to zero and distribute these weights over the remaining nodes. This action is required in order to achieve a total sum of one for all weights corresponding to Java3D morph nodes. And two strategies are used for this:

1. Add the weights the the maximum weight
2. Add the weights to the remaining non zero weights

The speedup for the two strategies is the same as we are using the same number of morph-targets. It is about 23% with threshold 0.2, a higher threshold leads to animations of lower quality. In figure 4 you can see the different framerates with different thresholds as the avatar is reciting a poem (using an AthlonXP 2100, GeForce 4).

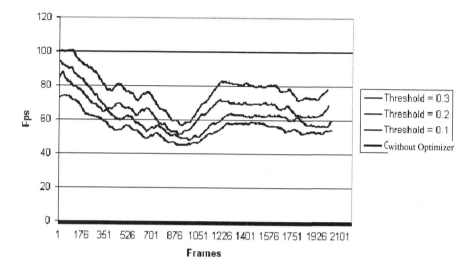

Fig. 4. Optimized weights results

4   Mesh Reduction

Another approach is to use mesh reduction methods to adapt the complexity of the graphical output. We modified the data structures of the avatar in order to accomodate mesh reduction. An edge collapse algorithm with different error metrics was implemented, we used:

1.   Energy function
2.   Method of Melax
3.   Quadrics

The energy function was introduced by Hugues Hoppe working on mesh reduction and progressive meshes. For details see [6] and [7]. This method is much slower and more storage consuming than the other methods. It works well until the avatar reaches 300 faces. Hoppe himself suggests some improvements in [8].

The Melax scheme was invented 1998 from Stan Melax, see also [9]. It is very fast and produces good results for around 480 faces.

Another common approach for an error metric are the use of quadrics, like in [10], [11], [12]. It is both fast and produces good results around the complexity of 100 faces. Thus quadrics seems to be the best error metric for the mesh reduction of our avatar.

In figure 5 you can see the graphical output of different mesh reduction methods.

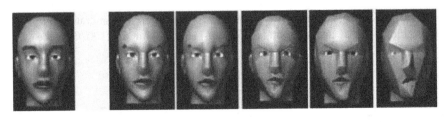

Original 782 faces   Quadric with 582, 482, 282, 182, 82 faces

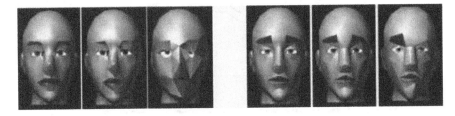

Energy with 582, 482, 282 faces   Melax with 582, 482, 282 faces

Fig. 5. Avatars with mesh reduction

Our first approach with mesh reduction was to identify the benefits of the different methods. In the future the best ones will be modified and performance measurement will be done.

5 Improved Java3D Morph Node

In Java3D a lot of graphical values are manipulated from the morph node. In this optimization strategy only the animation relevant features are modified from the new morph node. Less varied values are not taken into consideration depending on the actual animation. These are for example: color or not moved vertices. The results will lead to an acceleration of up to five times faster in the morphing process.

A new Java3D-Class *FastMorph* was implemented to replace the existing morph class. The new class uses some precomputing, better initialization and modified method calls. The number of the used method calls are reduced and the geometry arrays are accessed in a direct manner.

Thus the first approach to speed up the morph-node was the internal method calls and data structures. We refined all this and gained a 200 % acceleration.

The next step was to optimize the morphing of the geometric values. These are:

1.   The coordinates of the vertices
2.   The colors

3. The normals
4. The textures

Here, it is possible to either deactivate the morphing of all the values or give a tolerance for the morphing. Thus little differences between consecutive values are not considered. All fixed values are precomputed and stored in a special data structure. For the values under a specific tolerance a constant value will be computed, for example the balance point of the geometries. During the morphing process only the remaining changing values are computed. In table 1 you can see the speed up with different tolerances and deactivated values. The first row represents the system output with the original Java3D morph node.

Table 1. Performance of the fast morph node

Tolerance Vertices	Tolerance Colors	Tolerance Normals	Run-Time HotSpot [ms] (factor)	Run-Time IBM JVM [ms] (factor)
not available	not available	not available	58.0 (1.0)	69.5 (1.0)
0	0	0	32.5 (1.8)	24.0 (2.9
0.005	0	0	31.0 (1.9)	23.5 (3.0)
0.01	0	0	29.0 (2.0)	22.0 (3.2
0.01	0	0.01	28.0 (2.1)	22.0 (3.2)
0.01	0	0.1	21.0 (2.8)	17.5 (4.0)
0.01	deactivated	0	24.0 (2.4)	18.0 (3.9)
0.01	0	deactivated	13.0 (4.5)	10.0 (7.0)
0.01	deactivated	deactivated	10.0 (5.8)	7.5 (9.0)

One result of the new morph node is that the Java3D-machine is operating more graphical operations than the morph method on its own. This overhead remains regardless of the acceleration of the morph process. You can see this in figure 6 where the morphing costs (update) are around 1% of the whole computing time. To obtain a better acceleration other parts of the 3D-renderering must be modified or another 3D-system should be used (for example OpenSG) [13].

6   Future Work

Our future work will consist of the implementation of the pseudo-3D, the 2D-renderer and the adaptation engine and the integration of all components to a full system for conversational user interfaces. Additionally there must be a variety of optimization-methods to enable all renderers to be controlled from the adaptation engine. This optimization methods should be verified in different use cases, different graphical plat

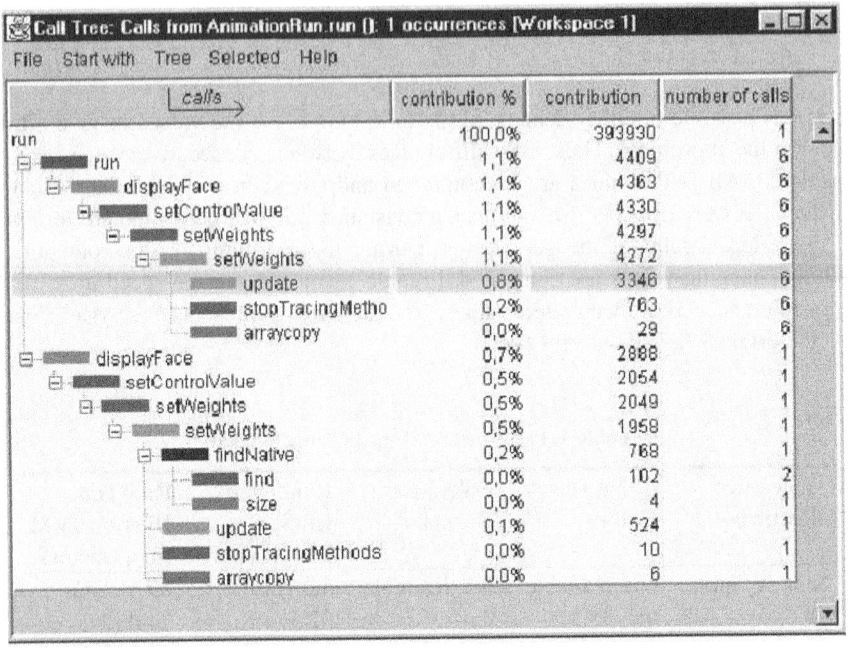
Call Tree: Calls from AnimationRun.run (). 1 occurrences [Workspace 1]
File Start with Tree Selected Help
calls
contribution %
contribution
number of calls
run 100,0% 393930 1
run 1,1% 4409 6
displayFace 1,1% 4363 6
setControlValue 1,1% 4330 6
setWeights 1,1% 4297 6
setWeights 1,1% 4272 6
update 0,8% 3346 6
stopTracingMetho 0,2% 763 6
arraycopy 0,0% 29 6
displayFace 0,7% 2888 1
setControlValue 0,5% 2054 1
setWeights 0,5% 2049 1
setWeights 0,5% 1958 1
findNative 0,2% 768 1
find 0,0% 102 2
size 0,0% 4 1
update 0,1% 524 1
stopTracingMethods 0,0% 10 1
arraycopy 0,0% 6 1

Fig. 6. Computing time of the fast morph node

forms (Java3D, OpenSG) and devices. Also there must be optimization methods for the 2D and pseudo-3D cases. Another problem is the visual fidelity of the graphical optimization. One possible solution are user tests with the completed system to achieve empirically data. At least there should be efforts to port the renderers to existing hardware devices like laptops, PDAs, and smart phones. Possible platforms for this are the P800 from Sony-Ericsson [14] or the series-60 platform from Nokia [15].

7 Conclusion

We have presented the idea of a scalable avatar used for conversational user interfaces. This avatar will run on different systems and environments and will be adapted to the actual context of the user and performance conditions of the actual device. The starting point for the main idea for a scalable avatar was the implementation of an avatar platform connected with a 3D-rendering system.

This paper gives an overview of the possible optimizations for the 3D-rendering. This includes the animation via weights and morph targets, mesh reduction and new morph nodes for Java 3D. The challenges for the future work are the development of the new renderers (pseudo-3D and 2D) including new morphing methods which should look pleasant and require less performance. For the 3D-renderer new graphical output systems will be tested and geometrical reduction methods will be optimized.

Acknowledgements. This work was partially funded by the German "Bundes-ministerium für Wirtschaft und Arbeit", BMWA through the Focus Project MAP [http://www.map21.de].

References

1. P. Maes, Agents that Reduce Work and Information Overload. Comm. of the ACM, 37 (7). July 1994
2. Cassell, J., Sullivan, J., Prevost, S., Churchill, E. (ed.): *Embodied Conversational Agents*, MIT Press, Cambridge, MA 2000
3. Gerfelder, Müller, Spierling: „Novel User Interface Technologies and Conversational User Interfaces for Information Appliances", Extended Abstracts of ACM CHI2000, The Hague, Netherlands 2000
4. Different avatar sites, 2003:. http://www.mrl.nyu.edu/~perlin/head/ http://www.cse.unsw.edu.au/~inca/, www.anthropics.com, www.planb-media.de
5. Alexa, M., Behr, J., Müller, W. (2000). The Morph Node. Proc. Web3d/VRML 2000, Monterey, CA., pp. 29–34
6. Hugues Hoppe, T. DeRose, T. Duchamp, J. McDonald and W. Stuetzle. Mesh Optimization. University of Washington, Jan. 1993
7. Hugues Hoppe. Progressive Meshes. In SIGGRAPH 96 Proc., p. 99–108, August 1996. http://reserach.microsoft.com/~hoppe/
8. Hugues Hoppe. New Quadric Metric for Simplifying Meshes with Appearance Attributes. 1999, http://reserach.microsoft.com/~hoppe/
9. Stan Melax. A Simple, Fast and Effective Polygon Reduction Algorithm. In Game Developer Mag., p44–49, November 1998.
10. Michael Garland. Quadric – Based Polygonal Surface Simplification. Mai 1999.
11. Michael Garland and Paul S. Heckbert. Surface simplification using quadric error metrics In SIGGRAPH 97 Proc, p. 209–216, August 1997
12. Michael Garland and Paul S. Heckbert. Simplifying surfaces with color and texture using quadric error metrics. In IEEE Visualization 98 Conference Proc., p. 263–269, October 1998
13. OpenSG Forum: http://www.opensg.org/, 2002
14. Sony-Ericsson, P800 Mobile Phone: http://www.sonyericsson.com/ , 2003
15. Nokia, Series 60: http://www.nokia.com/ , 2003

Physical Animation and Control of Simulated Creatures

Olivier Parisy and Christophe Schlick

LaBRI (Laboratoire Bordelais de Recherche en Informatique - CNRS UMR 5800)
Université Bordeaux 1
351 cours de la Libération
33405 Talence, France
{parisy, schlick}@labri.fr

Abstract. In the course of generating life-like movements of artificial live beings, the integration of a physical simulation in their animation process is a way to get interesting and realistic results. But the complex control problems associated with physical models challenges its usability from an animator point of view. In [14], we described a software platform which addresses the issues of the generation of those physical models. In this sequel paper, we detail more deeply this implementation and give some highlights on the way it can be used as a framework for control systems generation.

Keywords: Physical Model Generation, Physical Simulation, Animation Control, Behaviour, Artificial Life.

1   Background

In the process of generating life-like computer graphics models, representing a realistic animal or human being from a shape and texturing point of view is an essential basis. But even with a lot of work invested in this first step, the quality of the final result will be greatly influenced by the tools used to animate it.

Many methods have been developed to simulate the movement of living creatures in computer graphics; one can refer to [12] for a wide survey on this topic. We will present some representative works here in an increasingly higher-level control order, and from a computer animation generation point of view; we will then show how they can be articulated with behavioural and more generally artificial life tools.

1.1   Movement Generation

Probably the more intuitive way to get realistic animations of living creatures is simply to record their real movements. Lots of tools were developed for this "motion capture" purpose, using miscellaneous sensors or, more recently, direct video analysis [19]. The realism of the results is not disputable, but these data are, by nature, difficult to reuse, because they cannot be transposed to a different model or scene easily.

Complementary to this movement acquisition and deformation approach, a whole family of methods aims at synthesising animations. A first way to do so is to define the value of some characteristic parameters of the model at some given points in time

A. Butz et al. (Eds.): Smart Graphics 2003, LNCS 2733, pp. 231–240, 2003.
© Springer-Verlag Berlin Heidelberg 2003

("key frames"), and then to interpolate between them to obtain a continuous value: this is commonly performed on the angular values of joints in an articulated model. It is then simple to use them to compute body parts positions. But in most situations, it is more interesting to control precisely end-effectors (hands, feet) positions than joints flexion; *inverse cinematic* algorithms have been designed for this more difficult purpose [12].

But either tools, being automatically- of animator-controlled, provide no guaranty as of the realism of the resulting movements. For this purpose, a physical, *dynamic* approach can be used, based on a physically-realistic animation [20,9,11,12]. These tools make the specification of an animation difficult, because their input is a set of forces varying over time. This can be alleviated by using *inverse dynamic* algorithms but those are very expensive, and exact solutions do not always exist. Hence many algorithms focus instead on the optimisation of *space-time constraints* [6,9] : instead of specifying exact trajectories, the animator specifies a set of constraints on it, which a solver will try to respect by finding the best-fitting solution.

The previous techniques are useful as generic animation design tools. But many interesting movements involving life-like creatures are predictable and regular; following this logic, algorithms producing them have been designed. The common characteristic of these *motors* is to use a small set of high-level parameters (speed, mood, etc) and to translate them to continuously variating parameters which can, as an example, be used to drive a direct cinematic model. Commonly automated movements are walking [8], running [5] or grasping [7].

Most of those algorithms work in an open-loop fashion, like automata: the resulting animation is totally specified by its initial set of parameters. But if the evolutions of the environment are too complex or are not known beforehand, these techniques and more generally off-line approaches such as space-time constraints cannot be used anymore; it is then more realistic to design closed-loop algorithms which, given the current world state and a goal, will continually compute the needed actions to fulfil it [12]. Those *controllers* can be hand-crafted [11], but it is usually a painful process; they can also be automatically generated using optimisation methods [21,18,13,9].

1.2 Behaviour Simulation

A complementary way to consider live beings animation is to study its goal-driven nature, and to implement their characteristic perception/decision/action loop. Convincing simulations of animal groups can be obtained using minimalist perception and decision process, as the famous Reynolds' animations showed it [15]; this approach is called *reactivity*, or by metonymy behavioural animation [2]. More generally, a wide range of behavioural models can be defined; we can classify them using their type of perception and decision-making.

Perception can be defined as a set of *sensors* which deliver a low-level information such as a light intensity or a distance [21]. They may seem realistic, but extracting informations from them may be difficult which usually restrict them to reactive systems. At the other opposite of the range, symbolic perceptions can be provided; here, the decision-making process has access to a symbolic description of the environment, more or less restricted.

The other part of a behavioural system is the decision-making process. We already described the reactive one, which is based on the idea of a short, simple loop between perception and actions [16,4,17]. But more complex models can be defined, such as ethological or cognitive ones, which are based on the study of animal or human behaviour and abilities [3,20].

1.3   Our Approach

We have shown how the live beings animation issue has been addressed over time using increasingly higher-level concepts, towering with closed-loop control systems. Those especially prove of a great help when dealing with physical animation tools, which involve complex forces manipulation to get proper results. Indeed, non-trivial control systems and animations can result from artificial life techniques, and they can be more efficient than an human being in exploiting a complex set of low-level parameters to achieve a given goal [21,9]. This is especially true when the structure of the creature can be evolved and optimised, too [18]; but in most situations (games or animations development, as an example), the geometrical and visual characteristics or the creature will already have been designed with traditional techniques, and one will want to "make it alive".

Our goal is to study this specific need by developing a framework which, by integrating a physical animation system in a classical animation model, will supply us with a set of low-level parameters on which optimisation techniques can be used. This can of course already be performed in existing commercial animation packages by linking to the creature model a physical one. But it must be carefully handcrafted for this purpose, and this involves competences totally different from those usually required from an animator.

On the opposite, the tools we present totally automate physical model generation, releaving the animator of any need to understand the details of the underlying simulation. This can then be used as a basis for animation controllers generations through optimisation methods, a topic we are currently investigating.

Related works were presented in more details in [14], but not implementations issues; the rest of this paper will be dedicated to their discussion.

2   Animation Framework

2.1   Initial Model

We choose as a basis for our work a widely used animation model, the skeletal one. It is based on two kinds of objects: a skin, which is a classical textured surface, and a tree-like set of bones similar to those used in kinematic simulations. An influence is specified by the animator for each bone, which defines how it will deform the surface portion it is linked to; more specifically, for each control point of the surface a weight is specified for each bone controlling it. So instead of directly animating the surface by deforming it or manipulating its basic components, the animator only needs to interact with the underlying skeleton (this can be done using motion capture data, hand-crafted keyframes or any other source of data). Hence, skeletal animation can be seen as a specific kind of high-level surface deformation, similar in this regard to FFD and other modelling tools. Similarly, it provides smooth-looking deformations because surface is not only moved but also locally deformed in the process.

As it is, this animation tool is already usable in a wide range of ways, and much simpler than a low-level one. But as described previously, we are interested in its indirect control using a physical model. This process is twofolds; we first need to build a physical model as close an approximation to the skeletal one as possible. Then the behaviour of this physical model is simulated, and feeds the resulting articulation poses back to the bones of the computer graphics one.

2.2   Physical Model Generation

So far, we only described a physical model as something that could approximate an animated skin and its underlying bones animation mechanism. Actually, a wide variety of simulation tools representing physical objects and their behaviour exists, the most generic being soft bodies simulators. They are able to render deformations resulting from the interactions between physical bodies, but this incurs at a great computational cost. Moreover, even if we afforded it, our animation model would not be generic enough to render those local deformations. We hence chose a more specific tool, the articulated rigid bodies. Note that, as described in [14], the choice of physical and animation models is deeply coupled, and that our specific selection is a try at getting a good compromise between animation quality and credibility, in one hand, and computational cost, in the other hand. This last contraint is widely influenced to the way we expect our framework to be used, as will be described in 3.

Articulated Rigid Bodies. The Articulated Rigid Bodies (ARB) model is a compromise between soft models and rigid ones. It simulates the movements of a set of bodies which are themselves rigid, but articulated with each other. Because it models efficiently interesting real-life objects (such as mechanical tools and industrial robots), a great deal of research has been invested in the efficient simulation of that particular class of models. In most simulators, links are organised in a tree-like structure; it is often generalized to include closed, DAG-like structures.

It should be clear at this point that a mapping from a skeletal model to an ARB in not a too far-strenched approximation. But as much the bones structure is similar to the links one, as much the continuity of the rendered skin is incompatible with the discrete nature of the basic components of ARB. Hence, an algorithm able to properly approximate this skin with a set of rigid bodies is needed.

Surface Segmentation. This problem could of course be easily resolved by associating to each link a simple rigid body model, such as a cylinder, as a rough approximation of each limb. This technique is actually used to coarsely model manipulating robots, as an example. But in this situations, there will be no guarantees as to the quality or credibility of the resulting movements, not only because the physical model will not react properly to the forces applied to it, but most importantly because it will interact in completely different ways with the ground or other objects.

Hence, the goal of our surface segmentation algorithm is to associate to each bone of the initial model a mesh approximating as well as possible the skin surronding it. This extraction is made in a multi-pass process, each getting its data from the previous one.

Unrefined Meshes: We first associate an unrefined mesh to each bone; it is defined as a part of the set of triangles which have at least one vertex controlled by this bone. If a triangle is controlled by more than one bone, it is allocated to the deepest in the skeletal hierarchy. This way, the union of the surface of those meshes is the surface of the original skin; this will be an invariant during all following manipulations.

Meshes Cutting: We then compute a cut plane for each bone; it is located at its (local) origin, and oriented according to its rotationnal part and that of its children. Figure 1 shows the original model (on the left), and (on the right) the set of cut planes (displayed as gray disks) associated with its articulations.

Fig. 1. Original Model – Cut Planes

Proceding in a child-first (postfix) way, each unrefined mesh is then cut along its associated plane; the subpart in the parent side is added to it, and the other one is kept by the bone. The interesting thing about this operation is that it is the only one that involves actual triangle splitting, and this triangle/plane cut operation can be computed in a much more robust and efficient way than generic CSG operations.

Meshes Refining: Once this is done, we refine the result by redistributing subparts: in some situations (figure 2, on the left), some undue parts (ie, actually belonging to a child) may be transfered to its parent. The reciprocal problem is also very common: taking as an example the model and its associated cut planes shown figure 1, the planes associated with the root of legs intersect with the creature body. This leads to the association of some parts of it to the leg mesh, as shown figure 2 (on the right).

Using connectivity tests, both situations are checked for and corrected if needed.

Finally, meshes are defined as the union of those subparts, and transformed to the local coordinates of their associated bone.

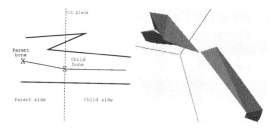

Fig. 2. Some Cutting Problems

Topological Reconditionning: The meshes resulting from the previous algorithm are usually perfectly usable from a computer graphics point of view; but they lack properties which are needed by most of the following integration algorithms. Specifically, meshes are expected to be closed manifolds, meaning each mesh edge must be shared by two triangles exactly. This involves at least the closing of holes and splitting of some edges, but also the handling of a wide range of degeneracies such as internal faces. In all its genericity, this surface reconditionning problem is an active research field and efficient algorithms are usually complex and not necessarily freely available.

Our solution to this need is a median approach: we try to automatically fix as much of the above problems as possible, and this is usually sufficient. But should this fail, we resort to a very robust method consisting in the generation of the points cloud associated with the degenerate mesh vertices, and then on its processing to extract the convex hull of this set. As stated, the problem of this technique is that it will loose concave details of the surface; but this turned out to be a proper approximation for a wide range of models, their individual limbs being usually mostly convex.

Volume integration. The previous algorithm brought us meshes associated with each bone; these are the basis of our simulation, representing the surface of the rigid bodies comprised in our physical model, but this information is not enough. What we also need is the physical parameters associated with each of those bodies, and describing how they react to forces. They are threefold; m being the mass of the body, G its center of gravity and M_I its inertia matrix, we have:

$$m = \int_V \rho(M)dv \quad G = \frac{1}{m} \int_V \rho(M)M dv$$

$$M_I = \begin{pmatrix} \int_V (y^2 + z^2)dm & -\int_V xydm & -\int_V xzdm \\ -\int_V xydm & \int_V (x^2 + z^2)dm & -\int_V yzdm \\ -\int_V xzdm & -\int_V yzdm & \int_V (x^2 + y^2)dm \end{pmatrix}$$

We found no simple algorithm for the computation of those integrals over meshes; available simulation packages most often use basic bodies (cylinders, boxes) whose integrals are analytically known, and to our knownledge algorithms used in large CAD or simulation packages (Cathia, Autocad) have not been published.

We first tested some basic ideas, based on the observation that physicists seem to often approximate complex bodies as the union of simpler ones. We tried to sample our meshes in a similar way, using subdivision and sampling. But they were either very memory and time consuming, either rather inacurate, especially on complex meshes. It was also unclear which level of approximation could be afforded to keep realistic physical data.

3D Delaunay Approach: We hence finally developped a totally different algorithm based on the idea that boxes were not the natural way to decompose a mesh; from an algorithmic geometry point of view, simplices (here, tetrahedrons) are. Our problem is simply a generalization in 3D of Delaunay triangulation, for which numerous robust algorithms already exist. Because those return a set of tetrahedrons whose union is the original volume and which have pairwise empty intersections, the sum of integrals on the items of this set equals the integrals on the initial mesh. Interestingly, we will show that the familly of integrals we are interested in are easy to efficiently compute in an exact way on tetrahedrons.

If we make the hypothesis that ρ is constant along the volume, the problem is reduced to the computation of integrals of the $\int_V f(x, y, z)dv$ kind, f being a polynomial function. In the specific case where three edges of a tetrahedron form an orthogonal basis, the computation of the integrals is then easily performed by decomposing them on the base axis. This method cannot be applied in the generic case, so we will use a property of integrations stating that if $g = (g_1, g_2, g_3)$ is a diffeomerphism associating to each point p of a volume V a point $g(p) = (g_1(p_x), g_2(p_y), g_3(p_z))$ of V', we have:

$$\int_{V'} f(x, y, z)dv = \int_V f \circ g(u, v, w).\,|J|\,.du.dv.dw$$

Where J is the jacobian of g and M_J its jacobian matrix. It can then be shown that a M_{T_0T} matrix associating to any point of the T_0 tetrahedron defined by $(O, \boldsymbol{i}, \boldsymbol{j}, \boldsymbol{k})$ a point of the T tetrahedron defined by its four vertex (S_0, S_1, S_2, S_3) always exist (if T is not degenerate); it is easily computed using matrix algebra. Hence, g can be expressed as a matrix product with M_{T_0T}, and it is then easily shown that $|M_J| = |M_{T_0T}|$. Knowing that M_{T_0T} is invertable by definition, $|M_J|$ cannot be null, hence g is a diffeomorphism.

Then, by using the previous property, we get:

$$\int_T f(x, y, z)dv = |M_{T_0T}| \int_{T_0} f(M_{T_0T}P)dv = \int_{T_0} h(x, y, z).dv$$

Using iterated integrals and geometrical considerations, we show that:

$$\int_{T_0} h(x, y, z).dv = \int_0^1 \int_0^{1-x} \int_0^{1-x-y} h(x, y, z).dz.dy.dx$$

We will not detail here the integration results because of space constraints; but using the previous properties, they are easily computed using any algebra system computation framework (the maths are simple, but intermediate expressions are lenghty).

Links Extraction. Once rigid body approximations of the model volume influenced by a bone have been computed, the last step to generate an ARB is their proper linking. It would at first seem that the conversion from animation bones to physical links is a simple bijection, but it is not necessarily the case.

Theoretically, a given bone have six degrees of freedom; actually, the positionnal part of the bone is usually fixed, which means that a given bone have at most three rotationnal degrees of freedom. This can be represented by a classical ball-and-socket joint, or by a combination of lower degrees of freedom links, depending on what is available in the chosen simulation package.

Links Constraints. Real articulations seldom use the whole range of their degrees of freedom; they are usually restricted to one of its intervals. Modelling that in a physical simulator is not as easy as, as an example, with a keyframe system, because the movements of the links are a consequence of the simulation, and not the basic manipulable parameter. This implies that constraints on links must be modelled as forces applying to them when they approach limit orientations.

The model actually used to define those forces is specific to each simulator, if it either implements this. But if this is the case, it is worthwhile to try to compute limit angles for our links. As an example, when recorded movements are available (even produced using motion capture or key frames), they can all be converted to physical links parameters. Then, by taking the minimum and maximum of the generated data for each degree of freedom of the model, rough limits can be computed.

This subject is complex, because actual constraints between links are interdependant for real live-beings articulations [1]. Models have been defined to account of this [10]; they could probably be integrated in a physical framework by computing proper return forces.

3   Model Control

We described a framework which enables an animator to get physical movements based on a computer graphics model. This is done in an automatic way, but in itself the result will not necessarily prove useful. Indeed, movements are now realistic, but hard to specify: the animator must think in terms of forces injected to his model. This is intuitive in some situations (modelling of collisions), but in most situation we have the same problem as the one we solved for model conversion: competences unusual from a computer graphics point of view are needed to exploit this framework.

This leads to the idea that a control mechanism should be added on top of the physical simulation: using its current state and a goal, it would compute proper forces to perform expected movements. Similar closed-loop controllers have already been described in section 1.

To address the previous issue, we are interested in computationnal tools which would help animators in designing control systems on top of our physically-animated computer graphics models. As a testbed for this problem, we are currently working on a typical situation in a physical environment: if no forces are applied to it, a physical model will simply fall to the ground and will only be restrained from auto-intersection by its links constraints, as defined in 2.2. As an example, figure 3 shows a physical model of a skate before simulation, then the same model at rest.

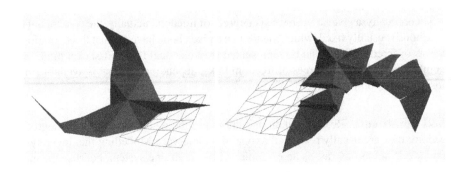

Fig. 3. Initial Physical Model – Model at Rest

What we would like is to generate a controller which, associated with this model, would be able to keep its initial pose by injecting internal torques counterbalancing the external collision forces. Basically, what we are looking for is the set of functions that, for a given link state and an expected base pose, compute the proper torque at that given time to reach it in a minimal time.

It is an interesting problem by itself, because it necessarily involves a closed-loop controller properly tuned to the specific simulated model. It is also an useful base for more complex tasks, such as pose reaching [6,9] which is a basis for locomotive controllers.

4   Conclusion

The work we present here fits in a wider project consisting of the development of as automated as possible tools for realistic animation. The associated framework was presented in [14] and this sequel paper aims at presenting in a more precise way the most important implementation choices and issues. Hence, solutions were presented for rigid bodies extraction, physical parameters computation and links conversion, and more generally automated physical model generation.

Using a physical simulation as a basis for realistic animations generation is an interesting, but very challenging task. We hope that this presentation of the main issues we met while developing such an animation framework will be of some help to anyone contemplating the design and use of similar tools.

Even if this framework is completed and works in a robust way, it should be clear by now that it is only the starting point for higher-level investigations on efficient control tools and their generation. As already described, our short-term concerns are pose keeping and reaching; they will be followed by locomotive controllers, and finally more tasks- and ecologically-oriented behaviours such as predator-prey systems and other kinds of creatures interactions.

References

1. Paolo Baerlocher and Ronan Boulic. Parametrization and range of motion of the ball-and-socket joint. In *Deformable Avatars*, pages 180–190, 2000.
2. Bruce M. Blumberg. Autonomous animated interactive characters : Do we need them ? In *Computer Graphics International (Proceedings)*, pages 29–37. IEEE, 1997.
3. Bruce M. Blumberg and Tinsley A. Galyean. Multi-level direction of autonomous creatures for real-time virtual environments. In *Computer Graphics Proceedings*, pages 47–54, 1995.
4. David C. Brogan and Jessica K. Hodgins. Group behaviors for systems with significant dynamics. 1995.
5. Armin Bruderlin and Tom Calvert. Knowledge-driven, interactive animation of human running. 1996.
6. Michael F. Cohen. Interactive spacetime control for animation. In *Computer Graphics Proceedings*, volume 26, pages 293–302, 1992.
7. Brett Douville, Libby Levison, and Norman I. Badler. Task-level object grasping for simulated agents. *Presence*, 5(4):416–430, 1996.
8. Ronan Boulic et al. Human free-walking model for a real-time interactive design of gaits. In N. Magnenat-Thalmann and D. Thalmann, editors, *Computer Animation*, Tokyo, 1990. Springer-Verlag.
9. Radek Grzeszczuk and Demetri Terzopoulos. Automated learning of muscle-actuated locomotion through control abstraction. In *Computer Graphics Proceedings*, pages 63–70, 1995.
10. L.Herda, R. Urtasun, P. Fua, and A. Hanson. Automatic determination of shoulder joint limits using quaternion field boundaries. In *5th International Conference on Automatic Face and Gesture Recognition*, Washinton DC, USA, May 2002.
11. Michael McKenna and David Zeltzer. Dynamic simulation of autonomous legged locomotion. In *Computer Graphics*, volume 24, pages 29–38, 1990.
12. Frank Multon, Laure France, Marie-Paule Cani-Gascuel, and Gilles Debunne. Computer animation of human walking : a survey. *The Journal of Visualization and Computer Animation*, 10:39–54, 1999.
13. J. Thomas Ngo and Jo Marks. Spacetime constraints revisited. In *Computer Graphics Proceedings*, pages 343–350, 1993.
14. Olivier Parisy and Christophe Schlick. A physically realistic framework for the generation of high-level animation controllers. In *Smart Graphics*, pages 47–54, Hawthorne, New York, USA, 2002. ACM Press.
15. C. W. Reynolds. Flocks, herds, and schools: A distributed behavioral model. In *Computer Graphics*, volume 21, pages 25–34, 1987.
16. Craig W. Reynolds. Not bumping into things. In *Notes for the SIGGRAPH '88 course Developments in Physically-Based Modeling*. ACMSIGGRAPH, 1988.
17. Craig W. Reynolds. Competition, coevolution and the game of tag. In Rodney A. Brooks and Pattie Maes, editors, *Proceedings of the Fourth International Workshop on the Synthesis and Simulation of Living Systems*, pages 59–69, MIT, Cambridge, MA, USA, 6-8 July 1994. MIT Press.
18. Karl Sims. Evolving virtual creatures. In *Computer Graphics Proceedings*, pages 15–22, 1994.
19. Bradley Stuart, Patrick Baker, and Yiannis Aloimonos. Towards the ultimate motion capture technology. In *Deformable Avatars*, pages 143–157. Kluwer Academic Publishers, 2001.
20. Xiaoyuan Tu and Demetri Terzopoulos. Artificial fishes : Physics, locomotion, perception, behavior. In *Computer Graphics Proceedings*, pages 43–50, 1994.
21. Michiel van de Panne and Eugene Fiume. Sensor-actuator networks. In *Computer Graphics Proceedings*, pages 335–342, 1993.

Author Index